Me, My Fatł

Normandy to Hamburg:
A Tankies Story

by

Calum Meadows

Dedication

To a magnificent generation of men and women who must never be forgotten.

Acknowledgements

To Ian Jolley, whose 60th birthday Ancestry gift got the ball rolling. Bovington Tank Museum for its inspiration and archive section, which helped fill in many gaps. John Lipscomb, who geed me along over our garden fence while I wrote the book during the COVID pandemic. Muckleburgh Military Collection and Michael Savory, who allowed me to use the Bernard Montgomery D-Day letter. Ian Morrison, who shares my WW2 passion, including Calvados and a memorable bottle consumed in Normandy. Tess, whose unwavering love and support is always there, whatever I do. And finally, to all the glorious men and women of that extraordinary generation who inspired me and should inspire us all.

Contents

List of Photographs

44th Royal Tank Regiment (RTR)

As part of a belated effort to build up its armoured force, the War Office converted several territorial infantry battalions into armoured units. The 44th RTR was formed in 1938 from the 6th Battalion Gloucestershire Regiment, which had served with distinction in the First World War.

Initial training was at Ashton Court Manor in Bristol, where the tank strength was unimpressive until the arrival of 'Matilda', a heavily armoured but slow infantry support tank.

In July 1940, the Regiment moved to Lavington Beeches on Salisbury Plain and continued to train, focusing on an anticipated German invasion. As part of the 1st Army Tank Brigade (later 4th Armoured) in the 7th Armoured Division (Desert Rats), the 44th RTR sailed to Egypt on April 27th 1941. They fought there until returning to Britain in January 1944, when the next chapter in their incredible history was about to be written.

Introduction

I am Calum, with one L, the only son of Peter and Jean Meadows. I was born on a remote tobacco farm in Malawi, formerly known as Nyasaland, before we moved on to Rhodesia (now modern-day Zimbabwe), where I enjoyed an unconventional early childhood.

My father grew tobacco, and my mother, a retired professional singer, was a farmer's wife who doted on us both. We lived in difficult political times but I only remember happiness, heat, and sunshine – lots of it. My friends were native African children with bright eyes and wide smiles conversing in a local dialect called Cha-Lapa-Lapa. I was fluent in it.

They were wonderfully carefree and adventurous days for a boy growing up in the African bush; it was a joyful place to live, where we ate *sadza*, climbed trees and annoyed our elders. Life was that simple.

So-called conventional times arrived in January 1963, when my family uprooted and moved to England. I had heard of England, an alien country called 'home', where my parents were convinced a safer and more prosperous future lay ahead.

It was a risk. My father was forty then, my mother a little younger, and as for five-year-old me, all I remember is confusion. Snatched away from my smiling friends and vast bush playground, everything I knew had gone including my home, a thatched, white-washed house with cool stone floors and wire-meshed windows. It had been my castle.

A poky flat with dim lighting and tatty red lampshades replaced it, and a dark, perpetually cold climate in a country full of grey people didn't seem that prosperous.

Two things stick in my memory about that place. First was my father putting his hand through a sash window. A few savoury expletives, which were new to my growing vocabulary, and fountains of blood suppressed by gingham tea towels remain etched in my mind. The other was my excited mother perched anxiously at the top of our threadbare, red-carpeted stairs. Any time soon, Pop, wearing his trilby hat and with his beige mackintosh folded neatly over his arm, would return from his first job interview in London. He got the job.

To save money, we moved to the countryside into a dingy, damp caravan propped up in the corner of a shady apple orchard in Suffolk. The locals were sullen and life was stark; even the Bramley apples had maggots in them.

My parents weren't happy, either; I could feel it. I wondered how bad it could get as they grappled with their decision and lack of genuine desire to move to this miserable new country. They had no apparent skills to suggest that this brave new lifestyle could be attained, so life was a real struggle.

For me, the emptiness inside was exacerbated by being eternally cold, a feeling I still have today, intensified by this adopted and broken country called England. Africa was my home.

We eventually moved into what my parents called a proper house with real windows, where a contented but different life began. It was safe, and my mother once described it as 'idyllic'. Maybe it was for her but it wasn't for me, which brings me back to the genesis of this story.

Mum died in 2004, followed by my father ten years later. Both had lived extraordinary lives as young individuals and later as a couple. I had always felt there was a story to be told and, at the same time, an opportunity to create a record of their exploits for my wider family to enjoy.

Some initial genealogical investigations gradually drew me towards my father and his war years. It was heads or tails; I could have started with Mum because her life story was as remarkable as his. But I decided on Pop and the escapades that had kicked off on D-Day and took him through France into Northern Europe and then, eleven months later, Hamburg. They deserved proper examination.

In June 1940, aged seventeen, Pop joined the 9th Battalion of the Royal Norfolk Regiment, known then as the Home Guard. Two years later, and newly married, he volunteered for the Royal Armoured Corps.

According to his enlistment papers, his occupation at that time was shoe designer, which surprised me, but unlike many of his contemporaries, he didn't lie about his age. In his defence, his father owned Meadows of Norwich, a shoe factory specialising in ladies' dress shoes, but that is where my justification for Pop's creativity has to end: he wouldn't have known a stiletto from a sandal. I understand that HM Queen Elizabeth did though, having once been a customer of theirs!

Other exciting revelations in his enlistment papers warranted investigation. It was stated that he had a scar at the base of his left index finger. Did he really? I'd never noticed it – and how would I have, since a gold signet ring, the one I now wear, hid it for most of his life. I have no idea how the scar got there or why he disguised it, but perhaps it was a trophy from his favourite pastime and one he was allegedly good at: fighting.

As I scrolled through the document, something else intrigued me and made me laugh out loud. According to the military tape measure, Pop's height was 5' 4½". Now that was a revelation because, in all my time with him, he claimed to be a significant 2½" taller than that!

When I started my project, my goal was to write a book one day. There was no hurry, and I fully expected my initial investigations to keep me busy during my early retirement. Writing a book would be a new venture, but creative writing classes at school and the compilation of numerous business reports in my work life – more fiction than fact, it has to be said – gave me the confidence to at least give it a go.

My initial research came from predictable sources: Pop's service record, provided by the Ministry of Defence; two hundred pages lifted from the 44th Royal Tank Regiments' official war diaries, and a well-thumbed copy of *A History of the 44th*, published in 1965. They helped to point me in the right direction. However, despite this information, numerous photographs and visits to the Bovington Tank Museum archives section, I still didn't have enough to write a book.

The other challenge was the man himself. Like many veterans, Pop rarely spoke about 'the War'. That part of his life seemed to be sectioned off in a memory vault stamped NO ENTRY.

Some of his contemporaries, and indeed his brother Val, had a different view. Captain Percy 'Val' Meadows, CBE, MC, was an intelligence officer with the Gurkhas in Burma during the war.

He enjoyed military reunions and the chance to reacquaint himself with the 'boys'. Had Pop been the same, my task would have been much easier, but he wasn't. Instead, he shunned all such opportunities 'to dig up a dismal past', as he robustly put it. Perhaps he was correct; I completely understand his point of view.

These men, a sublime generation, experienced events and saw things that no one ever should. In the chaos of battle when boys had to be men, they did some things that had to be forgotten. It must also be remembered that most were not professional soldiers; like me, they were ordinary people drawn from all sections of civilian life. And unlike the whining complainants of today's entitled generation, they did not grumble or protest. Neither were they ashamed and, more importantly, they did not wish to be seen as heroes.

'We simply did our duty, son,' Pop used to say.

On rare occasions, he dropped his guard, especially when nagging grandchildren probed him on the darker sides of war. 'Have you ever stabbed anyone, Grandad?'

Plonked on his office desk as a paperweight sat a German dagger with a swastika at the base of its leather-bound handle. On the far wall hung a ceremonial Nazi cavalry sword. Like a fishing lure, this loot (or 'booty', as he put it) teased their curious minds.

'Have you ever killed anyone, Grandad?' That was always a show-stopper.

A good time for a grandpa interrogation was after a big Sunday roast when Pop was primed with at least one large sherry and two glasses of Chardonnay, which had to be oaked Australian. The boys would question him relentlessly as I listened intently, trying to make as many mental notes as possible. 'One day I'll find time to use these stories,' I told myself.

Despite their exhausting cross-examinations, Pop was brilliant: he never gave the boys too much detail and revealed nothing overtly sinister to frighten them. Mum, who hated violence and found *Bambi* sadistic, used to step in to spoil it for the boys at a certain point. Her sensible 'granny check and balance' tactic worked every time.

'Peter, I think the boys have had enough, don't you?' Typically, she would be serving afternoon tea with one eye fixed firmly on Pop when she said this. The cake was another clever ploy of hers and it worked every time: chocolate cake always did.

I'd grab a slice and reflect, 'What about the guy he looted the dagger from? What happened to him?' And then back to the boys' question: 'Did you ever kill anyone?' I had asked that when I was their age, and his answer, even then, had always been the same.

'Did I ever kill anyone?' he'd say as if surprised. 'No, because I was just a tank driver.' A convenient answer for tiny ears, I thought.

But there was a supplementary probe, and it was a blinder: 'Did you ever get shot, Grandad?'

'No, but I did lose three tanks.' That grabbed their attention. 'The commander said, "One tank is unfortunate, Meadows, and two tanks concerning".' After a pause for effect came the punchline. '"But three is just downright careless".' He laughed a little too hard, possibly a distraction strategy to erase the memory.

When Mum passed away, I gently suggested that he might like to draft some memoirs, not just about the war but also about Africa and the broader aspects of his life; it would keep his brain active and help fill the void. My real motive was a selfish one: after years of tantalising glimpses, I needed some red meat on the bones of his anecdotes.

Albeit lacklustre, Pop at least gave it a go and the resulting A4 scrapbook provided a few gems to work on. It also gave me another idea.

I would retrace his journey through north-west Europe and try to combine historical facts with stories from his war years. I would put myself in his 'tankie' boots to do this. Dates and activities would be accurate and some names changed, but I would have to ignite my imagination to fill in the gaps.

Trooper 7952180 hit the Normandy beaches on June 9th 1944; my mission was to live his war again.

As enjoyable as these bonding sailing expeditions were, I cannot remember any without an episode of severe ocean sickness. Once the pristine white sails caught the wind and *Vegabond* began to smash her way through the waves, all hell would be unleashed. However, I also remember my father's face at this time. Perpetually brown and turned windward, his eyes would be screwed tight as he entered his meditation world. He was truly exhilarated; this was his sanctuary.

For me it was different. My guts felt as though they had been cut out by a blunt knife, lobbed onto a trampoline then bounced on by Demis Roussos. First I went cold, then warm and clammy. As my waxy white skin gradually turned green, something sticky and awful slowly crawled up from my intestines.

'Focus on the horizon,' came Pop's calming advice.

It made no difference. As the nausea grew, so did the severity of what was coming next. Then, in no order of consumption, a tsunami of bacon, sausage and egg was hurled into the sea – and, like the gift that keeps on giving, it came again.

Blissfully ignorant of the commotion below, *Vegabond*'s majestic sails powered us unrelentingly forward. In desperation, I occasionally turned away from the toilet bowl of churning sea towards my father. Just a hint of sympathy would have been nice, some recognition of my suffering – anything. Not a hope; only a metronomic shake of his head while he lit another cigarette.

'Fucking sausages?' Me, not him; he rarely swore.

Our fry-up always got the blame as I flicked straggly dregs of it away. This gut-wrenching sequence continued all day until my wasted body eventually flopped onto the shore several hours later.

These are bittersweet memories and I smile as I recollect them now. What finally rescued me were my young sons, James and Dominic; family weekends meant these jaunts became rare. Thank God.

I eased my car towards yet another roundabout and a myriad of rapidly blinking traffic lights. 'Yeah, yeah, designed to piss everyone off!' I gave them the middle finger and a startled old biddy in a clapped-out Mini gave me a look. 'Oops! Not you, sweetheart. Sorry.'

As a follow-up, she responded with a vigorous Churchillian victory sign. My congratulatory applause prompted a double-handed 'V' back, and her feistiness made me chuckle.

I bet my old man hadn't had this problem; in June 1944, he would have driven his tank over her! His first tank was an American-modified M5, categorised by the British as a Stuart 6. Due to their agility and speed, they usually operated alongside heavier tanks and were mainly deployed for reconnaissance work.

Pop later found himself in the medium-class and more powerful 34-ton M4 Sherman, but with these big beauties came a sinister and unenviable badge of honour; notorious for catching fire when hit, and because they 'lit first time, every time', the Allies soon started calling them Ronsons.

If they were medium-class, then what was a Tiger tank, I wondered. It was a rhetorical question and I knew the answer: they were super-heavyweights, almost twice the size.

'And what did our guys think when they first saw these things?' I addressed this question to the sat-nav lady.

My visits to the Bovington Tank Museum, especially the Tiger section, always left me numb. Every feature was gigantic, most notably the cannon – all 88mm. Forget *Top Gun* and boys in fast jets or flashy sports cars and the midlife-crisis brigade; this weapon was the ultimate penis substitute. It made our 75mm todger look like something left in a pair of budgie smugglers after a New Year's dip in the Serpentine. Or should I say Doggerland?

All those years ago, my father probably went along this same road, but his trip was very different. It led him to the docks at Gosport, where his war began, and into a future full of uncertainty.

'Comprehend that if you can, Calum,' I told myself.

Life for me has been safe and embarrassingly easy. At least my current mission would help me better understand my father's generation's sacrifices. I would make it my business to trace his footsteps and learn more about what had happened to him after Sword Beach, D-Day+3, on June 9th 1944.

This particular day was June 8th 2019, however, and the vehicle taking me to my embarkation point was a silver four-wheel-drive Freelander weighing around one ton. These lumps of plastic and tin are often called 'Chelsea tractors' by some of the grumpy locals in my corner of Norfolk.

'Owned by pricks,' is another noteworthy observation. They are luxurious and, for the tweed-clad holiday-home invaders who drive them, they come with matching upholstery and boots big enough to house a poodle parlour. I wondered if the locals included me in their remarks.

Unlike Pop, who sardined into his tank with three crewmates, my trip was comfortably solo. Earlier that day, my wife Tess had said goodbye and reminded me that the expedition would be emotional.

'Have you got tissues?' was the last thing on her checklist. She always asks that when I leave the house: mobile phone, water and tissues, always in that order.

Glancing down at the dashboard, I saw it was almost 19.00. My ferry was due to leave in precisely three hours, so there was ample time for final checks and a fuel stop. Even though filling up in France cost about the same, it somehow felt better to buy British.

Petrol prices would not have been on Pop and his companions' minds as they prepared to board Landing-Ship Tank 75. Once refuelled and packed with live ammo, their last task was to seal and waterproof the hatches with grease, window putty and reels of black Denso tape. All tanks in his regiment were petrol-driven, replacing the diesel engines that had powered most Allied tank squadrons until then. Seventy-seven tanks made up his battalion, predominantly Sherman M4s, supported by three troops of Stuarts known as Honeys.

'Why did they call them that, Grandpa?' one of my sons asked.

'Because their ride was "as sweet as honey".' It was one of the easier questions for Pop to answer.

The wind was gusting hard, and heavy rain was splattering noisily against the car windscreen. Using the back of my hand, I cleared a patch of condensation and dropped my side window down an inch to let in some air. Surprisingly, an urge for a cigarette hit me; I'd kicked that particular habit into touch several years ago.

Pop used to light up and then roll the tip of his cigarette between the rubber door seal and glass. With his eyes half on the road, it was an art form not to get any ash blowback or burnt rubber. That seemed to be his only consideration; forget about crashing the car or the antisocial aspect of smoking because such concerns didn't exist back then. I'm sure the sat-nav lady would have commented had she been around when he was at the wheel.

'Bloody brilliant.' Confirmation of my looming doom presented itself as a cluster of saplings in the middle of yet another roundabout swayed energetically in the strengthening squall. The vibes for a calm crossing were not good and were being made worse by the temperature gauge. Just twelve degrees made it cold for 'flaming June'. What a laugh. They were the same conditions as D-Day seventy-five years earlier.

My mind drifted back to our nautical days. Having reminded me to keep my eyes on the horizon, he always followed up with, 'Don't let it beat you, son.'

He probably didn't consider throwing up a sign of weakness, but he was competitive and would see it as defeat. Perhaps all this bonding stuff was just a game between him and the elements? I never asked.

Pop's funeral was on a blustery but bright December day in 2014. I said a few words and was sad but not anxious. It was emotional, though, because his life story was remarkable. After a brief eulogy, I recited a short poem I'd written to the congregation of family members and a few close friends. They all smiled politely in the right places.

All was good until, wedged into the same pew in the same soulless crematorium where I said farewell to my mother ten years earlier, a wave of loneliness slammed into me, a unique loneliness that an only child feels when their last parent dies.

The mourners included my half-brother and his family. Pop married June Howell in 1942, and Anthony was born in July of the following year. War had gathered pace by then, and at just nineteen, my father was already an impatient man. Being in the Home Guard was not good enough for him and, rather than wait for the formalities of conscription, he volunteered for the Royal Armoured Corps.

They say timing is everything, and on this occasion his was bad. Months spent apart from his wife during his training proved divisive and things ratcheted to terminal once he reached the front line in Europe. Unlike the subsequent fifty-year love affair with my mother, Pop's first marriage was brief and unhappy.

His ex-wife was alive and absent from his funeral, which was to be expected, and my mother and his three brothers, including a twin, had also predeceased him by then. That left just one sibling alive, Gloria, who was too old and sick to travel from her home in Toronto. Unfortunately, in most people's eyes – though probably not for him – they had not spoken to each other for years.

My little poem wasn't a Rupert Brooke or even a Pam Ayres; it was just a page of random reflections best describing my dear old dad at that moment: a man I loved dearly but a father I never really got to know. I can't pinpoint why, but he scared me a little. Mike and the Mechanics' song 'Living Years' gets me every time; it has a chorus line that does the damage: *It's too late when we die to admit we don't see eye to eye.'*

Often gregarious in the company of others, always outspoken and bloody-minded, he was also a very private person who preferred his own company. Though we loved each other and he was my superhero, something always blocked our connection. It was nothing severe or sinister, but sometimes his shutters came down and he seemed unable to open up. This was the same with everyone except Mum.

Pop was old-fashioned. He was a no-nonsense, slap-you-on-the-back man's man and proud of it; man hugs came to him much later in life. He wasn't even a tactile person when I was little; a cuddle on his lap felt like a treat. We did things together but the closest we got to bonding, apart from the sailing years, was going to the cinema or 'pictures', as he called them. I treasured this because he was all mine for a couple of hours – and we usually included a trip to the local Chinese restaurant.

Although I wouldn't say it now, we all called them 'Chinkies' back then. Sweet and sour pork balls with sticky sauce, egg fried rice, and chicken chow mein; the order was always the same, including the large, crispy spring rolls and prawn crackers served in faux wicker baskets. I loved the crunching sound as Pop devoured them but couldn't indulge myself. An inconsiderate allergy to crustacea inherited from my mother means that fine-dining on lobster and crab will always pass me by.

'Mind your fingers,' Pop would say as the waiter slid red-hot, stainless-steel plate warmers onto the plastic tablecloth in front of us. Our instant reaction was to touch them. Coke and ice for me and a small pale ale for him followed next.

Satiated by gallons of monosodium glutamate, and fizzing from the sugar hit of our pineapple fritters, in we went to the cinema. Passing the large billboards outside that tempted us with the next showing, Pop would quickly dart off to buy us Maltesers and wine gums.

Double-headers were standard then and James Bond was always a favourite. I remember *Thunderball* and *Goldfinger* in one such billing when Sean Connery was the leading man. Pop liked him because he was faithful to the books; he didn't much rate the softer representations of 007 that followed. God knows what his take would be should a non-binary, politically correct manifestation ever get the gig.

I loved sitting close to him, and watched intently as smoke patterns from his cigarette drifted across the cinema screen. The smell was intoxicating, too; like an addict, I anticipated his next match and waited for the salty, sulphuric hit as it fizzed into flame. He would take a deep breath as my young nostrils prepared for another lesson in passive smoking. I couldn't get enough!

On the way home, we would do a Barry Norman critique of the film and look forward to our next outing. These were special times for me and, I think, for him.

'Maybe I didn't try hard enough?' I shifted uneasily in my seat and straightened my back. Remembering that silly funeral poem made me cringe and squirm, and I wondered whether the congregation had thought it banal. Did they even listen? Probably not. Perhaps they were still recovering from Toto's song, 'Africa', or the warbling of Michael Bublé, one of his favourite singers, who had kicked things off.

'Why didn't we talk more, Pop?' I tried not to think about those lost opportunities, especially in the later years. 'Why didn't I make time?'

There were valid reasons: life, family and work, but that justification didn't help much, and that excuse taunted me. And then there was that killer verse.

I wasn't there that morning
When my father passed away
I didn't get to tell him
All the things I had to say.

It wasn't until I sat at his bedside that we got to know each other better. It was 2013, and the accident happened between Christmas Day and New Year's Eve. We had been out for Christmas lunch and, rather than visit him two days later on the Canaries' match day, I had decided not to go.

The dreaded phone call came to say he had fallen. We never did find out how long he had been on the cold bedroom floor covered in blood. If only he'd been wearing the red panic-alarm button hanging behind the door when he fell.

'It's just so irritating, son. I don't need it,' he'd insisted.

Much the same story applied to his expensive, state-of-the-art hearing aids; he didn't need those either. That was funny, because he rarely heard the doorbell or the phone ringing.

I smiled ruefully at the memory of one frantic phone call that went unanswered. I had feared the worst as I travelled the seventy miles between Cambridge and Norwich at what must have been a land-speed record.

Screeching to a juddering, handbrake-assisted stop outside his house, I saw that the kitchen lights were on. Interesting. And then I spotted him, washing up at the kitchen sink in his short but magnificent glory.

I could only see his head, but the old bugger was very much alive, and if raves for nonagenarians existed then this was the place to be. As he squinted through the steamed-up kitchen window, that old rocker Mantovani was blaring from his clapped-out music centre in the lounge.

He gave me a double thumbs-up and wandered outside to greet me. 'Are the Canaries playing tonight, son?'

'No, Father, they're not. I've been calling you for days.'

11

'But I've been in all week.' He scratched his head and gave me one of his quizzical looks.

'Try wearing your bloody hearing aids, then!'

'What was that?'

I repeated the question.

'I can hear perfectly well without them, son. Cup of tea. Maybe something stronger?'

Pop survived a grubby hospital ward ridden with norovirus, and quarantined from the world by thick plastic sheets and NO ENTRY signs. I questioned the frazzled nursing staff why a sick, ninety-one-year-old man could be left so exposed to this 'winter sickness bug'. The answer was well-worn but truthful: 'Bed shortages and staff sickness.' Nothing has changed much.

Severe bruising and dehydration but no bones broken was the prognosis. His spell on the floor had been defined as long, bringing with it potential problems. The nurse chose her words carefully as she explained that last part to me.

Thankfully, he was transferred to a quiet cottage hospital near Norwich for rehabilitation. The care there was exceptional and his strength gradually returned. While that was great to see, we all knew the truth: Pop could never manage on his own again.

'At the next circle, take the second exit.' The annoying American sat-nav lady broke my train of thought. It amazed me that a Yank was telling me in a so-called British vehicle that I had to exit from a *circle*.

'Roundabout, you irritating tit!'

I imagined how the passing road signs would be in German had Pop and his muckers failed to stop Hitler seventy-five years earlier. Arguably, and more amusingly, was the lollipop lady in the distance; she would probably be wearing lederhosen. It was a childish thought, but I laughed out loud.

'Now, now Calum, let's have some political correctness, please,' I said to myself. Like Pop, I found the absurdity of 'PC' ludicrous, together with our woke-infected nanny state and its snowflake-infused cancel culture. I'm told our society has progressed but 'the world's gone effing mad'. The old man would have agreed, and so would my dashboard friend.

We eventually found a 'patient-friendly' nursing home nearby that didn't smell of pee. Sadly ironic, and I never told him this, it was where his mother, Gladys, had spent her final days.

Pop was only there for eight months and, apart from the occasional dash around the block in a wheelchair, he rarely left his room. But he didn't grumble or complain and he never asked me to take him home, which, to be honest, made things easier. Importantly, he seemed happy. I don't know that for sure; he was probably content rather than happy because the 'Peter Meadows stiff upper lip' always masked his true emotions.

To state the obvious, talking about 'the War' was always difficult for my father. What surprised me was that this life-defining chapter in his life had seemed insignificant. I got that, but I also found it unbelievable.

I remembered his words again: 'Simply doing my duty, son,' he used to say. 'It was about serving your country and doing the right thing.' For him, it was straightforward. If pushed, he would add, 'It was also about good versus evil.'

Occasionally he questioned later generations, including mine: would they have the same resolve, and where were the world politicians to lead us through similar challenges? That was a great question.

At the time of my journey there were two prominent men in the world news: Boris and Trump. I entertained a contentious thought: maybe they could lead us. Then I realised I'd gone completely bonkers, shook my head and continued towards the ferry port.

I saw Pop the night before he died. His ruddy face, which had always exuded health, was transformed into a hideous white death mask, and his skeletal frame was scrunched up. He looked like an alien; this man, my rock, was now a corpse in waiting, and it was shocking to see.

But although his physical deterioration was quick, it was not enough to completely extinguish the Peter Meadows' flame. A week or so earlier, as I'd rounded the corner that led up to his room, his unmistakable voice boomed out from a bathroom, 'Why don't you jump in with me, Dora?'

'Peter, I can't do that,' came the mock-horrified reply.

'Why on earth not?'

'I'm a married lady.' More splashes and a pause.

'Remember, Dora, where there's a will there's always a way, my dear.'

A fly buzzed around his gaping mouth as I sat with him towards the end. Irritated by its persistence, I flicked it away repeatedly as I worried about what would happen when I left.

The bright and mischievous twinkle in Pop's eyes had been one of his trademarks, but that night his eyes were tightly closed. He was in pain. Occasionally they flickered open, revealing two black holes that startled me. Gone was the spark that had lit them; all that remained was a vacant stare.

We had the usual one-way conversation, and I struggled to find new things to say. If only he could have told me one of his stupid jokes. Instead we held hands in silence and waited.

The nurses were kind to Pop; with me, they were direct and honest but gentle. There was no hiding place from how things would eventually turn out, and they assured me he wouldn't suffer. I think the drugs helped, and I remember him pointing towards invisible objects as they floated around his room. This fascinated him. When he muttered incoherent questions and I asked what they were, he would point again, laugh weakly then fall silent. Sometimes after one of these episodes he looked sad and closed his eyes. Demons from the past or morphine-induced hallucinations; I don't know.

Finally Pop decided that his time was up and his body shut down for good in the early hours of November 26th 2014. I wasn't there for him when he died; I had returned to Cambridge with the promise of a telephone call if things deteriorated overnight but it didn't happen. I did get a very kind but obligatory call the following day, though, and the finality of it chilled me. He was dead.

As a young child, I worried that I would be alone one day and tried to calculate what point that might happen. Well, this was the day: my parents had gone forever. Both were as dead as the telephone line humming in my ear when Matron put the receiver down.

I carefully picked up the sea-sickness tablet strategically placed in the coin well behind the gear stick. Taunting me throughout my journey, this small white pill was a reluctant reminder of things to come. The traffic light was red, so I grabbed the bottle of water wedged between my thighs and washed down the tablet.

Green light. I shifted into gear and had enough time to complete a few more mental checks, plus a one-hour forward adjustment to the clock. Done. My tickets and passport were tucked into a black leather wallet stowed in one of several travel bags heaped up behind me. Comforted that they were easily accessible, I headed towards the dock area and for my journey's next – watery – leg.

To foster a road-trip frame of mind and to stoke up memories of Pop, my playlist included a few no-brainers. Bruce Springsteen's *Born to Run* blared out of the speakers, making me laugh at such a clichéd track, but it felt good, and then Ray Conniff and his singers came to mind. Being a particular favourite of my parents in the day, I found their classic track and put it on.

'Up, up and away in my beautiful balloon,' the line started.

'Well, that's enough of that. Very sorry, Pop.' I cut it short as another familiar voice interrupted proceedings. 'And you can shut the fuck up too.'

Five minutes later, the inevitable over-officious hi-vis clad man appeared. With exuberant, conductor-like hand gestures, he directed me towards the back of a short queue. The man, probably called Kevin, eased into his next choreography: Usain Bolt's victory stance.

'You'd think he was parking a bloody Jumbo jet,' I muttered to myself.

Acknowledging my enthusiastic host with a matey thumbs-up, I accelerated gently into the empty lane. From nowhere a boy, no more than six years old and all coat and furry hood, faced me. Our eyes locked as I yanked fiercely on the steering wheel. Kev dived the other way in a blur of yellow hi-vis and black wellies.

Everything happened so fast. As I waited for the inevitable bump, the clicking vibration of ABS brakes kicked in – but the only bump that came was my head thumping violently against the handgrip above the driver's door.

I remember an explosion of pain and tasting blood from my lip as my sat-nav friend told me I had reached my destination.

Bruce's voice continued to boom. The teasing feeling of relief was premature because, as I relaxed, a blinding white flash followed by a deep stab of pain drilled through my skull and into my brain.

Darkness and agony were all I felt until a soft, fluffy blanket of cotton wool and calmness wrapped around me a few seconds later.

From Peter Meadows' memoirs

I joined the 44th Royal Tank Regiment in Worthing several weeks before D-Day and discovered they had already served in the Western Desert. Later they landed in Sicily and then moved on to Italy, crossing the Sangro Moro and into the Rualti engagement.

The regiment returned home to prepare for the D-Day landings after this. Although it had Shermans, I was posted to the recce troop with Stuarts, known as Honey Tanks. Although lightly armoured, they were very fast.

The 44th had already spent months of reorganisation, re-equipping and training. Instead of the usual diesel-driven tanks, the new ones were petrol aircraft-engined Shermans, which we thought would be underpowered and highly flammable. Later on we were issued the new 'Firefly' with a seventeen-pounder instead of the 75mm main gun.

Once we had all our tanks and vehicles waterproofed, fitted with wireless sets and checked, everything had to be stowed away, including high-explosive and armour- piercing ammunition.

We threw a very successful 'all-ranks' dance at the Assembly Rooms in Worthing and, in turn, were given a reception by the town's mayor.

General Dempsey, the future commander of the 2nd Army, came to visit, as did Monty, who talked to us about the battle ahead. After several delays, we eventually arrived in Gosport on the evening of the 8th of June, forty-eight hours later than expected.

The Awakening

I felt like shit. My right temple seemed to be recovering from a hammer attack and a salty taste of fresh blood coated my tongue.

'Well spotted, Meadows. Steady as she goes.'

I eased the right stick back, one of two that dropped like stalactites from the bulkhead above me. Another dab from my right boot prompted a roar from our twin Cadillac engines as they thrust us back on course. Apart from a split lip and busted head, an urgent question needed to be asked: 'What am I doing here?'

Everything felt natural and authentic, but it couldn't be. The welcome rush of warm summer air felt good and distracted me momentarily, but in the distance loomed a bank of dunes. As they got closer, anxiety started to build inside me.

'Sorry, chaps missed that bugger.' The apology was casual, and it came from someone invisible above. Not for the first time, our eyes up top had been late to spot a bomb crater – this one smoking black – to our starboard. Piling into one of those would not only be painful and embarrassing, but only one person in our crew would carry the can: yours truly.

I decided to say nothing and concentrated on the vast expanse of golden sand before us. Sprinkled with black dots, it brought fond memories of Blakeney Point at the end of seal pupping season. In winter these dots would be Atlantic bull seals, late into shore for last-minute mating rites. As we got closer, it became evident that the objects here were less innocent than those lardy lumps of lumbering nature.

'Give your foot a rest, driver.'

Reducing our speed from 20mph to a walking pace relieved the squeaking from the springs in my leather-covered seat that was acting as a shock absorber on my backside. We began to plot a course through the twisted remnants of battle and thoughtfully placed sea defences. At another time these deterrents, with their pointy spines and serrated iron blades, would have formed trendy art installations among the flipped-over vehicles and exterminated life forms.

'Deftly done, Meadows.'

I had only one question for the faceless voice above: 'Deftly done, yes – but how?' I decided not to ask.

Intense artillery fire from our warships preceded by Allied aircraft destruction had left bleak reminders everywhere, even away from the landing beaches. And the smell? Seals give off a uniquely evocative industrial aroma; the stench filling my nostrils now was harsh and metallic.

In uneasy silence, our tank with its four-man crew continued to carve its way towards Ouistreham, a port at the mouth of the river Orne. Something subconscious told me we were four miles east of Sword Beach, our battalion's original landing point. Strange images of Pegasus Bridge, gliders and the battle at Merville Gun Battery flickered through my mind like old movie stills. Confused at first, I quickly corrected myself: they came from my book research. It was one of many light-bulb moments to follow.

'Brake, swerve and accelerate,' was the day's mantra from above, followed by, 'And mind that bloody hole!'

So far, so good: it worked. A tug on either lever steered us left or right; pulling back on both levers slowed us and eventually stopped the tank.

'This *has* to be a dream, doesn't it?' I desperately wanted to test this concept but puke prevention had to be my priority for now. That and coping with an exploding head and fist-sized lumps of ice jammed with razor blades gnawing their way through my guts.

The others heard me groan as my head smacked against the metal bulkhead again.

'No helmet? Dear oh dear.' The voice was new and came from the same intercom system. 'Worried about the rug, Peter?'

Rug? I hadn't heard that expression for years. And where was my helmet? The voice was Scottish and belonged to our gunner, Nigel Morton. I didn't bite; a lesson learned in my other life was that sarcastic Jocks were to be ignored. But here was another question: why had he called me Peter?

The pain pulsed harder now, and furry black floaters started to bob across my eye-line. *Great*, I thought, *especially when I'm driving*. Shaking my head made it worse. *Go with this, Calum, whatever this is.*

Wisps of seagrass and scrubs of yellow-tipped gorse topped the dunes that rose in the distance. They were steep, and when my boot increased our revs the tank's automatic transmission smoothly dropped down a gear. Up we went to level out – again impressive – and then down again effortlessly.

I glanced to my right and saw a beret-clad head peer through the bow-gunner's hatch. Wearing black sunglasses and with a cigarette drooping loosely from the corner of his mouth, Wolfie Smith from the Tooting Popular Front confronted me. His headset clamped tightly over his regimental beret made this urban warrior look more contemporary in 1944 than in the television series *Citizen Smith* of the 1970s.

The sea was on my other side but not a typical sea – this one was inky black and brooding sulkily. Something else looked different: the waves. Grey foam smothered the usual frisky white tops like a blanket. It looked dead, and with an early evening sun glinting off the surface, globs of multi-coloured froth folded into the surf as waves rolled gently up the beach.

'Psychedelic. It's as if the sea has a hangover, I murmured.'

'Hangover? You better not, Meadows.' It was the commander's voice again. 'Not sure what you mean by "Sico-Derrick".' That comment had to be ignored.

At first the dark shapes twisting on the surface looked like tricks of light, but with each surge and retreat the churning of an incoming tide unveiled more grotesque secrets. Visible on the shoreline was a white horse; once magnificent and proud, it lay dead and defeated as we passed. As a final humiliation, a gun carriage remained harnessed and sunk in the sand like an anchor behind it.

'Horses? Why use horses?' I asked.

'That's all they've got,' came the reply.

That was not strictly true, though much of the German artillery at the time of D-Day was horse-drawn. Better than that, their mechanical mobile transport divisions included bicycles!

Squinting into the glare, we could see more debris floating among the wreckage. In lakes of engine oil, torn life rafts and other battle detritus played peekaboo with dead soldiers who were bobbing in the shifting sea between them.

It was three days after D-Day, and bloated corpses were continuing to flop ashore clad in their haplessly named Mae West life vests. The lucky ones had left this world as they came into it, screaming and petrified but at least in one piece. Most of these bodies were in bits, ripped apart by machine-gun fire or disintegrated by exploding mines. Whole or otherwise, they slopped around in an obscene witch's porridge of blood and mulch. Perhaps the saddest thing was that, in the hopeful minds of those who loved them at home, these men were still fighting for their lives.

My only other experience of seeing death this close had been my mother's. Thankfully predictable and relatively dignified, she had passed away quietly in a sterile hospital bed. None of that dignity could be seen today, just total carnage and a brutal end to so much wasted life.

As for me, nothing felt right on any level. The 'where, why, and when' questions kept coming. The 'where' was easy: Normandy, I thought. The other questions were still firing blanks.

In terms of my physical well-being, everything around me appeared hazy, jerking along in vintage cinematic motion; if this were not concussion or a dream, it had to be an immersive combat simulator. Wrong: computer games were never my thing.

'Just make it go away,' I said.

'Shut up and keep her steady. Stop drifting again.'

Wolfie Smith gave me the internationally recognised sign for wanker as he acknowledged the voice from above. His real name was Tony Auden, and I wondered if I could ever explain my nickname for him. But for now, my job was to keep us on a straight and not-so-narrow path as we bounced along Sword Beach.

For me, the nearest to driving a tank had been in the early 1970s. Mac Beanland, a friend of my father's, had let me drive a tractor as part of my weekend job on his small tenant farm in Essex. My usual job was to look after the pigs; he called me 'Pigman'. At sugar-beet time I reverted to 'Sugarman' and drove a tractor and trailer while he synchronised his beet harvester alongside. This was sometimes tricky because its giant chute lobbed heavy bombs from a conveyor belt onto the growing mountain of soon-to-be sugar lumps behind me.

The only matter of importance was self-preservation by not stalling; health and safety, especially helmet-wearing, were not considered seriously in those days. But it was fun for a twelve-year-old boy 'living the dream', and a lump on the head was nothing. I loved my time on French's farm amongst the mud, the pig's blood and gore. I didn't realise then, but Mac would be an inspiration for me in later life.

As an orange ball of a summer sun slowly sank towards evening, all of us onboard our bucking hunk of creaking metal carefully scanned the sandy terrain around us. 'I want your eyes out on bloody stalks. Do you hear me?' That voice again.

We all said, 'Yes.'

Our troop was following in the tracks of two Sherman Crab tanks; these were from the Hobart Funnies' stable and the brainchild of Percy Hobart, Major General Sir Percy Cleghorn Stanley Hobart to be precise, leader of the 79th Armoured Division.

Flail tanks, as they were also called, were incredible machines and led the initial thrust on D-Day. Chains or huge strips of iron attached to rotating drums smashed their way through beach defences, decapitating life and limb and detonating land mines on their way. Once cleared, the Royal Engineers' escape channels were marked with white tape that guided our ground troops to safety. Theoretically sound on paper, the mayhem and chaos of that day meant this plan didn't always deliver the safe passage that was expected.

Aside from Crabs, there were other ingenious 'funnies' too. Churchill flame-thrower tanks were probably the most hateful of all; fondly known as 'Crocodiles', they had one simple and horrific purpose in life – incineration. As these dragon-like monsters trundled towards their foe, they spewed jets of fire and created deadly infernos fuelled by the tanks of petrol towed behind them. Maybe only carpet bombing or the ultimate bomb dropped on Hiroshima superseded the one-on-one devastation caused by the Crocodiles.

Then I thought of napalm. For pure evil, the elixir of death from Vietnam topped the table.

The funniest Funny was the infamous Duplex Drive, an amphibious tank. Nicknamed 'DDs', these were often Shermans packaged in thick canvas skirts. Loaded onto landing ship tanks that carried twenty, or landing craft tanks holding just four, they launched into the sea like boats. The seven-foot-high shroud wrapper was tall enough to displace enough water for a 34-ton weight to float. Clever stuff. Two propellors powered this strange craft on its two-mile dash to the beach. Well, that was the thinking.

What did the Germans make of this wonky, alien craft? The theory was brilliant but, as they neared the shoreline on D-Day, many DDs sank in choppy waters well short of their intended landing spot. This was especially true for our American cousins on Omaha and Utah beaches. American historians later claimed their reception was more hostile than the Brits and Canadians received on Juno, Gold and Sword beaches.

Whatever history wrote about Percy Hobart, nothing could deny his hero status. The man was an unconventional thinker; that brought him into conflict with the MOD, which retired him before the war. It was a fellow maverick, Winston Churchill, who recognised the challenges of Normandy and recalled him, a masterstroke from the grand master of eccentricity and unorthodox thinking!

'No Boche in sight, sir,' claimed my bow-gunner friend.

Our task – to spot signs of a German counter-attack – had been quietly successful. On the far side of a burnt-out Jeep, probably Canadian, another recce tank stormed from our troop. Clouds of sand and oily-black exhaust fumes billowed from its rear as it built up speed to climb the next dune. Everything about it was the same except for the turret, which was missing. A brutal-looking 50mm Browning machine gun replaced the usual 37mm main cannon that rotated 360 degrees on the old turret rim. This modification made these tanks lighter and faster, perfect for our type of reconnaissance work. We were called the 'Wanderers', and I watched as one of these adapted speed machines with our name painted onto its side powered ahead of us now.

'No obvious tracks, boss. There could be mines about?' I wasn't sure whether this was a question or a statement, but he agreed with my observation.

'Once we get over this, we'll head home.' Our orders to reach Ouistreham had been altered. 'And try to miss the bunkers, Meadows. I'm fond of my teeth.'

It was probably said in jest, but I visualised him as a pompous, public-school type who liked to dish out orders. Time would tell.

Despite being locked into this weird state, I was buoyed by my acceptance that this was a dream and most of my concerns began to diminish. Although my temple was throbbing, life would return to normal after a nice cup of tea. Tea sorted everything out.

My instrument panel's circular dials confirmed that the two water-cooled V8s were also performing well. I gave the accelerator some welly and felt the automatic transmission kick in. As we braced ourselves for the now well-rehearsed descent, things seemed nicely in order.

'STOP! Cut the engines. Cut the fucking engines.' This was delivered in an almost manic squeal; nothing was casual about this command. In unison, both tanks shuddered to a halt, their engines already shut down. We had no time to let them idle and cool first, so they coughed and spluttered in mechanical disappointment before falling silent.

As we waited for the dust to clear, I made out a dark row of life-sized objects stretched out in a line in front of us. The intercom crackled but no immediate order or comment came through. Then, just like tumbleweed in a Western movie, a bundle of dry gorse bounced along the sand.

'Unbelievable,' was all I could say.

'Jesus. Both crews stay as you are.' The order, more controlled this time, was as uncertain as the image in front of us was surreal.

A quick count and I saw ten British soldiers lined up in an orderly row. There was nothing exceptional about that apart from the red, white and blue deckchairs they were sitting in. And although each man was pointing an Enfield rifle directly at us, the dark-purple hole drilled neatly into the middle of each forehead confirmed that they were also very dead.

'Probably made by a handgun.' Our commander's observation instantly dismissed my idiotic thought that Hindu *bindi* ink or a strange tattoo had made these marks.

Grim reality quickly sank in. The same was true for all the men, except for an officer who sat at the end to the far right; instead of his mouth, a gaping black hole the size of a small ashtray replaced it.

'High calibre and close up,' muttered Wolfie.

Even a novice like me could agree that had been necessary to blast through teeth and then out through the backbone of his skull. The man's brains dangled like butcher's offal on the wooden struts of his beach chair and fresh blood dripped onto the killing ground beneath it.

'Wanderer 2. Cover us.' The next order was directed at us. 'My crew, dismount when I give you the all-clear.'

Lieutenant Peter Reeves was the commander of our tank and the troop leader. An uncomfortable silence followed when there was no immediate response to his order. We usually used three radio frequencies and ours was currently set to B, which connected all the tanks in our troop. Eventually, a reply came back. 'Message received, sir.'

Reeves was tall and skinny with a nerdy, prefect-like demeanour that confirmed my earlier assumptions that he must have been a prick at school. My harsh assessment continued as he stood, feet wide apart, on the deck before me. He might have been a professional soldier but he was as green as the volunteers watching him and waiting for his next move. Not one of us would have swapped ranks as he prepared to jump down from our tank.

'Take it easy, boss.'

'It's why I've got the stripes, Meadows,' was his response to my rather pathetic warning.

They were also the last words he said. He landed heavily on the sand beside us and almost instantly his body jerked upwards then folded in two. A brief pause followed before it puffed out and burst like a giant balloon.

I heard fragments of flesh, kit and splintered bone smash into the hull; simultaneously, a blast of heat forced me down onto my seat. A few seconds later, as my ears fuzzed like an untuned wireless, a cool mist of something moist and repugnant slowly descended. I wiped my right cheek; the reddish-brown smear across the back of my glove was blood.

'Bouncing Betty?' asked Tony.

24

'A big bouncing fucking Betty,' replied Morton.

Our support engineers had missed this one. Shrapnel 'S' mines were perhaps the most gruesome anti-personnel mines. No imagination was needed when eighteen ounces of TNT crammed with 380 ball bearings exploded beneath your feet. To prove the point, all that remained of our disintegrated troop leader was a steaming pile of twitching fabric and flesh; most of his bottom half had vapourised into nothing.

This devastation made its little sister, the Schu-mine, look almost benign. On a good day they only took your foot off, along with most of your bedroom tackle. Ironically, had Reeves landed on a Teller mine, he might have lived; it took more than 200lbs of body weight to detonate those dinner plate-shaped nasties.

'Sometimes the sneaky buggers plant them two or three deep,' Morton continued. 'If our lads miss the one on top, the ones underneath get you!'

'Who on God's earth invented something like that?' No one bothered to answer Tony Auden.

Two of the dead troopers had tipped forward in the explosion and one of their helmets was spinning around slowly. At first sight, it was comical. The only feature that distinguished these men from shop mannequins were the holes in their heads and the gooey mush of brains and pink slime that oozed onto the sand below them.

I looked back at our lieutenant. I'm not sure why; maybe it was for some macabre confirmation. All that distinguished him as human was his mangled head and half an arm poking out from his uniform.

'Tanks start up and back up twenty. NOW.' This time, the instruction came from the other tank.

'Gunner on Wanderer 1, take command and move up onto the next bluff,' was the order that followed. This time it came across on the alternative 'troop radio' frequency.

'Message received, sir. On our way.' Nigel Morton had already made himself comfortable in the vacant commander's seat. 'Meadows, get this bugger up there pronto and wait for instructions.'

The climb was easy, and as we slowly ground our way onto the next ridge our engines hardly grumbled. Wanderer 2 was on my right flank and we both reached the summit at the same time.

There were six of them, Jerrys, and they were marching directly towards us in pairs. Each soldier carried a rifle with a bayonet fixed onto the end of it. My heart palpitations fell back in line when a small white flag fluttered into sight attached to the lead officer's gun. I reckoned they were only a football pitches length away, and although in surrender mode they didn't look that submissive to me. I also knew from my research in my real life that this could be a deception ploy. Would they suddenly drop to the ground and then all hell would unleash from their hidden artillery?

'Crew on 1, dismount and intercept. We'll cover you.'

Morton led the way. It surprised me how agile he was and, considering what had happened to our commander, how cavalier. Despite this, he couldn't prevent the sigh of an old man as he dropped onto the ground.

We all carried Stens, our battalion's machine gun of choice, and made some hasty safety checks. These guns were famous for their unreliability; stories of how they burst into unexpected life soon became folklore. After a thumbs-up from Tony, who was braver than me, he went next. We aimed our feet next to Morton's landing spot.

'Okay, folks, this is our first face-to-face with the Krauts. Let's see what the bastards have to offer.' This comment came from the other tank's commander. Morton acknowledged it with a clenched fist.

The Germans were moving quickly and we could see their features more clearly now. They all looked significantly older than us except for the determined-looking officer in front. He had the white flag and was at least half their age.

'Don't be deceived,' muttered Tony.

I agreed; although they looked messy and unfit in long grey-green coats and oversized helmets, they also looked mean.

'Polish or Russian. Not sure. Could be PoWs,' spluttered Morton, now both agitated and excited. 'The one in front is different. He's SS.' Due to his bulbous red nose, which now seemed to be glowing, we later nicknamed Morton 'Big Nige'.

'Follow me, ladies.' His order, girly and high-pitched, failed to disguise his nerves. Above a row of yellow teeth, Big Nige had one of those loose-looking faces with no chin and slack jowls. Heavy bags of skin underneath his eyes made him a dead ringer for Clement Freud's dog-food bloodhound, Henry. Some might say that with those muddled teeth Tombstone might have been a better name.

His was a complete contrast to the face about to greet us. The enemy officer stood to attention as his men shuffled to a faltering stop behind him. He was a tall, good-looking man with the customary Germanic blond hair and blue eyes. He was also far too relaxed for my liking.

'*Hande hoch. Hande hoch.*' Big Nige gestured with his gun. His mock Jerry accent was so surreal it made me smile.

Initially, the men hesitated because they had to drop their weapons first to obey this command, but then the rifles thudded onto the ground one by one. I chuckled; the scene playing out could have easily been lifted from an episode of *Dad's Army*. Was this really happening?

'Karabiner 98ks,' said Tony. The stocks were made of walnut, shiny and looked new. These rifles were popular, together with the Gewehr 98/40; we would see them a lot in the campaign ahead.

All but one of the soldiers obeyed Morton's order and, with sad reality restored, my grin soon returned to its usual grimace.

'I am an officer of the German army and demand that I keep my firearm,' said their leader without fear. His men liked that.

'Drop your fucking gun. NOW!' My response surprised everyone, probably me the most.

Without moving his head, the officer's focus shifted to me. A distinctive badge on the collar of his tunic confirmed he was indeed in the notorious combat branch of the Nazi Party's Schutzstaffel organisation. I would be in trouble if this situation flipped around. On the front of his black cap, a formidable Waffen SS skull stared my way, too. Simply translated, that badge meant 'dead person's head'.

'You heard him, Twinkle Toes.' Morton's attention had been drawn to the officer's immaculately polished jackboots. His greatcoat was unfastened and fell to about shin height. Peeking out from beneath his tailored waistcoat was the unmistakable butt of a pistol. 'And I'll have that big boy.'

I knew immediately what it was. Although Walther P38s were standard German issue, this gun was a Luger. The officer had his arms crossed, blocking access to it, a bold move that gave his men confidence. Slowly, they started to spread out and retreat. These soldiers were not Waffen SS; their uniforms were different and certainly not designed by Hugo Boss like his. They were probably the Wehrmacht's regular army.

'And don't you fucking move.' I switched my attention back to the group, softening my tone though it still had an edge that worried them.

'Any more surprises? Let's have them now… *Bitte.*'

Directing the muzzle of my Sten towards the group, I realised how incredibly ballsy a gun in your hands can make you feel; however, this confidence disappears when you realise that the safety catch is off.

They did not move. Maybe they knew about Sten guns, or perhaps the 37mm tank cannon worried them more? The officer nodded and soon handguns piled onto the rifles.

What came next chilled me. Most of the knives had standard six-inch blades but size mattered because the more significant the reveal, the meaner they looked. King of the pile was a two-foot-long machete with a red-leather handle. Its blade was not the primary revelation but its owner. If you'd had to guess the boy's age, his two-sizes-too-big uniform would have put him at a generous sixteen. He was almost cherub-like; despite the pubescent giveaway of pox-ravaged skin, King's College choir would have welcomed him.

'And what do we have here, Adolph?' The voice was terse and belonged to our de facto troop commander from the other tank. Shoving me to one side, he blundered towards the waiting officer.

Sergeant Billy Moxton was the same height as the tall German but had the stature of a bull. Telly 'who loves you baby' Savalas, the iconic lollypop-sucking detective, could have been his twin. Like Kojak, his head was buffed and shiny, but a Mohican strip of bleached white hair ran down the middle. It was like looking at a punk from the 1970s, and I didn't know whether to laugh or cry.

Clean-shaven heads were not unusual in the war, especially within the American marine and paratrooper ranks. It had nothing to do with style or fashion, just the practicalities of being able to make running repairs to head injuries on the battlefield.

I wondered if the bleached strip was a zip to his brain, if indeed he had one. A private thought, of course. Moxton's look was all about intimidation and it worked, but who was it meant for: them or us? And I had another question: how the hell had he become a tank commander?

He leaned in close and scrutinised the thumbnail-sized gold pip stitched onto the officer's shoulder. Admittedly his look of disdain entertained me. 'Why is an obersturmführer,' Moxton turned my way, which was unnerving, 'a lieutenant to you and me, leading a rabble of shit like this?' He spoke slowly, his voice a loud Cockney baritone.

'No idea, sir,' I replied, not far off falsetto.

'This idiot is SS.' He turned dramatically to the others. 'But these buffoons are Wehrmacht.'

Gesturing towards the group, the wanker sign he made with his wrist made them fidget while their boss remained still. With arms crossed like an impatient mother, his broad toothy smile alarmed me.

'Something funny, Fritz?' Moxton asked.

The German remained impassive; he didn't reply, but he did start to chuckle. In a blur of movement, Moxton stepped forward, chopped the man's arms down with his fist and fumbled inside his black coat. 'Who's a naughty, NAUGHTY Kraut, then?'

There was the Luger again. I heard a loud crack as the sergeant's elbow smashed into the German's face. The man stumbled back holding his jaw, but although badly stunned he remained steady on his feet.

Slowly, with composure restored, the German straightened up. His smile was worrying enough but what intrigued me and made it worse was his desperate attempt to suppress his laughter.

'Still find it funny, my son?' Moxton was not smiling.

A streak of blood seeped from the officer's nose and ran down the side of his chin onto the lapel of his tunic. The ferocity of the blow and his reaction to it suggested that things were about to get out of hand. I felt the urge to say something; I was not sure exactly what, but someone had to step in.

'I love the sport of killing pigs. Especially English ones.' No intervention was needed; the German had saved me. Another tumbleweed moment followed.

'Do you now?' Moxton nodded.

'*Ja*. Like the pigs over there.' He pointed to our mannequin men. At this point, any of us with misplaced sensitivities quickly binned them as we waited to see our leader's next move.

It didn't take long. Moxton nodded and slowly traced the barrel of his Sten gun up the middle of the German's torso, stopping at his throat. 'English pigs, eh?'

'*Ja. Fette schweine.*'

Without warning, the officer made a grab for the gun. It spat into life, and the unexpected *rat-tat-tat* blast of sound was brief and terrifying. As the front of his coat shredded into a red mush of fabric and flesh, he twisted away and collapsed to the ground in a dramatic, movie-like fall. His knees went first, followed by the rest of his body as it convulsed into jerky fits.

No one moved or said anything until Moxton unlocked the moment. 'Blimey, these guns have a life of their own?' He flicked the safety catch back on and looked at us. Was it shock or denial that masked his face?

Then he said something that startled us all. 'Now bugger off. Our boys will pick you up later.' He pointed over the heads of the Germans towards the bluff. Not one of them moved as they continued to stare at the twitching remains of their officer.

'Watch my lips,' I said. 'Fuckinzee offen. Pronto.'

King's Choir knife-boy was the first to go. Hesitant at first, his initial steps soon turned into a foot-spinning Woody Woodpecker cartoon sprint.

'There is, of course, an alternative, you know.' The sergeant looked at the remaining German troops who remained frozen to the spot and then back at his Sten, which was still leaking wafts of blue smoke. He stroked it suggestively.

'Jesus, sir.' Morton took a half-step forward.

The Germans turned and frantically scrambled up the sandy mound out of sight. 'Look at them go,' jeered Moxton. His attention was now on Big Nige. 'The gun just went off, ' he shrugged innocently. 'It's not my fault, honestly.'

Tony, who had been unusually quiet, shuffled alongside me. Standing in a row like naughty schoolboys, we waited as our sergeant scanned us, seeking acknowledgement. We didn't say anything; no one dared challenge him. He could be right; these guns had a mind of their own. We also knew the likely truth.

'So that's going in my report then. Understood?'

We nodded and made feeble attempts to ignore what had just unfolded. Weirdly, Nigel began to whistle the 'Skye Boat Song', whilst I undid my bootstraps and fiddled with them. Tony hummed along out of tune and nodded stupidly. He flicked a freshly lit cigarette onto the sand and promptly lit another.

It was then that I realised the need for some serious headspace; this dream was way out of control.

'Okay, boys. Fill your boots.' The other crew had been invisible until their boss beckoned them over. They jumped down from their tank and strolled over, oblivious to the example set by our commander. Seemingly cloned from their unconventional leader, and like bizarre characters from Cirque du Soleil, their appearance was terrifying. These men were not scavengers; they were consummate professionals; as they made considered selections from the weapons on offer, we watched them closely and learned.

'Don't be shy, boys. Tuck in.' Moxton gestured expansively towards the carpet of loot and lit the stubby end of a cigar. I carefully stepped over the dead officer whose pistol's safety catch was off. *So, he would have used it*, I thought.

No one seemed to want the gun so, making it safe, I slipped it into my thigh pocket. My Webley 38, strapped to my chest to prevent snagging, would have to stay in its holster for now. Apart from the kudos of a Luger, the real advantage was that they fired the same nine-calibre bullets. 'Very useful, this multi-cultural ammo,' I said.

Moxton looked up and nodded. 'Yep, it's great killing the bastards with their own, believe me.' I believed him.

It felt strange to have two pistols in my armoury, and how to accommodate them both was a nice problem. General 'Bandito'

31

Patton from the US 3rd Army famously wore his on his hips like John Wayne. A lovely temptation, but I was no four-star general.

Without a flicker of emotion, Moxton removed the dog tags from our mannequin men and announced that they would be buried in the morning. He did the same for the SS officer, putting his tag into a small khaki bag resembling a trophy bag. At his command, and without question, we mounted up.

Laager is an old Afrikaans word for 'protective wagon circle', a holding position, and ours was about ten miles away. The other two tanks from our recce troop soon re-joined us and confirmed that the elite Panzer Lehr training division was very close; evidently, their day had been as eventful as ours; in collaboration with a troop of roving Shermans, five Panzer 1Vs were engaged.

'And two "brewed up",' said one of the commanders when asked about the score. Radio banter ping-ponged backwards and forwards while we shared our highlights, and the mood became more upbeat when we knew that none of us had encountered any casualties. That is, apart from the mannequin men, which tempered any homeward-bound euphoria.

Because the journey back to base was uneventful, it gave me my craved-for headspace. It was a time to think about the reality of my situation: death here was a real deal, for sure. I had seen it close up in all its graphic detail. The pounding in my ears and my other senses of touch, taste and smell confirmed that a full sensory house had been achieved that day.

Horrendous as this incredibly dark place was, I also found a paradox; the exhilarating muddle gave me an incredible high. Excitement and fear combined can make a potent cocktail. I also knew there was a war to navigate if I was to return home to my everyday life. My priority had to be survival.

Today had been our brigade's first significant contact with the Boche. I chuckled, remembering one of Pop's well-worn clichés: 'I've never cared about Germans beating us at our national game because we've beaten them at theirs – twice.'

And today, it was 1–0 to us!

From Peter Meadows' memoirs

We had got mixed up between several convoys landing at various beaches. By the last light on June 9th 1944, we were all harboured safely. The 44th Royal Tank Regiment was part of the 4th Independent Armoured Brigade and unfortunately Brigadier Curry was killed during the landing. He was replaced by Brigadier Carver, at twenty-eight years old the youngest brigadier in the British army.

That evening, we were concentrated in a village called Amblie. I forgot to mention that the first tank off the LST (Landing Ship Tank) completely disappeared underwater, so we had to sit and wait for the tide to go out. So ended our first day in Europe.

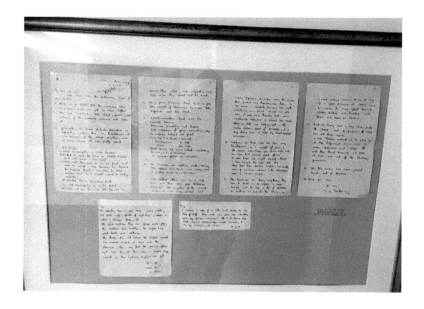

1. *General Montgomery's letter to his Chief of Staff, June 9th 1944. This is on display at Muckleburgh Military Collection, Norfolk. A translated copy can be seen at the end of the book*

My dear Simbo

You may like the following news of our battle

1. There is no doubt that the Germans were surprised, and we got on shore before they had recovered. The speed, power, and violence of the assault carried all before it.

2. Generally, the beach obstacles presented no difficulty; where they were troublesome it was because of the rough weather — and on some beaches it was pretty rough.

3. D.D. Tanks
   (a) Used successfully on UTAH beaches.
   (b) Failed to reach the shore on OMAHA beaches and all sank — too rough.
   (c) Were not launched on 50 DIV front as it was too rough; were landed "dry" behind the leading flights; casualties to 9 TRE sappers high as a result, and to leading infantry.
   (d) Landed "dry" on Canadian front.
   (e) Used successfully on 3 DIV front.
   Generally it can be said that the DD tanks

proved their value, and casualties were
high when they could not be used.

4. As a guess prisoners about 6000 so far.
They consist of Germans, Russians, Poles,
Japanese, and two Turks.

5. British casualties about 1000 per
assault Division.
American casualties not known.
High propation of officer casualties, due
to sniping behind our front.
Two Inf Bde Comds wounded.
   Cunningham   9 Bde
   Senior   151 Bde
Good many Inf C.O.s killed, including
HERDON, O.C. 2 Warwicks.
No general officers are casualties.

6. The Germans are fighting well; Russians,
Poles, Japanese, and Turks, run away, and
if unable to do so, surrender.

7. Our initial attack was on a wide
front, and there were gaps between
landways. The impetus of the assault
carried us some way inland and

many defended localities were by passed, these proved very troublesome later. In one case a complete German Bn, with artillery, was found inside 50 Div area; it gave some trouble but was eventually collected in (about 500 men). There is still one holding out — the radar station west of DOUVRES; it is very strong and is held by stout-hearted Germans.

8. Sniping in back areas has been very troublesome, as a result of para 7. The roads have been far from safe and we have lost several good officers. I have been all night myself, though I have toured the area all day. There have been women snipers, presumably wives of German soldiers; the Canadians shot 4 women snipers.

9. The Germans are doing everything they can to hold on to CAEN. I have
   . decided not to have a lot of casualties by butting up against the place; so

I have ordered second Army to keep up a good pressure at CAEN, and to make its main effort towards VILLERS BOCAGE and EVRECY and thence S.E. towards FALAISE

10. First US Army had a very sticky party at OMAHA, and its progress at UTAH has not been rapid.
I have therefore ordered it to join up its two lodgement areas and to secure CARENTAN and ISIGNY. It will then thrust towards LA HAYE DU PUITS and cut off the Cherbourg peninsula.

11. The two armies have now joined hands east of BAYEUX.

No time for more.

Yrs. ever

B. L. Montgomery

P.T.O.

P.S.

The country here is very nice; green fields; very good crops; plenty of vegetables, cows, cattle, chickens, ducks, etc.

The few civilians there are appear well fed; the children look healthy, the people have good boots and clothing.

The locals did not believe the British would ever invade France or come over the Channel; they say that the German officers and men thought this also — which may account for the tactical surprise we got.

B. L. M.

0900 hrs
9 June

P.S.

I enclose a copy of a letter sent today to my chief of staff. This will give you my situation and my future intentions. It is of course very secret; please acknowledge receipt personally to me by wireless — of M SEC

B L M

Taking Stock

D-Day was eleven days old. Like recent mornings, I expected to wake up in another life, the safe and untarnished one. Holed up in a field bordering onto a village called Amblie, the churn inside my gut and a nauseous recognition told me something entirely different.

Things, circumstances – everything had changed. Holiday brochures might boast words like 'Amblie, a quintessential, sleepy French hamlet tucked away in beautiful Normandy', but these were not regular times.

Thin plumes of grey smoke twirled into an overcast light, a depressing consequence of earlier Allied bombing sorties. And the smoke was different: it didn't come from carefully tended bonfires carrying the sweet fragrance of burnt garden clippings; this was the by-product of stinking, rotting flesh, human and animal, and it overwhelmed me. I found a name for it immediately: *putrification*.

We had seen the occasional animal carcass fizz and pop in the summer heat, and one soldier – we thought he was German – squashed to a pulp by the grinding tracks of heavy armour. Our tanks, their tanks, it made no difference. The utter horror, and the rancidity of decomposing matter lingering in the air like a cloud of death, would impregnate our memories forever. It was yet another stark reminder of what the clumsiness of war does to humanity.

Whilst the 'warm-up' bombing did an excellent job devastating the coastal towns of Normandy, the retreating German infantry and Panzer Lehr divisions also left their mark as they bulldozed and bullied an escape route away from the advancing invaders. Amblie was in the way and took the hit as both sides blitzed her in the mayhem of those early days. Her old, once-invincible buildings continued to smoke and steam as she lay mortally wounded almost two weeks after the first Allied onslaught.

A message to myself: 'Serious thinking time, big boy. Time to sort things out.' One minute I'm on a pilgrimage in my father's memory; the next, it's 1944, and I'm on a beach in France.

I looked around for anything familiar, something to give me hope. From my vantage point, a lump of military metal called a tank, it didn't look good. I could only see high hedges and a smattering of battle debris. Worse was that smell, so intense that it made me retch.

An orchard full of apple trees surrounded me, which was okay – but where was the fruit? I watched as wasps agitated from branch to leaf; they seemed as confused as me. Apart from their angry buzzing, the only discernible sound was an unmistakable *kraak* of sporadic gunfire in the distance.

'How the hell did I get here?' Each question prompted another: 'And why?'

My body felt utterly wasted and something peculiar was happening to my hands again: the tremors. To steady them, I had them wedged underneath my chin by my knees. The drive wheel of our tank was a good place for this and I curled up in a protective human ball against it.

I thought about the beach episode and our dead soldiers, our lieutenant's evisceration, the German escapade and Sergeant Billy Moxton. There was a lot to think about.

Officially, my nightmare had started sometime during our reconnaissance deployment on Sword Beach. From my dad's memoirs, I'd read about losing a tank as it drove off a landing ship into the sea. Although the water was shallow enough to disembark safely, this one dropped straight into a submerged bomb crater and sank like a stone.

Apart from that, and the knowledge Pop had landed on D-Day +3, there was little else I could draw on for now. Like the fuzzy white noise of the TV test card in the old days, my mind was in scrambled overdrive.

My eyes felt like frozen marbles; the only way to ease the pain was to keep them away from daylight – hiding them beneath the rim of my regimental beret helped. I also needed sunglasses like Wolfie's, but finding some was a task for later.

Moxton and his crew came to mind again. What the hell was that about? Thank God they were nowhere to be seen because I was about to enter into a conversation with myself. 'Think, man … fucking think.' Hugging my knees helped me to rationalise. 'So, what do I know?'

The answer was simple: nothing. Even better: 'What do I *think* I know?' That was a far more difficult question to answer.

As ridiculous as it seemed, I had found myself transported back seventy-five years in time. That was the easy bit. I allowed myself a brief chuckle at the memory that I had never appreciated the movie *Back to the Future*, and my two sons had ridiculed me ever since. But living in the future and dropping back in time, my predicament now seemed absurdly similar.

I chose the following words carefully: 'Calum, son of Peter, finds himself trapped inside his late father's body.' Explain that one to a psychiatrist. And what about 6' 2" into 5' 4"?

I bit my gloved fingers and thought of Herbert Lom in the Pink Panther films. Like him, I'd gone mad. Few answers, more questions, and they kept on coming.

Although I was in complete control of my mobility, expressing anything related to my real life seemed impossible. I could not articulate anything related to my life or any date between 2019 and June 17th 1944.

'The future hasn't happened so am I sitting in the past, in history?' This was another rhetorical question. I wanted to scream.

The watch. Glancing down at my wrist, I recognised it instantly. Worn by my father for most of my life, now battered and tired, it had lived in our kitchen drawer. I rubbed my thumb over its face; it looked new and the time said 5.15. That made it 7.15 French time, double-bubble BST. Churchill had added an extra hour to help maximise our daylight activities. Like so much in the Normandy campaign, this was clever. I pulled out the winder and moved the big hand forward.

There was something else: my father's gold signet ring. It was a coming-of-age present from his parents one month before D-Day, and it had been on my right pinkie for the last two years. Today, it was sitting on the second finger of my left hand.

The physical evidence of this change frightened me, plus the fact that I knew important stuff but couldn't articulate it. Hitler, for starters. He had committed suicide in a Berlin bunker, and the war in Europe ended victoriously for the Allies on May 8th 1945 – next year in my new time. And what of Hitler? The men around me only knew him as the tyrannical Nazi leader; the truth of the Holocaust and stories from the death camps would come later.

On August 6th, a nuclear bomb snuffed out the Japanese. I smiled, not at that, but apparently my formidable ex-mother-in-law was in Hiroshima at the time. The Japanese finally surrendered on September 2nd; if she had influenced that in any way, it would not have surprised me!

So the old man had survived, evidenced by his son who was now sitting on a tank in Normandy in the summer of 1944. 'That makes me safe?' It was sadly a misguided direction of travel for my newfound positivity. 'Alive, yes – but in France in 1944?'

I scrambled to my feet and methodically brushed down my denim overalls as if I were grooming a horse. This distraction gave me time to straighten my thinking. They were olive green and covered in a patchwork of zips and pockets. I noticed mine were turned up at the ankles like all the other little guys around me.

'Hallucination? That's it. I'm hallucinating.' I'd not done that for a while. 'Or is it some sort of coma?'

Desperation returned, and something else came to mind: sleep paralysis. As an occasional sufferer of this condition, could it be that? Best described as an out-of-body experience, it usually kicked in at some point between consciousness and sleep, and was always terrifying. The scary bit was that you were awake when it happened but paralysed and unable to talk or move. I had to make another weird assessment: could this be a form of sleep paralysis ramping up the fear factor scale?

It seemed ridiculous to do it, but a childish pinch-punch check told me I was alive. I could walk freely into the neat, square cornfield behind us (which was probably not a good idea) and nothing would physically stop me.

As I considered my next move, an early sunset bounced off the gentle slope leading up to a tall row of trees in the distance. The view would have been stunning on a typical day in any normal life, but today it masked a sinister truth: it was a potential killing field.

A gentle breeze caressed the copper-coloured barley beards; they were ready for harvest and I wondered if that would happen. Would the heavy blink of war ever reopen its eyes to allow farms like these to work again?

Thick bocage about ten feet high surrounded this field like all the others we'd seen recently. On the face of it, the fields seemed benign but the real story was different. No controlling force would stop me if I decided to move that way; however, a sniper's bullet, a land mine or a spray from an MG42 would probably blend me into a warm mush of mince and bone first. This was the reality, and I had to accept it.

First, though, a test was needed.

Tony and I fiddled over two Tommy cookers precariously balanced on an ammunition box. Health and safety considerations seemed ironic, given what we had witnessed in the last twenty-four hours. In an attempt to boil up yet another brew, the procedure thus far had been frustrating – literally a slow burn.

Our ten-man compo ration pack, minus tea, lay half-open beside us, providing most tank crews with two days' rations. The first out was always tea. A 'nice cuppa' with powdered milk had fast become our staple drink, and 'brewing up' in the conventional sense helped calm the nerves. Forget about chain-smoking; everyone seemed to do that anyway; hardcore tea drinking was the primary recreation in our tank regiment.

'Where's the Earl Grey?' I wondered. No one else would have understood.

Tommy stoves were solid-fuel burners similar to a baked-bean can on a base. After lighting a candle-like fuel block and balancing your billy can onto a circular rim attachment placed over it, you waited patiently. With luck, no wind and some gentle coaxing, the water eventually boiled.

These gadgets had another purpose: often they were our only heat source. We had been told not to expect a cook's kitchen, so the balls' ache of using these things to warm our rations would be in play for the next few days. We soon learned that, despite a diet of salt beef, potatoes and onion, life in the tank core would always be hungry.

'*Dark Side of the Moon* is the best album ever.' This got my first test underway; I could think of it, but I could not physically make that statement because it was in the future. I felt foolish and tried again. Not a squeak.

'Boris Johnson is a genius.' Good one. The same thing happened; Boris was contemporary to my real life. Perhaps that controversial word 'genius' was the real problem here? I needed to find another angle.

'Gracie Fields is a sex goddess.' And bingo; that lady, alive in 1944, worked. The conviction of my statement worried me, though, and Tony stared at me in a state of what can only be described as horrified perplexity.

My co-driver, bow gunner and Wolfie-lookalike, shook his head grimly. 'Fuck off, Pete. Are you a complete twot or what?'

Twot? The vowel would have been replaced in my other life, and my son Dom liked to up the ante and doubled up the word to make a new one, 'twunt'! How tame were 'nitwit', 'silly billy' and 'twit', other so-called derogatory phrases used by the men around me now? In a world of constant death and despair, that made me laugh.

Rummaging through a patchwork of pockets, Wolfie eventually found what he was looking for: a Zippo lighter. He flicked it open and lit up.

After a time of considered reflection, Pop would have agreed with what he said next. 'Hedy Lamarr.' There was a short pause while he took another lung-busting drag on his cigarette. 'Yep, Hedy Lamarr without question. Great tits.' He slapped me on the shoulder, picked up his brew and wandered off.

Tony was a wiry, shifty-looking man, a proper geezer type. His narrow shoulders were hunched to his neck, and greasy strands of black hair protruded from underneath his beret. With his customary dark shades discarded, I could see his restless dark eyes; they confirmed two things: Citizen Smith must have been modelled on him, and also Walker from *Dad's Army*!

I studied my surroundings more closely. Everyone seemed diminutive compared to my other life, and nothing emphasised this better than our tankie overalls, which looked like sacks on the lads hidden beneath them.

Then came a more disturbing revelation: I should have towered over these guys, but evidently I didn't. I seemed to have shrunk twelve inches. My feet confirmed this because they and the ground supporting them seemed worryingly close for the first time.

Any other surprises? Slipping off a glove, I ran a hand over my face. A moustache: that was normal, but it was more pronounced than my usual closely strimmed one. My fingers moved up to my head and discovered something else: backcombed, waxed hair. I had never done that, ever.

'Mirror, get me a mirror!' I called.

Tony huffed and strolled towards his kitbag perched on the back deck of our tank. 'You big poof.' He lobbed a chrome-framed travel mirror up to me. 'Don't break it, you ugly bastard.'

It was one of those small round mirrors that spun round. I flipped it over, wiped away some condensation and looked down. Instead of a fair-haired man of sixty-one with a white goatee beard looking back at me, it was someone else.

It was my father's lookalike. 'Jesus Christ.'

'I told you. Ugly as fuck.'

The man in my reflection had Brylcreemed black hair, dark skin and a silly Errol Flynn-style moustache. It looked like my dad. I *was* my dad!

Like many short men, Pop was always self-conscious about his height though, unlike an old sales manager who sprang to mind, he never had small-man syndrome. We called him Herr Flick, a character from the 1980s TV programme *Allo! Allo!* His real name was Alun Jones; he was from Cardiff and he limped. The paradox of this and my current situation made me smile.

'Peter is the name you were born with, so Peter is what we shall call you.' That was his response to my explanation that, although I'd been christened Peter, everyone called me by my middle name, Calum.

Nothing demonstrated better the kind of whiny, Welsh-wanker Jones was than the floor-length black-leather coat he wore over his shoulders like a cape. Presuming to be some sort of superhero, his look was designed to impress; it didn't, of course, and we mocked him ruthlessly. Even his faux-patent leather winklepickers squeaked as he scurried around our sales office in North Hampstead.

'Time is money and money is time. Let's not waste it.' This well-used cliché was cringeworthy enough, but he had better ones than that in his vast armoury. There was one he found weirdly hysterical: 'Have you noticed that all the people favouring birth control are already born?'

It had no relevance to anything at all. Nonetheless, it was surprisingly philosophical for Alun Jones and, as it happens, proved ironic in the end. Everyone knew he was shagging the MD's secretary including, it turned out, the MD. How she got pregnant was one of life's mysteries and almost the sole topic of conversation around the Klix vending machine. It probably still is. An immaculate misconception was one of our more polite assessments. Miraculous conception, more like. Soon Jones left the business in a flurry of packing crates and a blur of flapping coat tails. No one cared and there was no leaving party because he was one of life's dicks – a short one – and I think he knew it.

The other thing about short men can be their vanity. I wouldn't say my father was overly vain, but he looked after his body and jokingly referred to it as 'my temple'. He was not classically good-looking, certainly not in the Clark Gable mould, which was probably his generation's benchmark icon. Pop's look was more mischievous and rugged than handsome.

He was powerfully built and displayed what he liked to think of as a Mr Universe, Charles Atlas physique. Old black-and-white snaps depict a man trying desperately hard not to pose and failing badly. With tummy muscles clenched and sun-tanned chest thrust out, snug-fitting Speedos completed the horrific picture!

In my mid-teens, my father bought me a muscle-building device called a bull worker. This thoughtful gift was a physique-enhancing contraption with what can only be described as two thick elastic bands attached to either end. 'Designed to develop muscles that no woman can resist,' he said proudly, winking at my mother.

The blurb on the box stated this fact, and they were all the rage in the 1970s. Perhaps all my father wanted to do was to encourage his gangly teenage son in this vital aspect of growing up but, whatever his motivation, it didn't work. Muscles never came, nor did the women.

Excellent physique aside, Pop firmly believed that 'being small', as he ruefully put it, hindered him in life. 'Tall men are more successful,' he would state as a matter of absolute fact.

'Define success, Pop.' Of course, there were never any absolute facts, and I found it sad that he thought this way. I often wondered what sort of boss he would have made in corporate life: in my experience, probably a pretty good one.

Something else occurred to me: everyone here was young. At a guess, most were in their late teens or early twenties. Pop's birthday was on May 4th 1923, so it made me – him – only twenty-one. He must have celebrated his coming of age at Perham Down training camp in Wiltshire. Shrouded by thoughts of war and uncertainty, and immersed in the fallout from an already disintegrating marriage, what a strange celebration it must have been. Like his comrades, he didn't know what they were training for; he only knew that it was something big and about to happen very soon.

For a married man and new father, the saying 'the world is your oyster' would have required serious scrutiny. Pop's emotions must have been in turmoil, a mixture of fear, excitement and duty. And should they survive whatever lay ahead, their attitude had to be positive. It was easy for Pop because his glass was always half full. 'Everything was possible,' he used to say. 'The future was a blank canvas for all of us.'

All they hoped for was survival and that it was not a blank canvas body bag greeting them at the end.

Operation Overlord kicked in twenty-four hours late on June 6th 1944, and it would be the start of their journey.

My coming of age had been different: safe and traditional. Lots of booze, mainly lager and lime with vodka chasers, and some wacky baccy to help things along. We were on a converted car ferry in the Shetland Islands, the *Stena Baltica,* moored alongside an oil refinery construction site called Sullom Voe. North Sea oil flowed copiously in those days, together with loads of money, and I was living the dream.

My only concerns and responsibilities were insignificant compared to Pop's generation, who were training for war. For me, being a young man was about having fun and wasting money, simple as that. For example, could I make enough dosh to upgrade my trusty Mini to a lime-green Ford Cortina GXL with a black-vinyl roof?

Love also featured, so there were critical questions about an engagement ring and my stag do to consider—Clacton or Sunny Hunny? Clacton was my favourite because it had Butlin's. But as beautiful and intense as most romantic first loves are, mine was fragile and temporary; when it ended, Mum fussed, and Pop said little.

A blue sun strip on the windscreen of my 'little old NAR', the car's first three registration letters, affirmed another love: Radio Caroline. Forty-plus years later, it still is.

Life did have its adolescent complications but it was a doddle; how depressingly shallow and easy our lives were compared to those of my father and his contemporaries.

The year was 1979 and Pink Floyd's seminal album *Dark Side* had already been around for six years. Sitting cross-legged between two strategically placed speakers and listening to this mystical music 'stereo' backwards and forwards was my ultimate pleasure. Music for me is uplifting, mood making and medicinal. This record ticked all the boxes and was nothing less than sacred. Years later, the fusty smell and memories of my youth still tumble out whenever I slide the record from its sleeve. Life then was simple, just fun, money and Floyd. How perfect was that?

My father was not a great music fan before he met Mum but, like most departing troops, he listened and danced to Benny Green and Joe Loss's tunes, among others. Ivy Benson and Her All Girls Band would have been another. But this was before Mum's time with them and before he heard her sing in the flesh.

Pop liked movies, and before embarkation for Normandy he and his buddies watched films such as *Melody Inn* and *The Fighting Sullivans.* In the early days of the war, cinemas were closed to prevent negative propaganda from infiltrating a nervous and unsettled population. In later years, this ruling was reversed to help improve the confidence of our Blitzed people instead.

The booming rumble of artillery fire broke the moment. How far away, and to whom it belonged, we couldn't tell. Although

50

like muffled thunder without the warning flash of lightning, it still made me jump.

It was not a chilly day but the erratic sounds of war brought an involuntary shiver, and a quick look around confirmed that the other guys were feeling equally unnerved. Nearly all of them were either lighting up or flicking away half-smoked cigarettes; some even had two on the go. I saw one poor trooper puke into his billy can, and the overarching smell of vomit, excrement and cigarette smoke hung in the air like an adult creche without the Pampers.

From the direction of the gunfire, I saw coils of black smoke curled up over Caen, ten miles southwest of our position. Retrieving a stubby blue pencil parked behind my ear, I marked the proposed route and destination on our map. Knowing this was essential as a driver, I made a mental note, too. Wouldn't it have been great to hear that infuriating, much-maligned American voice again? Sat-nav technology seemed so long ago.

'We'll harbour here tonight, but be ready to mount up at 05.30 hours,' was our next order from the boss.

The expressions 'harbour' and 'mount up' made me smile; anything to do with a harbour meant boats to me, not a place for overnight tank parking. 'Mount up' was usually heard in Westerns; more recently, in the war film *Fury*, American tank commander Brad Pitt gave this order a lot – and annoyingly from a Firefly, which only the British had! The film's depiction of tank warfare did have poignancy, though; its location would soon be one of ours.

Our new commander was a lump of a man named 'Buffalo Bill' Turner. His predecessor, more chump than a lump, seemed relieved. 'Phew, survived that, then,' was all Big Nige said. He knew that being the man on top meant sticking your head above the parapet, and with that came a death sentence. The average life of a tank commander in Europe was short, and in certain battle zones, it was only about two weeks. Buff Turner had been a Desert Rat in the African campaign, breaking the mould in this respect.

It was difficult to gauge his age because most of his vast moon face was hidden behind a bushy black beard, but I guessed he was somewhere in his early forties. His head was shaved, and long whiskers just touched his chest, giving him a Moxton look; they were also ridiculously trendy and could have graced the cover of any fashion magazine in modern times.

Experienced, scary and stylish maybe, but he also looked battle-worn and tired. When he gave the order to mount up, his voice had a deep weariness. Our reply was more energetic, and he flashed me a cursory glance: 'Seen it all before' was my clichéd assessment. His eyes betrayed him and he slapped me firmly on the shoulder before turning away. Why he did this I don't know – maybe he felt a connection – but it felt good.

We were in the 44th Royal Tank Regiment, part of the 4th Armoured Brigade known as the Black Rats and part of the 7th Armoured Desert Rats. In years gone by, my reconnaissance troop would have been in the cavalry and riding along on horses, not in four bucking lumps of angry metal.

Three fighting squadrons, A, B and C, made up the rest of our battalion, and each had five troops of three Sherman M4s and one British-adapted super tank, the Firefly. An M4 fitted with a decent-sized seventeen-pounder was jammed into its turret to cope with our enemy's superior firepower. As one of many stories goes, the enemy tanks liked to watch as our shells bounced off them like tennis balls!

Our commanding officer, Lieutenant Colonel Gerald Charles Hopkinson, based himself at regimental headquarters (RHQ). Alongside him and other senior hoi polloi were the medics, engineers and Captain Huggins, our regimental padre. More about him later.

RHQ had four command tanks, one fixed with a dummy gun to disguise the fact that the CO's frontline office was inside its turret. This was absolute genius. The group included two Churchill heavy tanks and our recce troop.

RHQ's prime role was to direct combat activities and coordinate non-combative resources, such as engineering, ambulances and anything else with wheels. In our regiment, generally called a battalion, echelon groups A and F supported us. These guys were our lifeline and delivered supplies to the frontline.

What of our recce troop, the Wanderers? It was not a bad name – all troops had names – but ours showed little imagination regarding individual tank names. They were merely numbered 1 to 4, and I was the driver for Wanderer 1. Our job, to scout proposed combat areas and report back, was not envied by most.

'Free to roam but exposed and dangerous,' was how Pop had described it to me.

We also had a replacement for the unfortunate Lieutenant Reeves: Captain Freddie Smythe. I'd not met the man but listening to the others, almost predictably, his reputation was that of a 'useless posh toff'.

'Another kid who knows fuck all,' said the ever-eloquent Tony, who also hadn't met him. With interest, I noted that as well as 'knowing fuck all', Smythe was sitting in what had been Moxton's tank.

'And something else,' Tony added. 'He's a bloody dwarf. Jerry will use him as a fucking football.'

Speculating on that point, I reminded myself that the vertically-challenged club now included me as well. And what of the big guy? It had been a short-lived promotion for Moxton; if the jungle drums were beating in time, he and his merry men were now in a frontline Sherman troop.

Our battalion's seventy tanks had spread out on a broad five-mile front. This was good to know and it was also reassuring to hear that two infantry groups were supporting us, although we couldn't see them. We didn't know at the time, but F Battery 4th Royal Horse Artillery and B Company 2nd/60th Kings Royal Rifle Core were going to be our infantry brothers until the end of the war.

Our first combined test was an open secret: Caen. Turner had confirmed this earlier; until then, Amblie was our laager. Hunkered down in a scrubby orchard, the Wanderers were conveniently separated from the rest of the RHQ squadron by a stone-wall-lined brook that meandered through the village.

There were only a few apples in sight, and we soon found out about Calvados. Hungry locals had scrumped the fruit early and everyone seemed to have a stash of this craved-for and exceptionally potent liqueur. Our cigarettes and chocolate rations soon became hard currency to trade for what quickly became our favourite wartime tipple.

I was first introduced to Calvados when I was a chef in the late 1970s. Used in a rich cream sauce to complement a sumptuous pork-loin dish, it had star billing on the à la carte menu, along with Sirloin Steak Dunmow.

Trust House Forte owned the Saracens Head Hotel then; it was a time when melon boats and their sliced orange sails and Black Forest gateaux book-ended the fine-dining extravaganzas of the day. One glug for the pot and at least two for me, that's how I remember Calvados. And just how sumptuous was the pork dish? I can't say because I was usually comatose at the end of a hazy dinner service.

Mixed with petrol fumes and cigarette smoke, Calvados already had a fearsome reputation amongst the guys in Normandy. The high was impressive enough, but the hangover low was one to end them all.

Rumours abounded that we were about to join forces with the Canadians who had arrived on Juno Beach when the Brits landed on Sword Beach. Monty aimed to 'take' the city of Caen within twenty-four hours. Almost two weeks later, that still hadn't happened.

'Now you know how it feels.' The voice was loud and came from behind my left ear. Startling me, it troubled me on two counts: no one was there and worryingly, I recognised the voice immediately.

The only other person in earshot was Auden who was reclining against the mud-caked tracks of our tank, and he was at least ten yards away. Behind him, a plump male blackbird was sitting perfectly still on a bramble bush. Not renowned for talking to humans, his bird song was a surprise given the noise and chaos of the last few days. Profiled against a pastel blue sky, and with a distinctive yellow eye ring to match his beak, I wondered how something so beautiful could want to be here.

I looked around again and tried to source the mystery voice. Nursing another brew, Tony had his head back and eyes closed. Deep in contemplation or sleep, he was definitely not conversing with the blackbird or me.

'Life is harder when you are short.'

'What?'

There it was again: that voice and a strangely familiar statement. Only my father said that, and his voice was unmistakable: always loud with a slightly posh inflexion.

Panicked, I tipped away my brew. It took two attempts to climb onto the back of our tank, which was set in a defensive hull-down position. All the tanks in our recce unit were lined up in a wide but shallow ditch with guns pointing skywards towards the cornfield. Although technically prepared, the enemies' killing range of 2,000 yards versus ours of around 500 made us insignificant.

Pop confirmed this eloquently during one of our chats. 'With our measly 37mm pop-gun up against a Panther's 88mm cannon, we were pissing in the wind.'

The real workhorse in Panzer divisions was the Panzer Mark IV, a fact often overlooked in history books. An immense adversary with its 75mm gun, on a lucky day we matched up to it with our new Fireflies. Nevertheless, demotivating stories of our Honey tank rounds bouncing off them like ping-pong balls were already folklore. But the truth was sometimes different, especially regarding the infamous Tiger 1.

Their reputation had more psychological than physical impact on Allied tank crews because fewer than 2000 were built during the war. A combination of mechanical unreliability and a shortage of skilled operators meant that the number of 'reported' interactions was sometimes overstated. That said, in a head-to-head it was better to be sitting in a Tiger than cowering, scared shitless, in the confines of a paper-thin Sherman M4.

'Pop?' It felt stupid to whisper his name. 'Pop, excuse my French, but what the fuck is going on?' Nothing came back; of course, it didn't.

I was supposedly retired and living in a sleepy village that welcomes its visitors with a quirky sign saying, *Slow You Down*; now I had to work out quickly why things had changed in my life so dramatically.

The plan had been simple enough. On my return from a road trip to France, I would write a book about my father's exploits. As of this moment, my master plan had stalled badly. It was time to re-evaluate.

'Plan on track. Sort of.' A mental tick. 'The difference is I'm there. Here?' The second tick was fainter than the first, and confusion followed. 'So my plan is on track-ish. But I'm in France and it's 1944.'

Badly needing something positive to hook onto, I kept going. And then came the creepiest question of all: 'Am I him?'

Some residue from the waterproofing tape stuck to my backside as I rocked like an ape on my driver's-hatch lid. This motion helped calm me but even Sir David Attenborough, an expert in chimp behaviour, would have been scratching his head right now.

Tony glanced up. 'You okay, mate?'

I nodded. This sudden show of unexpected compassion was temporary. Diverting his attention back to things more important, and with a brew clamped precariously between his knees, Tony lit another cigarette.

Pop's voice again. 'Yes, Calum, it's 1944, and you are in Normandy. This is real, son. I don't understand how, but we've returned in time.'

I let that bombshell sink in. 'So we're in a time warp. I guess that's what he means,' I said out loud.

'Do what?' Tony looked up at me, all sympathy gone. Scrambling to his feet he wandered off, taking a trail of grey cigarette smoke with him. The blackbird was next to go. He had seen enough, too; abandoning me, he left to roost somewhere more peaceful for the night.

'Okay. Maybe you can help me predict things,' I said. Going with the flow was becoming my new strategy.

'Like you, son, I can't explain what hasn't happened.' The voice was there again, deep inside my head.

'But you were in Normandy, Pop?'

'Yes, and we're back there now, together,' he replied.

'So your life has rewound itself and taken me with you?' As I said this, I instantly dismissed it. That theory was too wild; he had been dead for six years.

'Not exactly,' Pop said. 'You bumped your head and somehow found yourself in my WW2 timescape.'

'Go on.'

'Son, to get free you must survive the war like I did.'

Going with the flow had indeed confirmed my insanity, but I did know things about his war. Our old conversations, the months of research and forests of scribbled notes marked with orange highlighter pens logged it all. But at this crucial moment, when I needed it most, I had forgotten everything. All that remained was a fuzzy void.

'And if I don't survive this, Pop?' The question hung in the air like a cricket ball inviting a six.

'Then, Calum, you will never go home.'

Six it was, straight out of the ground.

From Peter Meadows' memoirs

In the big plan, the 4th Armoured Brigade was not to be included in the storming of the beaches; we had been brought in three days later to be thrown against a massive counter-attack which was expected. As we were making a drive over the Odon, we lost one of our recce tanks south of Caen. About this time, five German tanks were spotted. The Fireflies opened up, brewed up two of them and damaged two more.

Intuition

Although there was bright sunshine, reveille at 05.30 hours was never the ideal way to break into another new day. After a fitful night's sleep underneath our tank, the fact we hadn't been called up for guard duty seemed to be a good result. 'Stand to' was in one hour. Morton fussed about on breakfast duty and eventually produced some depressingly tepid tea and a plate of teeth-shattering biscuits.

In a quiet moment I asked Tony, 'Do I talk to myself? You know, in my dreams?'

'You want to get that lump looked at.' There was a modicum of sincerity in his tone. 'We're all hearing voices, mate. It's all a fucking dream.' That eloquent appraisal had to do for now.

We gathered around Wanderer 1 and waited for our orders. With her fuel tank filled to the brim and a maximum load of ammunition and provisions on board, we felt relatively upbeat. The atmosphere around camp was different, though: a lethargy permeated it, and the familiar rumble in my guts reminded me of things to come.

It was similar to the pre-match nerves I experienced playing for Blues Sports in my teens when I claimed to be a goalkeeper. Cup games were the worst, especially against teams in leagues higher than us. While our slick opponents did impressive stretches and flexes in sponsored kits, we jinked around in our 'bank of dad' funded budget strips. No one ran too much either, and senior players liked using my goal mouth as an ashtray rather than wasting energy. As for displaying 'intimidating' ball skills in our warm-ups, I don't remember seeing many. Correction: our centre half was once stretchered off after attempting a Johan Cruyff turn!

In Normandy, we tried to live for the day but worried about the future, which made it an apprehensive time for tank crews. Multiply my pre-match nerves an infinite number of times – that was where we were on days like this. The camp latrine (or trench, to be precise) was never a favourite place to linger on a fight day;

nevertheless, it was the most popular place. The urge for another visit reminded me why.

'Fag, Meadows?' Reassuringly, it was not a statement. Nigel Morton threw a cigarette at me and I caught it under my chin. Having not smoked for years, my agility and speed surprised me when I flipped the cigarette into my mouth. Apparently I was a smoker.

Retrieving a Zippo lighter and a loose Woodbine from my top pocket, I cupped my hands and lit up. It tasted terrific. I inhaled my next drag even more deeply and the hit of smoke in my lungs felt so good that I wondered why I'd ever given up.

As my anxiety subsided and my bowels settled, a large, perfectly formed smoke ring wobbled into the fresh morning air. Like all smokers, I inspected the freshly lit cigarette tip and flicked away some imaginary ash. Life was good.

'Flash cunt.' Big Nige's attempt to copy me failed spectacularly and he gagged instead. 'Shame you can't drive as well as you smoke.'

In the distance, an earnest-looking 'Buff' Turner was slowly approaching. He looked tense, probably because of his orders' conference with the other commanders. O-group meetings agreed on the plans for the day; looking at his face, our day's briefing didn't look promising.

'He wouldn't make a poker player, would he?' moaned Morton. I agreed.

'More like King Kong, who's just lost Fay Wray,' Tony chipped in, referring to the famous scream queen of the screen.

But why would he look happy? For some of us, the next twelve hours would not end well, and Buff knew it.

'Negative, Calum. Think motivation and teamwork,' I said to myself. It would get us through this mess to safety.

'Peter, don't drive like a maniac today,' Buff said. I nodded. 'We do need to get a move on, though.' His reference to Peter annoyed me. I wanted to correct him but I couldn't.

'Something more important on your mind?' My non-reply annoyed him, but then he diverted his attention to the others. 'Come on, chaps, let's get this shit done.' He beckoned us closer and we formed a huddle as he walked us through the grand plan step by step. The proposed order of march was for our troop to lead in column formation, followed by A Squadron and RHQ behind them.

'B Squadron will be on the right flank, C on the left.'

'Like wings,' chimed in Tony.

Buff ignored him. 'Finally, coming up on the rear,' he looked at Tony, 'will be supply echelons of A and F.' Tony kept quiet.

This was a big move, and it came with good news: As the second tank up, we weren't leading the pack. However, the orders substantially changed things for our battalion. Our new objective, to capture the high ground overlooking a village called Cheux, meant we were now at the tail end of Operation Goodwood, Monty's mission to capture Caen. And evidently, with weak intelligence guiding us, there was still one whopping unknown: what of the enemy?

Tony seemed particularly edgy and asked about 'likely resistance'.

'We can expect some Panzer pushback and probably infantry back-up, too. That's all I can say,' Buff replied.

We shuffled and nodded gravely. Panzer resistance meant we had to be on our game; only a shoot-first policy would give us any chance of survival. I threw this into the pot when Turner prompted more questions.

'Exactly right, Meadows, so keep the banter down and use your fucking eyes.' After eye-balling each of us in turn, he continued. 'Listen to my commands, and if I ask you to do something bendy, DO NOT question me. Understand?'

Rules would be broken, and like Pop, I quite liked bending them. But then, so did the other side. Everyone nodded enthusiastically.

My attempt to give the boys a 'high five' fell flat when the briefing concluded. 'Fuck off, Meadows.' They looked at me as if I'd gone bonkers. This modern-day gesture of celebration was unknown in 1944, so we shook hands instead.

The 44th were not alone on this mission. Our newly acquired infantry brothers would deal with the leftovers after our initial softening-up job. Tony called this foreplay.

'More like rough sex,' grumbled Morton because we usually bore the brunt of any artillery fire that came our way. 'We always get it up the arse.'

In a typical scenario, tank battalions were always frustrated because although the infantry wanted us to clear pathways and take the flak, they didn't like tanks anywhere near them. We attracted heavy artillery and occasionally the wrath of aerial attention, too. We couldn't win.

Back to football. Once the referee blew his whistle, the adrenalin kicked in. Today was no different. Like on a match day, it was three o'clock when Buff ordered us to mount up. In no hurry, we clambered on board.

The driver's lid was already open, so I dropped onto my seat. Tony followed suit to my right and we heard the scrape and clump of boots as the guys above wedged themselves into position. Everything inside was cold – it always was – and it ponged horribly: petrol fumes, stale grease and dampness, and the rotten whiff of body odour infused with adrenalin that made us gag, especially in the early days.

'Let us begin,' prompted Buff, sounding like a vicar as he introduced our well-practised start-up drill. It was work time now, and our only thought was the job at hand; cocking things up would endanger the whole team.

The fact that I seemed to know my routine was positive and another surprise because starting up a lawn mower in my real life had always been a struggle.

'Okay, ladies, let's do the radio checks.' Turner went through the well-rehearsed procedure. He re-tuned and checked each of the three frequencies and then, in turn, our connections with him. Unfortunately our radios didn't synchronise with those used by the infantry boys and unless you were lucky and got a connection, there were few ways to correspond with these guys during a battle. We didn't even have carrier pigeons like in the Great War, so hand signals from the turret were the way to go. Thank God that Tony, with his impolite hand gestures, wasn't a tank commander!

For our infantry foot sloggers, communication with us was more heroic: messengers on motorbikes had to race alongside our tank then, gripping jousting poles, they passed notes up to any waiting hand. As battles raged and the terrain became scarred, like in scenes from *Ben Hur* (a film not yet made), a stuntman's bravery was needed to clamber on board.

61

Once the team checks were complete, we carried out our own. I had to test the steering levers and optics, and re-attach the windshield when travelling heads up. Once the engines fired up, the operating levels on my dashboard dials were next. Two engines meant double everything: oil pressure lamps, rev counters, starter motors, and ignition lights were all caked in grime and needed constant cleaning.

Buff gave us another quick summary of the day's plan and told us to start in a hatches-open position. I shoved the transmission stick into neutral and flicked both ignition switches on. 'Ready to go, sir.'

'Then start her up, Meadows.'

Pressing the accelerator pedal gently activated an automatic choke. It was essential to start both motors simultaneously because stalling them would only result in humiliation and ridicule. 'Come on, you beauty.' I pressed the start button.

The parking brake for a Stuart is incorporated into the two steering levers. With no manual gearbox or clutch to worry about, just a light dab of the accelerator got us going. The almighty roar from our twin V8s always impressed us. As this happened, clouds of dust and smoke billowed out from the only tank in front of us, Wanderer 2.

Despite the rules and regulations, any tank in any regiment at this stage would fill up with the smog of swirling cigarette smoke. My day's tally was already at twenty-something. Some doing. 'Twenty. And I'm a non-smoker?' I asked myself.

Our weekly cigarette allocation was one hundred, and occasionally our ration packs had an extra cylinder of fifty squeezed into them. Additional requirements meant using hard-to-get cash, or trading something of greater value. Cigars and American cigarettes were valid currencies but difficult to find.

I flipped a Woodbine into my mouth and fiddled behind the instrument panel for our team's spare Zippo. It was because we had two steering levers to contend with that 'flipping up' and lighting a cigarette one-handed became a skill mastered by most tank drivers.

Looking around, I saw missiles everywhere. A maximum load for us would be about 150 big rounds, plus 7000 for the machine guns. Like Shermans, and depending on the mission, Honeys usually carried equal loads of high explosives (HE) and armour-piercing tracers (APs). As it said on the tin, APs were solid-shot slugs and didn't carry explosives – they punctured through metal, supposedly.

As always, a few smoke bombs and a box of hand grenades were in the mix. There was one critical thing to remember: be careful. Damaged ammunition could be faulty and it would not help anyone's physical or mental well-being if it was sitting on your lap!

It made me think of the expression 'tommy cooker'. Germans had good reason to call Shermans by that name; a combination of wafer-thin armour, live ammunition and petrol meant that, if hit, the light show was generally fantastic. I wondered whether they had a name for our flimsy little Honey, little sister to the Sherman M4.

Stretched out ahead was a single-track road made of grey tarmac. It was in good condition, but with our whole battalion on the move what it would look like in an hour was anyone's guess. The road reminded me of the narrow country lanes I'd learned to drive on. Always proud that sales reps were the best drivers, Pop was my teacher and he taught me some handy, if not life-enhancing, tricks.

Racing lines first: practised on budget cross-ply remoulds, these tyres were legal back then and comprised of rubber strips stuck onto worn-out treads. With Pop's coaching and my lack of road grip, I got from Great Dunmow to home in nine record-breaking minutes. That was before I moved on to more expensive radials after a late-night incident at Duck End Forge, a notorious S-bend with a pond.

The other trick for hard-up students like me was Pop's fuel-saving tip: freewheeling. 'Switch the engine off, son, and cruise.' Modern-day engines would have a fit if asked to do that, and so would I if asked the same question!

Lined up on either side of us was the familiar sight of a tightly packed bocage; tall, green and dense, the secrets hidden behind it usually spoke to us in German.

'Perfect ambush cover,' droned Buff's voice down the intercom. That was lovely to hear, and our necks went into an owl-like contortion mode.

'Meadows, eyes on the road,' came the reminder. 'And mind the gap.' I'd heard that before.

Column formation training had taught us that at all times, at least a seventy-five-yard gap should be maintained between moving tanks. 'Minding the gap, sir.'

We were moving one up, and I could hear B and C Squadrons crashing through the trees on either side of Squadron A directly behind us. According to the manual, leaving a gap made it difficult for us to be hit, another comforting MOD fact. It was the one rule that was rarely broken.

A column disposition of four tanks usually travelled in a standard convoy; the troop commander led proceedings with his main gun set forward. The second tank – yours truly on this outing – had its turret traversed to a three o'clock position, and the third tank set theirs the other way. The last-in-line main gun was always directed to the rear. Although we rarely travelled with our main cannon loaded, it must have been disconcerting for the lead tank following behind because the barrel of our tail-end Charlie was pointing straight at them!

In theory, all angles were covered against any land-based attack. Our turretless Honey and its rotating machine gun was a welcome addition to the troop; another bit of good news was that a new crew was on board to replace Moxton and his band of brothers.

Luftwaffe attacks were always a threat, so our machine guns were set up similarly. With a gunner clinging on for dear life, Browning anti-aircraft guns mounted to the rear of each turret pointed out from similar clock-face positions. So far, though, we had only seen our planes, which were usually on bombing sorties before missions like this.

The intercom sparked into life, making me jump. 'Ladies? Remember, LOOK for trouble everywhere.'

We didn't expect any at this point, so we responded enthusiastically. The perception of being safe also gave me some time to reflect. 'I'm Pop, but it's me, Calum, in control.' It was all completely unbelievable but I got it. 'Anything reckless from me now and it's over.'

Was it, though? To check this theory out, I tugged back on the left steering lever and immediately slewed sharply to the left, hitting the steep grassy verge with a bump.

I instantly regretted that move. There were mines everywhere and, to make it worse, the first thing we hit was a wooden signpost declaring: *MINES, clear to 1 yard.*

A steep bank of twisted trees and bushes straightened us up as we forged ahead off-piste. Another rule, now broken, was only to manoeuvre your tank according to your commander's order.

Pulling hard on the other lever, we were soon back on track.

'What the fuck was that?' Buff demanded.

'Sorry, Buff, an accident.'

'Acci-fuckin-dent. What are you doing, boy?' He was more than pissed off, and the others were fizzing too.

Everything inside a tank is sharp, pointy and hard, so when it hits you it hurts. To my right Tony was rubbing his ear, and above me Morton was groaning about his front tooth. I would pay for this big time. Luckily, Captain Smythe, who was leading our troop, hadn't reacted to the extraordinary shenanigans behind him. If he had seen my impromptu diversion, inquiries would have been made. I needed to think fast.

'Buff, I thought I saw a Panzerfaust,' I said. Brownie points for a valiant try. 'So I went for him. Granted, it was stupid!'

A Panzerfaust was an anti-tank weapon like the American bazooka or our British-made Projector Infantry Anti-Tank gun (PIAT). At a distance of fifty yards, they were super destructive and could blow a hole through just about any armour. Their portability and lack of recoil also made them user-friendly and devastating in the dense foliage of Normandy. They had a downside, however: they only had one shot and that gave tank crews time to escape.

A Panzerschreck reloadable soon came along; that, and an additional fifty-yard range, made them probably the most feared enemy weapon of World War 2.

'Don't Buff me, son. "Went for him?" Do I look fuckin' stupid?' His response was better than I'd expected.

Tony continued to glare at me as he contemplated my likely downfall. I'd be dead by the morning for sure – sooner, if this lynch mob got hold of me.

'There are bleeding mines everywhere, ESPECIALLY off-road.' Buff paused. 'You moronic fool.'

To my relief, the intercom clicked off – but then it came back on again. 'Straight line, if you don't mind, driver.'

'Not sure he can, sir.' It was Big Nige's turn now, and I felt a sharp kick from his boot on the top of my shoulder. Tony didn't comment; he gave me a foolish grin instead and his trademark wanker sign.

Apart from my little mishap, the first day of our mission was uneventful. 'Could have been more fruitful,' moaned our boss up top who saw things differently. It did prove one thing, however: I was in control of my destiny.

We were all subdued on the way home and lacking in the usual banter. My 'moronic foolishness' was part of the reason, but reality had also set in. This was just the start; although this mission had been quiet, we knew it wouldn't last. The rabid nose of war would come sniffing our way soon.

I also felt incredibly depressed. Why was I there anyway?

We got to our overnight harbour in Bretteville-l'Orgueilleuse at around 17:00. Buff dismounted and headed towards the commanders' O-group conference with abnormal haste. He was not a happy man; the fact that he made no comment and that the tank was still moving when he dismounted was a clue to that.

We proceeded with our end-of-day chores in silence. 'Oh, dear, oh dear,' huffed Morton.

'Seems to be in a bit of a hurry,' added Tony.

'Someone's upset him,' countered Morton.

It was a bit like being back at school. Some poor idiot was in trouble and his classmates were in a feeding frenzy, waiting to see their teacher's retribution. Neither of the guys said much more – they didn't need to because the smug look on their stupid faces gave them away. Excitement, even arousal, were the best words to describe their reaction to the prospect of my imminent demise.

Big Nige was the worst. As he shook his wobbly fat head, spittle sprayed from his yellow-toothed gob. If only I'd yanked the lever back harder. 'Tut-tut, Peter.'

'You're both self-satisfied ugly bastards.'

'Oh, dear, oh dear,' he replied.

There were stormy waters ahead for sure, but at least I knew my predicament here in Normandy was real. And whatever it was, my destiny was sitting well and truly in my own hands. Intuition and luck might safely get me through this mess.

From the regimental book, *A History of the 44ᵗʰ RTR*

At last, on June 25ᵗʰ, we heard that we were to be used to help the 11ᵗʰ Armoured Division in a great drive over the Odon south of Caen in a bid to reach the high ground behind the city and cut it off. At the time, we were near the village of Sequevelle-en-Bessin. Here, we were joined by 'F' Battery 4th Royal Horse Artillery and 'B' Company 2nd/60th Kings Royal Rifle Corps. The latter had been with us in Italy and were old friends; the former we did not know so well except by reputation. Be that as it may, we were all to remain together until the end of the conflict. Their story is ours; without them, we could have achieved little.

Live Together, Die Together

The 26th of June started badly. News came that our brigade commander, John Currie, was dead, apparently killed in a mortar attack during his O-group meeting the previous evening. We'd heard the distant rumble but hadn't worried too much because RHQ had harboured two miles north of us.

That said, Buff was still there… The unthinkable thought was short-lived when I heard his voice boom out, 'Right, you horrible lot. Hands off cocks, on socks.'

We gathered around in our customary huddle and waited, me for what was to come, and the others for what they were about to witness.

'Two things first, ladies.' Here it comes. I waited. 'You've heard about our CO?' We nodded. 'Brigadier Carver will replace him.'

They didn't hang about in those days. Richard Carver, at twenty-nine, was the youngest of that rank in the British armed forces and he had a serious pedigree; the Duke of Wellington was a distant relative, no less. As sad as the news was about John Currie, he was just a face to a man we didn't know; on the other hand, Peter Meadows and his pending doom were far more important. Were we meant to say something respectful? None of us did.

With hands thrust deep into their pockets, Morton and Auden made circular patterns in the soil with their feet while Buff continued. I remained still.

'Secondly…' The silence, as the cliché goes, was deafening. This had to be it. 'Apologies are offered to our man in a hurry here.' Buff looked straight at me.

'Really?' Each voice hit a different pitch.

'Shall I tell you why?' His voice didn't sound that convincing and carried a hint of sarcasm. My brain raced into overdrive.

'Yesterday – who can forget yesterday?' His eyes hadn't left mine and that worried me, too.

'Bad day, sir, bad day,' flapped a concerned Morton.

'Panzerfaust teams were indeed operating, and that is when Richard Seaman showed us his driving tricks.'

He prodded my shoulder in an exaggerated show of approval—mock approval, the sort that in some circumstances, like in a pub, could quickly be superseded with a smack in the gob. Who the hell was Richard Seaman? Goalkeepers sprang to mind; I later discovered he was a British motor racing champion. Praise indeed—but did it mean I was off the hook?

'Chaps, we were bloody lucky.' I thought Buff meant me when he said that and it was my turn to nod. 'With Krauts everywhere, in the name of God, tell me what you see.'

I wanted to drop to my knees and slide along the grass in a goal celebration; the others tried hard to disguise their disappointment and muttered half-hearted congratulations.

'Son of Houdini,' mumbled Morton.

'Zero to hero,' confirmed Tony.

'Thanks,' I said modestly.

We listened to the rest of Buff's briefing. The last thing he said was an absolute killer, especially for the boys: 'Chaps, be more like Meadows. Use your eyes.'

Big Nige shook his wobbly face and clucked like a hen with an ostrich egg up his arse, while Tony smiled and gave me one of his discreet double-whammy hand signals – a middle finger followed by the usual.

As I looked up, Buff winked and slowly leaned over. I could feel his breath on my neck. 'You are fucking lucky, my son.'

We were back on the road two hours later and on the way to Cheux. Our troop was at point and the rest of the 44th followed in a convoy disposition rather than in our recent, more expansive formation. Our infantry brothers lagged behind except for a few scouts who clung onto us like limpets. That was welcome and perhaps a sign that nothing too dramatic was expected on this trip.

Intelligence reports from the local French resistance, the Maquis, usually fuelled the direction of our surveillance but we had yet to see them. These guys were terrain-savvy, well-armed, motivated killers. As a crew, we were fully aware of their reputation and welcomed the addition of another security blanket.

Due to reported sniper sightings, the other operational difference was our 'closed down' order. This way of travelling was arguably safer, but it meant conditions were poor inside the tank. In addition to engine noise and the monotonous clank of drive wheels and tracks, our mobile tomb soon felt like a furnace.

'And it hums like a dead skunk,' added Tony, with his stirring description of our environment.

Cigarette smoke made things worse. There were strict no-smoking rules, but naturally we all had one on the go. There were other regulations to disregard, too. The fact that no one wore a helmet surprised me, and to free up space the protective guard rail around our main gun's breech was conspicuous in its absence.

'Better used as a clothes horse,' suggested Morton when he yanked it out. Who else?

We had discussed helmets in one of our troop meetings, but it had already been decided that the black regimental beret was more comfortable. Practicalities and comfort over safety became policy in most British tank crews during the war. I admired the common-sense aspect of this decision and concluded that 'practicality' should be added to the training manual of my health-and-safety obsessed other life.

The Yanks had better 'everything', of course: comfortable tankie suits, quality boots, and proper helmets with built-in mics and earpieces, for starters. Our helmets were made of cork covered in canvas and rimmed inside with crude rubber strips that acted as shock absorbers. The best thing they did for us was carry water.

As for food, if our rations were basic then the Americans were prepared by a master chef on a bad day. Ours were also dangerous, and by that I mean they needed tin openers. All you did with a penknife-sized weapon was stab its stubby blade into the top of the can and forcefully rock it around the lid. Any lack of concentration often resulted in an added ingredient of sliced fingers.

Food also included chewing gum – Wrigley's! This seemed to be a relatively new concept to my new friends, who liked to trade a single boiled sweet for a strip of peppermint-flavoured gum. I *think* it was mint – the American version.

70

Pop didn't enjoy the pleasures of chewing gum, apart from his half-hearted attempt to quit smoking. That was well before nicotine patches or impregnated gum; his indulgence was Juicy Fruit. It proved a temporary distraction because his tobacco craving soon returned. He proudly announced that he was reverting to a 'healthier brand of menthol cigarette', as he put it. Even though the first time he smoked one, he nearly inhaled the extra-long filter attached to the end of it.

My favourite was bubble gum, the flat, round sort wrapped inside a waxy paper sealed with a twist at each end. The strawberry flavour seemed to last forever; it filled your mouth with a mixture of gooey juice and cost only one old penny. The skill here was to see how large a balloon-sized bubble you could blow before it burst over your face to make a sticky, pink face mask. Apart from virtuoso gum blowers, this was virtually impossible with Wrigley's unless you crammed your mouth full of chewing-gum strips.

I almost forgot the tabloid version of them all, bazooka gum: soft, four-inch-long pink rolls. All you did was twist off a chunk and lob it into your mouth. Sweet and sickly indeed, and an ironic brand name given where I was.

Sweets were great in my hormone-charged youth, and sexy, too. Especially chocolate. Who could ever forget that advert and its soundtrack? 'Only the crumbliest, flakiest chocolate tastes like chocolate never tasted before.'

And her? The poppy field, the mesmerisingly beautiful girl flouncing around with those gorgeous pouting lips? This was pure chocolate porn, and we all waited for it to come on telly between programmes like *Daktari* and *Danger Man*. When she eventually appeared, all hair, red lips and skimpy dress, we knew exactly what was coming next. Our thirty-second seductress suggestively slid back the yellow wrapper over six inches of flaky milk-chocolate. The subsequent jeering cheer could be heard from every living room window down the street as she nibbled at the end. What a noise! It was like England scoring the winner in a cup final. Brilliant ads like that would no doubt be banned by the whining, woke idiots of my retirement years.

Freddie Smythe's tank slowed as we reached the bottom of an incline where the road deviated sharply to the left. I eased down and stopped the regulation seventy-five yards behind him. Harder to hit? That made me laugh.

The problem with periscopes is that peripheral vision is impossible; all I could see was the arse-end of his tank framed by a rectangular field of view consisting of trees, a rusty farm gate and green pasture that sloped steeply up behind it.

Buff flicked the intercom to the RHQ setting B to hear Freddie Smythe's next order. It came soon enough. 'Okay, chaps, follow me into this field and then line up alongside.'

Smythe had one of those voices that didn't quite fit the face; it was certainly not posh. I'd only seen him at a distance, but his physical appearance was similar to that of Field Marshal Bernard Montgomery. That meant he wasn't that small, so the jungle drums were well off beat on that occasion. He was taller than Monty, with similar angular features and a greying, pencil-thin moustache underneath a pointy nose.

'Tanks line up in numerical order. One-hundred-yard intervals, please. Do you understand?'

I expected his voice to be upper-class, clipped and very public schoolboy. Instead, we got a 'don't fuck with me' drone, akin to Ray Winstone's, a hard man of modern British films. I liked him instantly.

Buff promptly acknowledged the order, along with the other two commanders in our troop. 'Heads up, please. Be ready to go in five minutes.' He was polite, too.

Smythe switched frequencies, presumably to brief RHQ, which allowed us to get fresh air into our cauldron of piss, shit and sweat. Morton decided to relieve himself into a shell casing, which he passed down to Tony 'for a top up'. Some spilt out. Why he did this, God knows; we had our own pots to piss in!

After a few expletives, Tony tipped it away. 'It's like a fuckin khazi in here.'

'And what a waste of brass,' I added sensibly.

'Knob.'

Five minutes soon became twenty as we waited for the order to proceed. Sitting in the open with our engines idling and 'heads up' was probably not the wisest thing to do with our time. The Maquis had already confirmed sniper presence, so my newfound appreciation of Captain 'Cockney' Smythe was under some scrutiny.

'I need a shit,' grumbled Tony.

'You can fuck right off. Not in here, you're not.' Buff's denial was a robust one.

How Tony could logistically have achieved such a feat flummoxed me. It was customary to crap into shell casings, but only in the heat of battle. Tony farted loudly instead as a welcome distraction of our order to move forward came over the net.

I don't know why, but I expected Smythe to get off his tank to open the heavy metal gate obstructing his progress. He didn't. His engines roared into life instead and we watched the gate ping off its hinges and fly through the air like a playing card, narrowly missing a ruminating cow and her calf.

He thundered through the new opening and surged up the grassy slope, leaving a trail of oily black smoke. As we burst into the field behind him, some of the cow's dead relatives lay bloated, their legs pointing to the sky like sticks. The scene could have easily been lifted from a *Monty Python* sketch.

Soon we reached our rendezvous point and spread out in formation as instructed. 'How much time do we waste waiting?' I mused.

It reminded me of conversations with my good friend, John Halsey, alias Barrington Womble, from the Rutles pop group fame. 'It wasn't all sex, drugs and rock 'n' roll, you know,' said Barry Wom. 'Time on the road can be boring.'

Yes – and fun, too, I recalled. As his occasional chauffeur and drum roadie, we spent lots of time doodling away doing nothing. Sound checks, loitering in motorway service stations and waiting were indeed rock 'n' roll. Another drummer from a popular music combo, Charlie Watts, once said the same thing. Apart from the musicians' company on these tours and being absorbed by their legendary anecdotes – enough to fill another book – I agree with those sentiments completely.

Our troop stretched out about four hundred yards. On the crest of a slope directly ahead of us was a dense hedgerow barricade, and on either side were tall conifer-type trees interspersed with clumps of bramble and what looked like thick hawthorn.

'Why the fuck are we here?' I asked.

'Shut up, Meadows,' Buff snapped.

I felt claustrophobic and sensed enemy eyes everywhere, Germanic blue and shielded beneath black helmets. Then, just for a millisecond, I saw a glimpse of something new. Dead ahead amongst the thick foliage, whatever it was shimmered like a heat haze. 'Buff, top left. Looks like … vapour?'

'Seen it.' Buff barked back to troop command, 'Could be a Panther extractor fan.'

The mayhem that followed was instantaneous as the tanks in our line woke up and let loose. Our guns blazed away at a range of about three hundred yards, their target the thick bocage ahead and its mystery vapour.

Panther tanks had two extractor fans about the size of maintenance covers above their 700hp Maybach petrol engines. When they were warm and in the right conditions, a visual distortion over the engine deck was sometimes created. It was a big giveaway but hard to detect, especially for a novice like me. Spotting this had been lucky.

The deafening barrage from our guns jerked us backwards, and soon the inside of our tank filled with choking cordite smoke coughed out from the emptying breechblock. We knew we could generally get four shots off to one of theirs, but we also knew their guns were far deadlier than ours; unless we hit a weak spot, our shots nearly always bounced off their thick skins. Even our M4's bigger guns struggled. It was a different story for the enemy: for them, hitting their target meant catastrophe for us.

As we edged up the hill, our infantry guests disengaged and dived into the canopy on either side. Tanks 1 and 4 were using armour-piercing shells with tracers, and we had high explosives up the spout directed by our big Browning tracers.

I took a glance at my bow side. Tony, fag behind his ear and lips bared over clenched teeth, hung onto his smaller 30mm bow gun as it let loose. These weapons had a range of about twenty-five yards and, with no telescopic lens, he had only his periscope and tracer bullets to guide him. Round after round rocked our tank back as missiles and bullets tore into the wall of bushes.

Wanderer 3 was in a hurry and sped past us on our starboard side; presumably their orders were to get closer. As if to make a point, the colossal machine gun rotating on top where a turret would generally be spat out empty brass shells as it jolted and juddered 180 degrees left and right.

We had hot brass casings inside our tank too, and they dropped around me as Morton triggered the main gun by stomping his foot. Commanders in Honeys had to multi-task as loaders and as Buff hand-balled the empty casings through exit ports some didn't always make it that far. I felt the heat from one brush my face and another bounce off my shoulder onto a growing pile beside me.

I calculated that our initial load of around 130 rounds would soon run out. Soon all that was left at the top of the hill was a twisted mass of smoking vegetation. Any sinister secrets waiting for us would have no chance.

'Close down, boys,' came the order. Our lids slammed down at record speed; the order was welcome and confirmed we were now in a 'kill or be killed' scenario.

Although overdosed on adrenalin, our team quickly reset into a deadly groove of controlled chaos. It was too manic to feel frightened: this was about survival, and a euphoric feeling coursed through my body. My job was simple: be vigilant, wait for orders and keep the engines running – the easy bit.

For at least ten minutes, streams of molten metal continued to gouge our target area; some bounced, some penetrated and a few exploded. But through all this, our enemy's exact whereabouts were still unknown. And it wasn't just us dishing it out: an AP tracer suddenly came our way and drilled itself into the turf about fifty feet in front of me. I watched the ground ripple and crease as the angry warhead furrowed towards us.

'Fuck, fuckety- fuck.' Buff had gone all Hugh Grant while Tony and I froze.

This unwelcome guest's velocity and sheer power buckled and then burst the surface as a thick wave of soil and stone swept over the front of our tank. We held our breath and waited for the big bang.

I couldn't see anything through my two optics, nothing at all. There was no bang either. I jammed my periscope backwards and forwards to clear the debris and shouted to Tony to do the same. He gave me a thumbs-up and looked petrified. What about me? What did I look like? I'd never seen my father frightened.

'Meadows, forward slowly,' Buff said. This was unexpected. *Forward. Are you taking the piss*? It was a private thought and I did as I was told.

The profile of a Panther Mark 5 is impressive; this one was much darker green than I recalled from my war research – and she was huge. Luckily for us, we had scored an unconventional bull's eye right on the tip of her main gun but, although ruptured and inactive, she had other weapons of significance and, more worryingly, she was still on the move.

As the giant machine slowly reversed to reposition herself, one side remained exposed. Morton struck again and congratulated himself. Boy, he was good! This time, he hit her sweet spot, a plate of thin armour above the track. A delayed lightning flash followed and an orange flame erupted from a man-sized split in her side.

'Bingo! Did we do all that?' our sharpshooter asked as we juddered to a halt.

As purplish-black smoke gushed out of a six-foot gash, I saw the flailing arms of desperation. The next play was grotesque, graphically reinforcing where we were. As Germans scrambled out of various escape routes, our tracer bullets ripped into them. These men were dark shapes, like floundering salmon; they were not human. One was on fire.

Then the last man appeared. He hung onto the defunct main gun and, as our bullets tore into him, his head bounced down the front of the Panther like a football. The rest of his body tumbled over to the other side, forcing me to look away.

Could I have done that? Did Pop ever do something like that?

'Nice one, son.' Buff liked what he saw, but his hyper-pitched laughter told another story. We had probably hit the fuel line or ammunition storage to get such a result, but what followed was depressing.

Tracer rounds were good and also very bad. They pinpointed the firing direction for a shooter but also gave away his position. British tracers were generally dark orange, making the scenario surreal. It was like a crazed computer game because the only part for me in this battle was to observe.

German tracers were different, so when a stream of bright green light ripped towards me, it felt like game over. But it was destined for Wanderer 3; as we watched, an AP rocket sliced through her hull, macerating everyone inside. Our initial relief quickly flipped to guilt as we watched the missile divert towards them.

Helpless to do anything, we saw another high explosive strike as it took out the big Browning and its two gunners desperately trying to return fire. Both men vapourised instantly.

'Gunner! Two o'clock!' screamed Buff. Our turret slowly traversed as Big Nige jammed his joystick to the right. 'Fire. Fucking fire!'

The turret of our mechanical cousin, the Sherman, took around twenty seconds to rotate; ours was shorter, but it seemed an eternity longer than that. The rockets came from the other side of the field, and all our attention focused on this new starboard-side threat. Meanwhile, the mashed remains of our comrades engulfed by flames and exploding ammunition would be scraped out of their metal tomb later.

'Six seconds to get out, that's all. After that, we send you home to Mummy as well-done steak!' I had overheard someone say this to a group of tankies in Normandy.

As one of three tanks in our troop, we moved up the hill in a well-rehearsed and sequenced drill: stop, fire, move, and repeat. While Nigel and Tony unleashed everything from our weaponry, I held us on course and steady. Machine-gun tracers from both sides criss-crossed, and the metallic, punching sound reverberated as they peppered our hull and deflected off. It made no sense, but the repetitive jackhammer sound of a bullet hitting metal made me duck sporadically.

Gripping the steering levers tightly, we surged and bucked up the slope. Then suddenly it stopped; the ear-blistering commotion faded as a call came in from troop command to hold fire. Between a canvas of verdant green and scorched bocage, plumes of swirling black smoke funnelled into the sky.

'Targets terminated,' announced Buff. I looked for confirmation and saw at least one machine-gun post, probably Spandau, a burnt-out Panther and an 88mm anti-tank gun unit. All had been deactivated.

'No one fucks with us,' boasted Tony.

'Too close for comfort, boys.' Buff knew it; we all did. Luck was the real miracle in this result.

We gave a lukewarm cheer as the tank came to a halt. She vibrated loudly, which was not a good sign, and her engine spluttered anxiously. A glance around confirmed that most things were in order in the driver's section, albeit topsy-turvy. No one said anything as we waited for orders. The dials and their levels seemed okay, but my left-side steering felt tight. This almost certainly meant track damage and urgent repairs.

Tony's report to Buff wasn't positive either. 'Periscope knackered, gun fucked, sir.'

'Reload everyone. Doesn't feel right.' It was the most deflating order yet.

'And that's us fucked, then.'

'Shut it, Meadows.'

Light on firepower and with our manoeuvrability seriously hampered, if our commander's hunch was correct, we were in trouble. We listened for the clunk of enemy limpet mines and held our breath. Ten minutes passed and then, through the smoke, five of our foot soldiers appeared. They held up their hands, palms forward, and gestured for us to stay where we were.

It was calm as they made their way down the slope towards Captain Smythe, who clambered down from his turret to greet them. He gave us the all-clear and we burst out of our hatches for air.

Drawn by the heat and crackling noise further downfield, our eyes diverted towards Wanderer 3. Fist-sized lumps of white-hot iron coughed out of her bowels into the battle-smoked sky, and even at two hundred yards the intensity of heat felt unbearable.

Tony and I slipped our goggles back on. Much worse than the heat was the smell of roasted human flesh; now familiar, this pungent, sweet aroma had been with us every day in France. A bitter mixture of bile and rising vomit stung the back of my throat and I fought the urge to gag. Nige couldn't help himself and hurled into an empty shell casing.

Huddled together on top of our turret, drawn like magnets to the scene behind us, we said nothing for a while.

'If the devil's a pervert, he's just exposed himself.' Tony broke the silence, and for once, it wasn't a joke. He was right, though; we had just watched hell in action.

An hour later, the order came through to make camp and soon a team of engineers appeared. They quickly got to work fixing our problems – or rather, thought about how to fix them. As the men pontificated and fussed, we brewed up and wolfed down some compo rations.

Our attempt to catch some sleep that night was important, but recent events and worms of self-doubt gnawing through our brains prevented it; that and the image of a glowing tank melting down behind us.

When morning eventually came, the weather matched our mood. Instead of being fine and dry as in previous days, a drizzle and low mist hung over us. The reveille at 06.30 hours did its best to disturb our troubled slumbers. Aching, exhausted and miserably numb, we crawled from beneath our tank into a dank, damp dawn.

'Another day, another dollar,' muttered Morton.

It reminded me of Glastonbury. My one time there had been enough, and I had been working. Part of my task as drum roadie for John was to drive so, as my silver BMW skidded its way down a muddy farm track towards the acoustic stage, a plethora of mud-surfing zombies hopped onto it.

'For the crack,' said one as he clung on for the ride.

'Capitalist cunts,' said another charming character, joining in the fun. Was it my flash car or the fact that John was wearing a paisley-patterned cravat and tweed cap? He liked to dress up for these things.

We eventually reached our meeting point and something with purple hair and pink jeans greeted us; this creature hung on, too.

'What the fuck is that?' That was all we could say as more apparitions of loveliness peered through the glass during our wheel-spinning trip towards the stage compound. In every direction weak puffs of damp wood smoke tailed up from desperate campfires, and slanting sheets of Glastonbury rain thrashed against our foggy windscreen. 'Let's go home,' moaned John as we took turns to clear it away and more gruesome sights exposed themselves.

Finally the tents, thousands of beige and pointy ones as far back as we could see, filled the gloomy horizon. We found out later that they were coloured tents camouflaged with mud and cow shit from the recently evacuated bovines.

Fast forward – or was it back? The vista was much the same in Normandy, but instead of semi-naked kids with Apache-like makeup, and spliffed-up parents wearing fake dreadlocks, 'just for the weekend, you understand,' we had soldiers. There were lots of them bunched together in sombre groups. But unlike the born-again hippies of Glastonbury, living the dream and wondering how much money had gone onto their credit cards, most of these men drank tea and smoked regular tobacco in contemplative silence. If only they could see what they were fighting for. Liberty and freedom, indeed – but for the Glastonbury music festival?

'All we need now is Paul McCartney singing "Hey Jude",' I thought. If only I could educate the guys.

So far, I hadn't managed to free myself from my tankie gear or get a proper kip. A combination of gunge-impregnated clothing, sweat and cold summer rain made the cosiness of our team cocoon fetid at best.

New guests had flown in, too: mosquitoes, not as cannibalistic as the midges in Scotland, but they were still irritating. The itchy red bites and oozing yellow pus added another layer of misery to our lives. Most of us were also nursing impressive hangovers. Although our day's exertions had been rewarded by heroic-sized slugs of gin and lime cordial, a feeling of lethargy and wretchedness in our troop was the flip side.

Our mood dropped further when we saw yesterday's horrific reminder behind the white marker tape. She continued to steam and hiss as our regimental padre and others carefully removed the grizzly secrets from her bowel.

'My God, take a look at that.' It was Big Nige. 'Second thoughts, don't.' One medic was using a spade and another had a gardening trowel to dollop a black treacle-like substance onto a canvas groundsheet.

The reputation of these medicine men grew daily; their compassion was remarkable as they worked fearlessly, often on both sides of the battlefield. From conscientious objectors to yellow bellies, as some Americans saw them, they soon became the bravest of all war heroes. Over 25,000 served in military non-combatant roles, and thousands lost their lives during the war. Few carried guns. Perhaps the most depressing irony was their distinctive Red Cross emblem, because some enemy gunsights saw those as convenient targets.

'If there are such things as angels, chaps, these are the guys.' It was Morton again, and the truth of his statement made me smile. I had also used this sentiment about MacMillan nurses at my mother's funeral.

Big Nige was on tea duty again and fussed while we slowly packed our bedrolls and prepared for the day ahead.

On his return from an O-group briefing, Buff looked tense and was unusually tight-lipped.

'What's the secret, then?' Tony asked the question, nudging me with his elbow and looking directly at Buff.

'No secret. But until that thing is mended, we're not going anywhere.' Buff pointed to the track segments lying alongside our injured tank. A couple of guys from the Light Aid Detachment team were continuing to agonise over what seemed to be an insurmountable problem.

'What say you, Meadows?' asked Buff.

'If these blokes can't do it, the engineers will,' I suggested knowledgeably. 'It looks worse than it is.'

'Confident statement, son.'

Agreed. What did I know? A glance around me confirmed there weren't any engineers to be seen. With our next push imminent, the other squadron and most of the infantry had decamped earlier. The engineers also appeared to be part of Echelon A, our tank supplies group.

Buff read my mind. 'I think they've fucked off.'

The steering stiffness was more than a mechanical fault; a small mine or large shrapnel deflection had removed a set of wheels, and how we had gotten up the hill was a mystery.

After a eureka moment, one of the LAD team, still scratching his shiny bald head and deep in thought, wandered over to us. He removed a straight wooden pipe from between his teeth, dabbed the bowl with his thumb and asked Buff a question. 'What time do you need this bugger?'

'We're due to leave at 14.00 hours.'

'Doable,' came a contemplative reply.

The man was short and wore a pair of round-framed spectacles on the tip of his nose; a bank manager or science teacher, perhaps. He nodded. Using a small penknife, he scraped the bowl of his pipe and flakes of charred tobacco fell as he wandered back to a maze of dismantled metal, rubber and rivets.

'Okay, ladies, get this thing spick and span. And then, may I suggest you do the same to yourselves.' Pointing towards the mobile shower unit, which had arrived overnight, Buff strolled towards it.

'It's like living in a cloud of nerve gas!' mumbled Tony, pursuing him.

As badly as I needed a shower, a new brew lovingly prepared by Morton trumped any ablutions. There were also a few routine checks required on the tank. Big Nige was on guns and radio, while Tony would focus on finding space for additional ammunition storage. Fuel, my job, had been replenished already so, apart from us having sore feet, our mechanical steed would be ready to go anytime soon.

As well as hot showers, another pleasant surprise greeted us: we had a cook's kitchen. That meant proper grub, lots of it, and although it tasted bland it was always hot. Breakfast was traditional and usually consisted of bacon, eggs, and beans, but for some reason, like all our food, its seasoning was heroic; it was either extremely salty or very sweet. I wondered if it was about preserving food in those days.

It was the same with porridge. When I first complained about this, the cook's answer was short and straightforward: 'Good for the shits and plugging up your arsehole.'

True, diarrhoea was prevalent. Modern-day umami or Chinese five spices, weren't around to flavour things up and I privately rejoiced that the health police in my nanny state were still many years off.

Most tankies were taking advantage of the washroom opportunity to eradicate the strong wafts of body odour from our miserable lives, but not me. It was a mistake to wait for the queue to die down, but I decided to look at the remains of yesterday's skirmish instead.

The battered Panther, now ring-fenced with the usual white marker tape, had a couple of curious admirers studying it. They were senior rank, so I headed off to check out what was left of the Spandau machine gun. MG42s (or Mausers, as was their actual name) were catastrophic weapons. Six-inch-long bullets fired at 1200 rounds per minute could slice a man in two. American soldiers aptly named them 'Hitler's Buzzsaw' due to their unmistakable *brrr brrr* rattle, making them one of the most feared weapons on the battlefield.

But the benefits of rapid-fire had a downside: Mauser barrels tended to overheat and melt. Like much German-made equipment, including tanks, they were over specified and expensive. It took about seven seconds to change a barrel and reload a belt of ammunition, inconvenient for a user but life-saving knowledge when they ripped up the turf in front of you. 'When the rattle stops, get the fuck out,' we were told. 'But if there's more than one gun, you have a problem.' Nice one, Buff.

'Sonny, if you've got your eyes on this, think again.' The voice was Scottish and cultured, probably from Edinburgh at a guess. It belonged to a staff sergeant who was kneeling in front of a black-coloured Spandau. He didn't look up as he concentrated on dismantling each part carefully.

'You can help yourself to any of those.' He gestured with his head towards the other guns stacked against a tree.

Already the proud owner of a Luger, my interest was in the Mauser P40 Schmeisser, a pistol-grip submachine gun. 'This one?' I asked, reaching down for it.

'Yep, that is precisely what you need, son.' He looked up and then did what everyone with a Wyatt Earp-style droopy moustache did: with a finger and thumb, he slowly made a couple of exaggerated downward strokes. 'Much more reliable than your Sten,' he said, 'and it takes the same ammo.'

It was slightly heavier than a Sten and made of steel and plastic. The magazine was more prominent and vertically fitted rather than fixed to the side like ours. I ran my hands over it and nodded my approval. It felt solid and very German; in modern times this would have been a good sign. 'I'll take this, then. Thanks.'

He nodded back and continued to take apart the big MG42. 'Have fun with it, son.'

The transaction was so casual about an object designed to terminate life, but I was equally blasé at finding something more efficient at doing the job. The only real gun I had ever owned was Diana, a .177 air rifle made of shiny wood and black steel. Naturally, I hadn't shot anyone – although that was not strictly true. I had shot George Hutton.

It was the summer of 1971, and he was the irritating brother of my best mate, Michael. George was older than us, about fifteen, and we were stalking him with our shooters.

Michael's gun was much flashier than mine, with a pump-action mechanism and a chamber holding beads screwed to the top. Mine was classic in design and more stylish. To load it, you had to break the barrel first; making sure the capsule-shaped pellet was the right way round, you carefully pushed it into the magazine chamber with your thumb. Granted it didn't have the machine-gun-like capacity of Mike's rapid-fire beany gun, but at least Diana looked like the real deal. She was also deadlier.

Planning for that fateful day had been meticulous and as we crept up to our target, we were professional hitmen. Being skilled in the art of assassination, the routine was simple: fire, terminate the target and escape. We didn't actually want to kill him, 'just hurt and maim, that will do'. It was written into our contract; at worst, our victim should only get a painful sting.

'Hopefully on his bollocks,' chipped in Michael at our final briefing. The hit had been rehearsed thoroughly, mostly on plastic Fairy Liquid bottles and old grain bags from the stables, though we had never managed to hit either in our practice sessions, a fact we had forgotten in our planning. What could possibly go wrong?

Diana's barrel rested on the fence post, a pre-determined vantage point identified from an earlier reconnaissance mission. I looked around for Michael. Where the hell was he? In the meantime, George had his back to me and was fiddling about with a wheelbarrow; in range at approximately thirty yards, this was a perfect time to finish the job.

When I spotted Michael, he was about the same distance behind me. That worried me. We had agreed on a thumbs-up signal to commence the hit, me with a deadly single shot and him with rapid fire from his pump action, but at this point in proceedings, we were meant to be side by side. I was confused. Our mission's motto, one we had agonised about over several cold Ribenas, was 'Live together, die together'.

With our objective set and strategy agreed upon, this sad but necessary assassination was for the good of everyone on our street. And to seal our bond, we were more than mates; we were blood brothers. That is what I thought.

'Maybe he will follow my lead?'

Remembering Pop's coaching, I held my breath, took aim and slowly squeezed the trigger. After enough time for an egg to boil, our target fell to the ground, pole-axed and screaming like a child. Really? How could my Diana go from pea shooter to bazooka?

Equally disconcerting was Michael's absence; where was he? Apart from his blubbering, writhing brother, I seemed to be the only other person in the middle of this crime scene. It was time to retreat, so I backed down our pre-arranged escape route and tripped over my friend's useless, discarded weapon.

Clean up the evidence, Calum. Forensics. I remembered Columbo, who always referred to forensics in those days. And then a sad truth dawned on me: the barrel of Michael's weapon was still cold. My comrade had bottled it.

I looked back at the target, who was now spread-eagled on his back in a four-pronged star shape. 'Jesus, he's dead.' There was only one person to blame. 'Diana, what have you done, girl?'

I scrambled through the bushes, hid our guns where we had once found the porno mags and grabbed my bike. It was unlocked and pointing in the right direction, ready to go. Everything was as planned except Mike's Chopper with the curved black seat and ape-hanger handlebars. That had gone already. What a surprise.

'I'm in trouble. I'm fucking dead,' was all I managed to say as I frantically peddled homeward. 'This time, I'm *really* dead.'

Worse than death was the thought of my mother. 'Mortification personified' best described her reaction when Pop shocked us with Diana on my thirteenth birthday. It was as if he had initiated me into the carnal delights of a stripper – or worse.

'How can any husband of mine,' smoke was coming out of her ears, 'bring something so evil into our home?'

Pop's admirable attempt to smooth-soap her failed badly. 'Owning an air rifle, my darling, is good discipline for a growing boy.'

'Did you have one?' was her choked retort as the veins bulged in the whites of her eyes.

'No, dearest. I wasn't allowed one.'

Until *Georgegate*, the only thing I'd ever hit with my gun was a few Smedley's carrot tins lined up on our garden wall. When I got really good, Pop propped up smaller sardine cans, the flat, oval sort you opened by twisting a key and rolling back the lid. Discipline and a cool head were indeed required, especially when the old man was watching.

'Lean forward, bring the stock back into your shoulder,' he ordered. I just wanted to fire from the hip and hope. 'Now line up the sights and squeeze.'

Ping. It was so slow you could almost see the pellet arching up and then curving down towards the target; sometimes it hit, more often, it didn't.

Teatime eventually arrived, and when nothing was said about a local homicide I began to worry. George could still be lying dead at the end of his garden. Why hadn't anyone found him? And what of my accomplice and loyal friend Michael? He hadn't telephoned, either. Then it finally sank in that his stupid brother wasn't dead: he must be in intensive care or with the police, giving them a description of his assailant. Me. I began to worry again.

The phone call from Eileen, the deceased's mother, came later that evening. I was upstairs skulking around in my bedroom and strained hard to listen. My dad took it; the conversation was muffled and the call short. I heard the phone ding as he put down the receiver. 'That was Eileen, dear. She wants to know whether you want some rhubarb.'

'That's nice, Peter.'

'George is bringing it round later,' Pop replied.

What? From his coffin? That was a shocker. Astonishment, mixed with disbelief and happy thoughts of rhubarb crumble, seared my mind. George was alive – but judgment day would soon arrive for me. Freshly briefed by the victim, Pop would deal with me first and then it would be Mum's turn. Like a manic gospel singer on acid, she would seek out and destroy the weapon of mass destruction hidden safely behind my wardrobe.

But it never happened. The only real consequence of this event was rhubarb, tons of it, and with every meal. To give credit to weasel-faced George, he didn't tell anyone about the failed assassination attempt. He had felt nothing through his David Cassidy T-shirt, which was another good reason to shoot the bastard. But he did have an excuse not to grass us up when we were cornered behind his dad's greenhouse the next day: it was called blackmail.

'You are mine now. If you don't play the game, I'll tell them my snotty little brother and his retard friend shot me.' As George gripped both of us by the throat, one in each hand, he seemed to have morphed into Fagan, all wriggly fingers, spit and saliva.

Thankfully, his attempts at extortion were short-lived. We spied on him again the next day and soon found a way out of our predicament. Like all inquisitive boys, we occasionally explored our parents' drink cabinets, and that was how we caught him red-handed. He thought he was alone and was sitting Al Capone-like on the sofa, glugging on a bottle of his old man's best malt whisky. Wedged between the fingers of his other hand, a half-smoked Montecristo cigar dozed gently.

No guns were needed this time, just stealth and a Polaroid camera. What an invention.

'Book him, Danno. Murder one.' That famous line from *Hawaii Five-0* seemed appropriate as the blank, waxy paper purring out of this fantastic camera gradually developed into a fully-fledged, proper photograph.

We had him bang to rights and took two pictures, hiding one for insurance purposes. 'Just in case you grab this one,' taunted Michael as he waved the first photograph in George's face. This impressed me; my friend had stepped up to the plate and showed some proper metal this time. We were even-stevens on the bribery front and, as my brave blood brother and prophet once said, 'Live together, die together.'

Regarding my father and guns, he rarely used Diana, claiming she was too small for him to hold, but he was good when he did.

Maybe – and understandably – firing guns had painful memories for him; he never said and I never asked. But one thing in this war so far was clear: me, my father and I still hadn't fired a single shot. How long could that last?

As I walked away, I saw a row of four temporary graves. Planted into each fresh mound of earth was a rifle, each one with a distinctive German helmet hooked onto it. One was flattened out of shape, another split down the middle as if an axe had hit it, and all four had metal dog tags dangling beneath them. At a later date, perhaps in the calm of eventual peacetime, these forgotten souls would be buried in proper war graves. I felt sad because their families couldn't grieve; they hadn't heard the news yet.

The rain had given way to a burst of misty sunshine. My calculations had been wrong: not only had the chance to clean up gone, and the shower unit had closed, but I could also see the cook's kitchen being packed away.

'Just brilliant. Cigarette, Calum?' I said to myself. 'No thanks, I really must give up.' I lit one anyway, and it tasted great.

Over my shoulder were the mangled remains of an 88mm German anti-tank gun. It was free-standing, not tank mounted, and it was the weapon responsible for the death of our comrades in Wanderer 3.

'Two crews dead, four mashed up in graves and four in buckets of paste. Who won that one, then?' I wondered.

The glowing tip of my cigarette pulsed brighter as I inhaled deeply and watched it creep towards my mouth. Another deep drag and it would be gone. My old man smoked all his life and, remarkably, when he died his lungs were healthy. So was his blood pressure, a miracle given the amount of salt he consumed. The Germans couldn't kill him, cigarettes didn't either, nor did sodium chloride. That was amazing because every plate of food he consumed was accompanied by a mound of salt the size of Kilimanjaro, supplemented by a top coat poured evenly over it.

I thought about the Germans: Kraut, Boche bastards. It had been slow coming, but finally I despised them. To confuse things, I also remembered my other life and the fantastic times I'd had working with my colleagues from Munich. And what about my

French comrades, our historic allies? That was never quite the same.

Increased activity around our tank prompted me to move. When I got there, the others were loitering around impatiently. 'Come on; we're late, you fuckwit. Get this baby fired up,' said a virtuous and scrupulously clean Tony Auden. 'Fuckwit': was that term used in the war years?

A few tanks from the C Squadron were indeed on the move. 'I didn't think we were going yet.'

'Timings have changed, son. New toy?' Buff nodded towards the Schmeisser hanging loosely around my waist.

'You know what they'll do if they capture you?' Not waiting for my answer, Tony continued. 'Firing squad.'

It was unusual for tankies to be kept as PoWs, especially when they were caught by the SS who preferred to shoot them. It was also common knowledge that having loot in your possession made things worse; wised up to this, troops disposed of their acquisitions when the SS were about.

Big Nige staggered like a drunk towards me; concentrating hard must have been difficult. Gripped tightly in his hands, a large bowl of murky water sloshed over the rim, soaking the front of his overalls. Balancing act over, he carefully placed the bowl's remains on the back deck of our tank. 'There you are, my son; you'll soon smell like an English rose.'

A slimy green bar of carbolic soap slid along the bottom of the washbasin. I had always liked Sunlight soap's sweet and slightly medicinal smell and immediately recognised the brand from my days as a salesman working for Unilever. But there were more pressing thoughts going through my mind. How many hairy bollocks had this lump of gunk washed? Please, God, make it none.

It was not quite the luxuriating shower experience I'd been offered earlier. Was this a thoughtful gesture from Nige or a subtle hint about my body odour? I dived both hands into the soapy soup and tried hard to avoid the gunge.

With RHQ and C Squadron, we had planned to move out and laager in Mondrainville. That meant crossing the river Odon, where an SS armour division was causing problems for another group of British and Canadian Allies. We found out later that they were the notorious 12th SS Panzer division.

'Nasty bastards from the Hitler Youth movement,' Buff said knowingly. He went on to explain that, having been brainwashed from the age of eight and commanded by fanatical Nazi officers, these were not friendly people.

I reflected on the tank firing squads mentioned by Tony, parked the thought quickly and hastily hid my newly acquired Schmeisser.

Except for scruffy urchins on bikes who offered us fresh eggs and milk, the next part of our trip was uneventful. Eggs supplemented our rations, and we gratefully accepted them, passing chocolate and sweets back in return. The bartering stakes went up a notch when the village elders offered us Calvados, although to be fair, most of it was given *pro bono* as we were their liberators. Because these interactions made us feel good, as did the Calvados, we lobbed tins of treacle pudding in return. Never cigarettes, though: they were hard currency and would only ever be exchanged for real luxuries like cigars or whisky.

Each passing village played out the same as we powered north in pursuit of our enemy. 'Just look at the girls,' howled Tony. There were certainly lots of them, and most were young and very pretty. That said, even big Nige might have been attractive in a skirt at that stage of the proceedings.

I slowed down for a better look as they blew kisses and showered us with wildflowers and fruit. Some wrote messages of thanks and tattooed our tank with chalk pictures. And while goodwill, laughter and mayhem surrounded us, we were all thinking the same thing. It was Tony who probably summed it up best. 'A good six inches. That's what they need.'

From the regimental book *A History of the 44th RTR*:
We moved on the afternoon of 26th June to form up near Norrey-en-Bessin. That evening, we started to push forward towards the village of Cheux but found the enemy in strength there and lost one of our light tanks commanded by Sergeant Conroy to an 88mm gun. It was too late to do more that night, so we leaguered where we were.

Hill 113

Moving house is always fun, and so is moving tank. Like an excited family, we unpacked the Honey and waited for our next orders.

Buff finally confirmed our habitat change just before sundown and like expectant parents, the anticipation was almost too much to bear. 'We are moving, girls, and going up in style.' Sounding like an estate agent, he explained that our new home would be more spacious and comfortable with 'some proper firepower.'

Sherman M4s were leased from the Americans and adapted for the British army; this included the introduction of twin hatches in the turret and a bigger gun for the Fireflies. Two hatches? I wondered about that. They had to make ambulances bigger to accommodate people in 'modern' Britain, so based on that, not many of us would have gotten into a WW2 tank.

'Harsh but true,' I said aloud.

'Hard for who?' replied Tony.

As our banter continued and the excitement grew, grumpy Nigel Morton tried hard to dampen the mood. 'Ronsons? They light first time, every time.' He shook his head morosely and made that irritating clucking sound again.

'Thanks for that, mate.'

'But you know what the Huns call them?' It was Tony's turn to have a go. 'Tommy cookers!'

'Fucking hell, chaps, I get you somewhere nice to live and all I get is this,' Buff retorted.

'I like it, sir. Please can I go and play with her?' My camp voice made the others laugh as they continued to heave their remaining bits of gear from our old abode.

'Anyway, you two dicks are going nowhere. Just Speedy and me on this one.' Buff gave a horizontal 'V' sign to Morton and Auden, who both 'ooohed' in unison. 'Meadows, get ready. You guys wait to hear from Captain Smythe. You're in his tank today.'

It turned out that our 'injury' was severe, so the forlorn-looking Wanderer 1 had been booked in for a makeover. The Royal Electrical and Mechanical Engineers team were on it, but for how long we didn't know.

The team split was mysterious. Buff and I were to join C Squadron, where Major Teddy Foster was the commanding officer; maybe a combination of my brilliant driving skills and Buff's talents as a commander had gotten us this gig. The real reason came immediately. 'A new M4 has come in.' Buff pointed at me. 'And he's the only free driver we've got.'

'Charming. Thanks for the "big up", boss.'

Buff led me towards our new pad, or as the infantry liked to say 'coffin', and like some saddo petrol head test-driving a new car, my pace increased when I saw her. American tanks and my German-made submachine gun – did we own anything British? Question noted, I fired up another Player's Navy Cut with a Zippo lighter! And could I drive it? The thought suddenly occurred that I had no idea how.

On cue, I heard Buff shout, 'Meadows, get intimate with her. These buggers are bigger and there's a gear stick to worry about now.'

Absolutely no pressure, then. There she was, a grey-green camouflaged beast slumbering in the sunshine. Apart from her size, the other thing that grabbed me was her name in two-foot-high letters sloshed across the side of her turret in canary-yellow paint: Daisy.

'Daisy? A fucking cow!'

We had seen plenty of cows, and most were dead, which was not a good omen. Most troops had names for their tanks, and apart from Wanderer, they were usually macho tanks like Killer, Bomber, or Rocky. Sometimes, sentiment came into it, and they were named after girlfriends or wives. C Squadron had decided to be different; theirs would be named after farmyard animals.

A quick look around confirmed my detective work. Oink was one; the almost funny Gobbler was another, and just behind her was a beat-up tank called Kosher. It took me a second to compute. 'Dead meat. Are you kidding me?'

Despite her name, Daisy was intimidating. Her size and impressive 75mm cannon made her look brutal. Oink and Kosher were deceptive creatures, too; they were Sherman Fireflies with longer seventeen-pound guns wedged into their turrets. This adaptation reduced space, so the lap-gunner position was eliminated to allow additional ammunition storage and larger warheads. In the early days Shermans retained their Browning fifty-calibre anti-aircraft guns fixed to the rear of the turret but after Normandy, thanks to the RAF, the frequency of Luftwaffe attacks had diminished. For practical purposes, the guns were often removed and replaced by smaller 30-calibre Brownings locked onto the commander's hatch. This proved controversial, however, because 'the men up top' were supposed to command, not fire machine guns!

I climbed onto the front of Daisy and hung onto her main gun. Welded onto the outside of her hull were links of metal track to give us an additional layer of protection. However, this extra 'padding' on top of three inches of armour plate was nothing compared to a Panther or Tiger tank. If you added their cannon's velocity and range over ours, it made this crude adaptation insignificant.

I dropped down into the driver's seat and something new jabbed me in the thigh: a Sherman had steering levers coming up from the floor rather than down from the roof. Buff had been correct; Daisy had a manual gearbox, which meant a clutch to master. Like a child, I pushed, pulled and fiddled with the levers and various other switches until a squeaky northern voice interrupted my fun. 'Who goes there?'

'Trooper Meadows. Driver … new.'

'Trooper Tom Smith. Bow gunner. Old,' came a cheerful reply. With that, a pair of long legs followed by a slim body dropped onto the bow-gunner seat to my right. Old? He looked about twelve as he reached over to shake my hand.

A little later we trundled out of camp. I was enjoying my new toy while the others wondered who was in control. It was June 29th 1944, and we were tail-end Charlies, part of Number 4 troop. A pair of armoured Dingo scout cars raced past followed by a Kangaroo, not the animal kind but a troop-carrier tank conversion. Rather than a serious fighting unit, I began to think this was a zoo.

Teddy Foster had given a heads-up order so the noise and churning dust made life uncomfortable. Oink was ahead and the amount of black smoke billowing out of her rear end made me wonder if this was normal for a Firefly. Kosher was in front of her, and the major was riding on Gobbler and leading the pack. Surely this couldn't be real? I smiled.

Although it felt strange to be driving a new tank, the Ford GAA V8 petrol engine had guts. Like in a Honey, the driving sensation was about immense power and how to harness it. It felt great; without sounding all Jeremy Clarkson, the buzz was similar to trading up in car size. It reminded me of car-swap time in corporate life, which was even better with promotion because it usually meant a better vehicle. It is an absolute fact that company cars are a matter of life and death to most salespeople; what better evidence than the intense bar-room conversations around mph, mpg and zero to sixty? The latter measure was sometimes attributed to our 'shagometer' ratings about the unlucky bar person serving us. I'm not proud of that.

Status was the other important thing about company cars. A full-spec Ford Mondeo was the archetypal rep car in the noughties, but it had absolutely no class. So when the keys to a silver BMW estate dropped into my hands or, as the dealer in the shiny suit corrected me, 'Tourer sir,' it was then that salesman's heaven arrived.

Everything in my new M4 was bigger, smoother and more responsive than the old Stuart; it had the same feeling as getting my new BMW. The difference was that I had been given this for doing nothing and without a hint of promotion.

'How's learner boy doing down there?' Buff, with his sarcastic voice, may have the responsibility but I was the one having all the fun.

'He's doing okay. Gears take some getting used to,' I replied.

'Yep, noticed that.' Buff was referring to a couple of my less-than-gentle gear changes. This manual gearbox had three forward gears, one reverse and no synchromesh. To engage smoothly, it was necessary to 'double de-clutch,' and Pop had shown me how to master this technique as we raced home from the pictures one night. We were in his blue Ford Anglia, registration ALH 785B, pre-seat belt days. His masterful demonstration was exhilarating and reckless as we slid around the country lanes of Essex. If Richard Seaman wasn't impressed, I was.

The other guys didn't seem too concerned – and 'others' included an additional member. We now had a commander, gunner (or, to be technical, a cannoneer) and a separate loader crammed into the turret. Everything else in an M4 was much the same, but space would be at a premium on this trip.

A Sherman should officially hold around ninety missiles, each about 18" long and weighing around 22lbs in old money. We had 130 on this trip, which cramped our style and added significant weight. Every nook and cranny had an HE or AP projectile jammed into it, plus machine-gun rounds and a few smoke bombs to use for infantry cover. Even my new Luger had to find another home behind the green dashboard on my left.

As usual, we didn't have the exact details of our operational plan for the 44th, but we knew a big offensive was in the offing. The whole regiment, apart from RHQ and us, had laagered in Evrecy twenty-four hours earlier. My route cards and destination points were already stuffed into my top pocket as a standard back-up procedure.

'Worried you'll get us lost, Buff?' I replied when he asked if I'd done them.

From his briefing, our objective was to protect the right flank of the 29th Armoured Brigade, whose mission as part of Operation Epsom was to capture Hill 112, four miles west of Caen.

'And there's more. We have to expand the bridgehead through Hill 113 to Evrecy.' Buff's tone was earnest, perhaps because it was our first significant mission as a brigade. My football match collywobbles returned, as did my stomach churn.

After several associated bowel-relief stops, we arrived at 09.30 hours and waited for orders. Almost immediately they came in: we were to move forward. 2 Troop were leading this mission, with our farmyard boys behind them; 1 and 3 completed the dart shape at the rear.

We pushed up towards a wooded area north of the village; the open fields and rutted cart tracks meant the going was as good as it could be in bocage terrain. Four Fireflies populated our squadron: two were with us in Teddy Foster's 4 Troop, and the other two sat in the middle of our slow-moving triangle. Some weird Sherman conversions with sharp iron prongs welded to their fronts joined the party, too. The guys called them 'Rhinos' and they were there to clear a pathway through the thick bocage and trees. Swarms of infantry were everywhere, and a squad of soldiers hitched a ride with us on our way up the hill.

'Cheeky bastards,' moaned my new bow gunner.

'Cheeky fuckers indeed,' agreed Buff. 'Always after an easy life.'

Nerves began to kick in and we felt on edge, but Oink and Kosher were visible and that helped to settle our stomachs as we ground our way forward. Fireflies were big hitters in the British Tank Corps and were introduced to combat the might of German 88s. In our case, I was unsure if Oink and Kosher intimidated or amused the Krauts. Maybe the bright yellow names splashed across their turrets were an ingenious deception of ours?

As we slowly bounced towards the meeting point, confidently fearful was the only way I could describe my emotions. Our orders were to set up in the hull-down position when only the commander's head and main gun were visible.

'They can't see you, but you can see them,' our man said with noticeable hesitation.

'Where did you read that, boss?' I asked.

'In the training manual.'

Like in cars, ours remained unread and was taped to the underside of my driver's seat.

'Twist?' The question came from Tom.

'Do what?'

'Twist? Cards?' He held up a deck. Tom, one of life's perpetual smilers, dealt both of us a five-card hand of poker. The cards were curled up at the corners and sticky, just like on Thursday poker nights in my other life.

Being shut down and stationary with your engine running for an hour was uncomfortable, and heat and petrol fumes worsened it. Hull-down also meant claustrophobia because the driver and his bow gunner couldn't see outside. Cards and smoking acted as a distraction; we got through a packet of Woodbines, which did little to enhance the fetid atmosphere.

'Jesus, boys, it's like pea soup up here.'

'Happy to swap,' replied Tom.

No answer. I'd learned the gunner's name was Chris and his loader was my namesake, Peter. If I strained my neck around, all I could see were the soles of their boots. I nodded and picked up another hand of cards from 'Smiler'.

Playing cards on manoeuvre was a big 'no' for some commanders but Buff seemed relaxed about it and occasionally joined in; he was good like that and even better at taking our money. We managed to get a few more rounds in, with Tom pocketing most of the pennies, before our radio sparked into life. Everyone sat up.

Teddy Foster was on the troop's B channel. 'Okay, chaps, off we bally well go.'

'Bally well' – so funny. What was bally short for, I wondered?

'Recce troop from A Squadron have lost two tanks. We've been asked to take up their position.'

Losing two reconnaissance tanks probably meant eight guys were dead. I worried whether Tony and Big Nige were in that unit, but with no time for sentiment, we put away the cards. Being an old hand in surveillance, I knew this meant we were first in the firing line.

Buff did nothing to soften the blow when he told us that the enemy was gathering in numbers on the other side of Hill 113. My pathetic attempt to break the ice was unappreciated. 'Krauts, look out. A stampede of cows and pigs is coming your way. And let's not forget Gobbler.'

'Outstanding, Meadows. Eyes on the road, please.' Buff's voice was calm and business-like.

We listened in on the brigade's frequency and heard Squadron A was encountering trouble on our left flank. The mood shifted from relatively chilled to highly agitated in double-quick time. Teddy Foster, second in line, ordered us to drop back.

Troop commanders often rotated the unenviable task of being a lead tank, so we were glad ours was second up on this occasion. In another wasted attempt to lighten the mood, I said, 'Fudge packers up the rear, sir.'

'Some of your words are lost on me, Meadows,' groaned a mystified Buff.

97

At around noon we smashed our way into yet another cornfield and continued to follow the track marks of Oink, Gobbler and Kosher in that order. Apart from the furrows carved through the crop by our tanks, the wheat looked golden and ripe for harvest. As we eased down a gentle incline, I wished I were controlling a combine harvester and not a war wagon.

More concerning was the sound of our engine: a loud vibrating rattle was coming from somewhere towards the back end of Daisy and the temperature gauge was showing red. 'Buff, we have a problem,' I told him.

'Yep, I can hear that. Let's stop and have a look.'

Ten minutes later, with steam coming out of her rear end, we identified the problem: a leak in Daisy's cooling system. The good news was that we could make a temporary fix.

'We'll get the vets onto it later.' Buff didn't seem phased. My limited knowledge of car radiators reminded me of raw eggs: if you cracked one into a leaking radiator, it plugged the hole. As I remember, that was another Pop 'top trick' that never seemed to work. And my suggestion that the solution may be in our repair manual fell on deaf ears.

'Forget bloody eggs – just top her up with water.'

Teddy Foster confirmed that the rest of our troop would make their way towards the ridge on Hill 113 and wait for us. That was less than thirty minutes away.

The sound of artillery fire was close. From behind the glow on a distant tree line someone, somewhere, was getting a good stonking. I couldn't tell if it was the Jerries or us dishing it out as orange balls of flame jumped into the sky. I felt uneasy again and noticed that Tom, squatting over the engine with me, had finally lost his smile.

The others had already tucked inside. Chris manually traversed the turret 180 degrees until our big gun was pointing towards the mayhem across the field.

'Get ready to go, Meadows,' ordered Buff.

We sealed the engine cover and were inside Daisy in less than two minutes; not quite a Grand Prix wheel change, but it was impressive.

Over the background noise of rumbling gunfire, my ears were buzzing. They had been like this for days. Like me, Pop had suffered from tinnitus. Perhaps the ravages of war noise like this had played their part? I'm pretty sure Deep Purple caused mine.

When I hit the road in my 'little old NAR', Pink Floyd's psychedelic twiddlings had to be temporarily parked in the karma of my bedroom because *Made in Japan*, the most incredible live rock album of all time, was the one for the road. Like all my LPs, I'd recorded this classic album onto cassette tape so the original vinyl could be locked away safely forever. We all did this; that's why fifty years later, most of my collection is still in mint condition. It was also when the rock stars of yesteryear started to moan about their royalty fees.

While Blackmore and Gillan did their thing, my speakers pogoed on the parcel shelf behind me and my tonsils got a strenuous workout. And what about those speakers? They were big enough to block out my rear view – but who used the mirrors anyway? – and loud enough to blow the rivets that held my NAR together.

'I can hear you a mile off,' Pop used to say before adding, 'and as Michael Caine once said, "the speakers will blow the bloody doors off".' His half-quote from the movie *The Italian Job* was a classic and one to savour.

'We are vulnerable here, guys; let's get going,' came the order from Buff. 'Close down hatches.'

'No shit, Sherlock.'

'Do what?' He wouldn't have understood.

Buff, in his commander's seat, always insisted on sitting 'up and out' of the turret hatch when we were in open ground. 'For extra visibility, gentlemen,' he would say.

Like us, he rarely wore a helmet, choosing to strap his onto the machine gun stand behind him. He dressed it with a set of goggles and our regimental scarf, a decoy ploy often used against snipers, though I think Buff's was more of a mascot. We called him Errol. Many commanders saw the helmets as a badge of honour, proudly showing off the subsequent bullet holes.

Later statistics compiled for British tank crews in Normandy demonstrated that half their casualties were caused inside the tanks, and 25% were hit outside, mainly through enemy shelling into camps. That left a quarter of all tank crew casualties 'partially' out; these were the commanders – another good reason why promotion to this lofty position was seen as the kiss of death.

We preferred to be 'heads-up' but based on the proximity of more fireworks going off behind us, we were pleased with the order to 'close down and move out'. I always felt happier on the move and was now feeling even more so because our temperature gauge was finally behaving itself. Peace and relative tranquillity had been restored.

'Shit. He's hit! Turner's hit!' Chris the gunner shouted.

An almighty bang burst my eardrums as something nasty thumped into the top right-hand side of our tank. A spray of orange flashes and sparks sprayed down over Tom. The force was so brutal that it shifted us off course to the left. Instinctively, I yanked the right lever back. Daisy didn't respond as black smoke quickly filled our driver's chamber.

'This is a brew-up, boys.' Thoughts of Ronsons, tommy cookers and seconds to evacuate flooded my mind.

'Can you turn this fucker forty-five degrees?' It was Chris. 'They got us to starboard and our turret is jammed.'

'I'll give it a go.'

Daisy felt crippled, but I tugged the right lever again and rammed the left one forward. As the gearbox crashed into first gear, Daisy's V8 screamed in agony. The temporary fix had been just that: the temperature dial was back on red. 'Please, girl,' I begged, 'don't let me down; just a little more.'

Slowly Daisy corkscrewed to the right. The oil light was also red, and we needed a few more seconds to get our gun aligned with the target area Chris had identified. At last it came into view through my optics. I assumed the others, like me, could see movement in the hedgerow only about 150 yards away. But with Buff silent, no orders came.

'Can you see the fuckers, Chris?' I shouted. He didn't reply. 'Can anyone see them?'

Chris introduced himself with a blast of fire from his coaxial machine gun. A stream of orange tracers marked the spot for his following action: to trigger our main gun with his foot.

Daisy rocked backwards and we watched the dense foliage erupt into a blanket of flame, smoke and torched undergrowth. Peter loaded and more tracers followed, some from Tom who was off his seat now. Standing as if playing an arcade machine, he roared like Tony had a few days earlier. With his smile gone and surges of adrenalin pulsing through his body, he was screaming like a maniac.

The noise was horrific, and the extractor fans struggled to clear the thick smoke inside Daisy. She shook as another high explosive launched into the trees and lifted them into the air. But we were brewing now, and as flames began to lick hungrily at our ammo storage, it was time to get out.

The order came from Chris. Tom had already gone, and I watched as the boots of our gunner and loader disappeared through their hatches above me. I heaved my lid open and grabbed my Schmeisser. As the others dropped off the tank, they faced the flaming bocage; instinct made me go the other way towards the open field.

Why the fuck did they do that? I crawled back towards Daisy's rear end. Unlike the contrasting carnage on the other side, the wheat field near me was untouched.

It felt strange. My last battle in a cornfield had been with my mates when we'd had them in Great Bardfield. Harvest time was when stubble fights were as real as it got for war-hungry kids brought up on Hollywood films.

It was especially exciting when the farmers burned off the unwanted straw left in neat rows by giant combine harvesters. Like our tanks, these huge machines, with lights like glowing eyes, were relentless as they trundled up and down twenty-four hours a day. Burn-offs usually occurred at dusk; ignorance meant it was believed that this practice was harmless.

'It's perfect for the soil,' Pop stated knowingly. 'It combats pests and weeds, you know.'

To a certain extent he was right, but the practice was banned in 1993 mainly for pollution reasons. Before then, climate change issues and eco-warriors didn't exist; the only environmental concern for me was saving Bengal Tigers or blue whales from extinction.

Mum was concerned, however. She got more pissed off than usual at harvest time (and it was the only time we heard her use that word), especially when her windows were freshly washed with vinegar and warm water, or her Persil-white clothes were hanging out to dry.

'Peter, please have a word,' she'd tell Pop. He didn't. Whether it was tobacco or wheat, the farming brotherhood was strong.

I loved that time of year. I thought about the stubble fight. Like the raves of the noughties, inside knowledge taught us the next field to be torched. There was no internet or social media, just old-fashioned, 'nudge-nudge, wink-wink' intelligence.

We gave ourselves thirty minutes of prep time before splitting up to build forts from our bicycles and go-karts, which were usually made from pram wheels. These forts made great defensive lines against enemy foot patrols and helped us eventually escape from whichever farmer was chasing us.

As thick lines of smoke and flames snaked towards us, sometimes ten feet high, we made our bombs from clumps of corn stubble we'd yanked out of the ground.

Moulding the clay-covered root ends into perfectly sculptured missile tips was a significant art form. Fuelled by teenage testosterone, we sometimes inserted stones and other sharp objects into them. This made things realistic and their eventual target impact more meaningful. That was ironic, because the German potato-masher stick grenades bouncing off our tanks in Normandy were similar!

Robert Bardsley, a living testament and legend to our ramped-up version of warfare, carelessly lost two front teeth in one such confrontation. And when things got dire, we lit the stubble ends from the flames lapping our ankles and hurled them at each other like Molotov cocktails.

'Peter, please say something! Someone will get killed soon.' Mother again. It was a fair point as she patched up another Germolene-impregnated wound after one of those late-night skirmishes.

Pop would nod earnestly and relight a bowl of his favourite St Bruno pipe tobacco. It was fun and total madness, but Mary Hopkin summed it up nicely at the time: 'Those were the days, my friend'!

'What am I waiting for?' I wondered.

The answer came, and it was an unmistakable sound; chilling and loud, a Spandau's rapid *brrr-brrr* rattle smashed through the relative calm. Metallic clanks followed as bullets rebounded off Daisy and others ricocheted into things more forgiving, making a thudding *oomph* sound.

I desperately wanted to hear the slower chuntering rattle of return fire from my colleagues, but it didn't happen. I pushed my face into the ground and the cool soil moistened my tongue as the mayhem continued.

Eventually it stopped; it was time to do something important. Were they reloading? Seven seconds to escape – but would it take them that long?

Dragging myself forward, I peered around the back of Daisy. Steam hissed angrily from the grilles above her engine, and drops of boiling water ran off the deck onto me. I wanted to scream, and I rolled over as the scalding pain of poached skin spread over my back.

The cool earth and adrenalin surge helped to calm me, but where was the offending machine-gun post? Peering round the corner of Daisy, I saw that Peter was there – partially. Fragments of his body lay twisted and dumped into what looked like a mangled mass of spaghetti meatballs. Eager flies had already settled on the remains of his scalp.

Two burning questions remained: why did they drop onto this side, and did Buff get hit first? Where was he? 'Buff?' I called quietly. No answer.

'Tom?' Still no reply.

The spitting crackle of sparks and the hiss of billowing smoke from the ruptured guts of our tank filled my ears instead. It looked like the work of a Panzerfaust, or possibly a self-propelled anti-tank gun – probably the latter, given our heavy shunt sideways.

For more than a minute, the Spandau remained quiet. Most machine gunners would want to see the result of their handiwork, and my concern was how many there were. The answer came when three German soldiers stepped onto the scorched field and casually walked towards Daisy.

I thought of the Schmeisser. *Bloody hell*. Morton's reminder of how the Germans dealt with looters flooded back.

The men walking towards me were young, and their green uniforms indicated Wehrmacht. Would they go gently with someone their own age?

My naivety hit a wall when a man appeared wearing the same uniform as our old friend from a few days earlier. His trench coat, remarkably like the one I'd bought from the Army and Navy stores in Colchester, flapped around his ankles. Mine was a standard issue in design; his was Hugo Boss like most things the SS wore.

I couldn't see his face but he was older and not as casual in demeanour as the boys behind him. He moved purposefully and was closing in on me fast.

This level of fear was a new experience for me. Only the combat game paintball came remotely close; although a thousand miles away from this scenario, being battered by hard, marble-sized slugs is scary and it hurts.

One experience of paintball stayed with me. As brightly coloured pellets fizzed over like tracers, our attackers on that day – especially one person – seemed obsessed with killing someone: me!

Billy Crake, a person who looked nuts on a typical day, was the man. With a captured flag held aloft and killer eyes bulging, he pumped round after round of dye-filled capsules into my cowering torso. At a range of two feet, clamped firmly underneath his right boot, a pattern of love-bite welts melded over my back and legs. They needed some explanation when my wife administered ice packs and antiseptic cream inquiringly, but not that sympathetically, a little later.

Another victim spent the night in A&E. 'Mad Frankie Fraser', named after the infamous London gangster, had leapt into the poor man's foxhole and, out of ammo, used the butt of his gun instead. Corporate team-building was all the rage in those days.

The men striding towards our tank, the leader in black jackboots, were not like him – they were the real deal. As with 'Mad Frankie', there weren't any rules; if captured, I faced a firing squad – and they wouldn't be using pretty paintball pellets.

As they got nearer, the excited chatter grew louder. It was amazing how unphased these men were having just wiped out a tank crew and with chunks of badly butchered human flesh in evidence everywhere. I could see now that they were just boys wearing oversized overcoats and lopsided helmets, which made them look comical.

At fifty yards, the one in charge snarled an order and the animated conversation behind him stopped. Rifles were raised, bayonets fixed.

My mouth turned dry and my hands began to shake again. *Not now, Calum.* I fumbled for the safety catch and, for the longest second ever, couldn't find it.

As the Germans advanced, their eyes and guns scanned in my direction.

Come on, you fucker. It couldn't end like this, surely? I felt the safety catch click off noisily, though the men didn't hear it. After a visual magazine check, I waited. *Quiet Calum.* I couldn't give myself away now. *What range did these guns have anyway?*

Michael and his brother flashed back. *About 100 yards for a Sten, but these?*

Then, at about twenty yards, the SS man saw me. He stopped suddenly, seemingly frozen to the spot. Primal instinct, or unadulterated fear, kicked in; this was my only chance. I pulled the trigger and kept it there. The gun kicked slightly to the left, but it was smooth and incredibly quiet for a sub-machine gun. It was also very accurate as its snout sprayed bullets left to right.

The unprepared men fell to the ground. Although it felt unreal, it was easy; I had been lucky. The Schmeisser did well and in no time, three humans lay contorted and dead before me.

It was ironic, a German-made weapon ripping German-made bullets into one of their own. I remembered the staff sergeant's words when he'd given me the Schmeisser.

But something more perverse coursed through my mind and it disturbed me: I felt good. Three seconds to snuff out three lives was not bad – and three Kraut families had been destroyed. But pinging my friend's brother with an air-rifle pellet had upset me more than watching a German's arm and shoulder detach itself.

As I waited for another opportunity, an intense feeling of animation took over. 'Come on, boys. Come to Daddy,' I muttered. It was irrational and frightening, but I repeated it, wanting more.

My hands continued to tremble. It was a risk, but I put the gun down and clasped them together. Why me? Why was I still alive? The realisation began to sink in.

As my euphoria dipped, my brief respite ended when I saw more movement at the edge of the field. Something flashed – or was it a reflection? *Of course. They'd been sent on a recce. Idiot.*

Pressing myself hard into the ground, I pushed back towards the other side of Daisy. A wave of heat wafted out from beneath her belly. Given the amount of ammunition we had on board, why she hadn't brewed-up yet was a mystery.

Leading up the hill was my escape route: two parallel tracks made by the other tanks from our troop.

I slithered into one of the ruts and inched forward. The channel was narrow, and the tall wheat stems on either side were threaded with wild oats and bright red poppies. This crop was taller than those in my modern-day life and provided the perfect cover. Shorter, weed-free and genetically modified might be good in some ways, but it was not great when trying to escape from Germans. That thought made me chuckle.

Buff, what happened to Buff? The others were dead, but where was he?

Any faint glimmer of hope extinguished itself when I saw him. He was there all right, upright in the turret and correctly positioned as any commander should be. He held a pistol and everything looked normal, but something important was missing: his large, woolly-faced head.

A second later Daisy disappeared too, obliterated by an 88mm shell. This time the goodies inside her erupted. I kept my head low and scrambled towards Hill 113.

Everything happened in a haze. Soon a 'Katy' ambulance, driven by Trooper William Robertson, scooped me up and rushed me back to the medical centre at RHQ. He quickly gave me a quick once-over and offloaded me; later research confirmed that his many exploits on 29th June 1944 gained him the Military Medal for bravery.

'Did it work, son?'

My old friend 'Sergeant Schmeisser' walked past as I jumped from the ambulance. 'Yes, I guess so. Got at least three.'

'Wouldn't know. Never shot a dickie bird.' His reply surprised me, but I read somewhere that most soldiers didn't discharge their guns during the war.

On being presented with a shaken but uninjured soldier, the doctor checked me over and promptly declared me fit enough for immediate duty. The sweet builder's tea thrust into my hand was soothing but turned to poison when an enthusiastic young officer wandered into the medical tent and posed the question. 'Indeed, he is, sir,' the doctor replied. 'He's all yours.'

So another brief respite ended; it had been less than an hour since I'd been collected from Hill 113. There was no time to grieve or reflect, which didn't help the situation.

Ambivalence was the best word to describe my feelings, and that worried me. Was it a result of being lost from my real world? Or did my father, like me, feel protected by a strange autopilot invincibility? Did he feel as ambivalent about snuffing out human life as I did?

'War is black and white, son, brutal on every level. There's certainly no time for sentiment,' Pop once said. Perhaps that's why I felt the way I did.

Shepherded from the makeshift surgery to allow in someone more deserving, I followed my new boss. He stopped abruptly. 'My last driver got it in the head,' he said. 'A complete bugger, but she's been cleaned up now.' Was it a bugger that his driver was dead or that the tank got splattered with his blood? He then told me that Major Teddy Foster wanted to see me.

'Asking after my health?' I asked.

'Unlikely.'

'Then I've done wrong, sir?'

He ignored my question and ushered me away impatiently.

An assortment of thoughts, mostly negative ones, scrambled my brain as I went to meet the major. He was sitting on a box making a brew on what the desert veterans called a Benghazi boiler. These were metal drums filled with petrol-soaked sand and covered by a metal grate. They not only put out substantial heat but were quick at boiling water for brews and heating food – definitely one up from the inefficient but faithful tommy stove.

Whatever heating method we used, everyone agreed that tea was the most crucial thing in our lives – that, and staying alive. Hot food and letters from home came next. The latter hadn't arrived yet, and who would write to me anyway? The lads regularly sent home field service cards, but these were multiple-choice questionnaires where all you could do was indicate how well you felt, wounded or not, whether you'd got your letter or not, etc. They were deliberately vague and designed to protect regimental plans if the cards fell into enemy hands. It was always better to send handwritten letters, but troop commanders occasionally censored them.

Even though they were estranged, I wondered whether Pop's wife would write. That would be an unwelcome problem – how would I reply? But letters might also give me answers to some of my questions.

I saluted the major crisply and waited. He did away with the usual formalities and gestured for me to join him on what I now identified as a large munitions box. It was unopened and therefore presumably alive with the stuff.

'At ease, trooper.' He lit two cigarettes and passed one to me.

At ease? We were about to go up in smoke!

'Two troop commanders have observed your efforts and fortitude, son.' I loved the word 'fortitude'. He continued in a posh west-country accent. 'Promotion will be forthcoming, once things settle down.' He patted me on the back like an obedient Labrador while I waited for him to say, 'Good boy.'

'Bally good job, Meadows. Bally good job.' There it was, another great word.

At school, a teacher called Jimmy Yule liked that phrase, too. The major not only looked like him but also spoke like him. Precise in diction, very loud and reeking of cigarette breath, Colonel Yule was a tall, dapper man who wore smart grey suits with matching waistcoats. He could only have been from the military. To complete his look, he had shiny black shoes with blakeys in their heels and a neatly manicured RAF-style moustache that sprouted proudly from his top lip.

We all knew his history and, although we respected him, we enjoyed taking the piss out of him too. Morning assembly was a good time for that.

As 'Jimmy Boy' herded us into some semblance of order, his favourite rant was always bellowed in regimental sergeant-major style. 'Get into ranks, boys! I say bally, well, fall in line!'

We would deliberately line up haphazardly to make him say it. The colonel had been a PoW at the infamous Colditz prison in

Leipzig; in my time at school in the 1970s, a BBC television series of the same name had made Jimmy a cult hero, especially with the boys.

Colditz was a high-security establishment and mainly hosted recaptured PoW escapees from other less-secure German prisons. These men were usually officers, and Jimmy Yule was one of them. Amongst many well-documented exploits, he was part of an illicit team operating a clandestine wireless set to receive coded messages from British intelligence.

Jimmy was also a virtuoso musician. Richard Crane and I once sang 'Bridge Over Troubled Water' in assembly while he tinkled the ivories behind us. 'Let me introduce you to the next Simon and Garfunkel popular music group,' he announced proudly.

Our mates sniggered in the front row and made predictable hand gestures to put us off. They cheered us for an encore, though, and with a limited repertoire, we sang it again. My solo was the third verse, 'Sail on silver girl'.

The musical group he organised in Colditz was a much more serious affair and became famous for creating diversionary tactics to help orchestrate prison escapes. Although the colonel absconded from other prisons, he preferred to be a 'conductor' in this one. Good old Colonel Jimmy Yule. He was a true inspiration and a man I remembered fondly.

Back to his kindred spirit, Major Foster; my respect for him was not quite the same.

'Fucking *observed*,' I wanted to say. 'Trying to help us would have been good.' Deciding not to go down that road, I took the praise instead; this could have been the shortest promotion ever. Promises of a commission in the field were mentioned next, and Colonel Hopkinson would be duly informed as a primary signatory to the formalities.

In conclusion to our 'little chat', as he put it, Foster closed the meeting by inviting me to report to Troop Leader Major Hales of B Squadron. 'Be a good chap and make yourself known to Hale and Hearty,' his idea of a joke. 'Bally good man. Bally good.'

Foster patted me on the shoulder and squeezed it hard before ushering me away. That was my cue to leave, and it was the last we saw of the major for almost four weeks. Having been wounded in a tank skirmish later that day, he had to be carted off back to England for repairs. We later learned that severe burns had been the problem (a common injury for tankies) and he would be okay.

Something else occurred to me then. Sitting on an ammo box by an open fire with a fag on? Bally idiot.

From Peter Meadows' memoirs

While endeavouring to capture Point 113, my tank commander told me to drive forward and down a long slope of fully grown wheat. Just as we reached some small trees, we were hit broadside and suddenly stopped. Looking up into the turret, I saw two pairs of legs disappearing so I decided to join them; although I had been given no command, the gun was still undamaged.

As I moved to the left side of the tank, another shell hit the other side where my comrades were standing and they were killed instantly. I realised how vulnerable I was; the only chance I had was to crawl up the hill using the path where the tank tracks had flattened the wheat and I would be unseen by the enemy.

The 44th tanks were lined up on the ridge in hull-down positions, and one picked me up and took me to the field ambulance. I had not been wounded, so the doctor made me a strong cup of tea while an enthusiastic officer came along and asked the doctor if I was OK to drive his tank, having just lost his driver. It was my lucky day for now; I had a new tank with a new tank commander.

On the Way to Vire

When I found Major Hales, it was coffee on the go rather than tea. He offered me one and a shot of something more potent from a leather-bound hip flask tucked inside his boot. The coffee tasted authentic, not the bland Camp coffee concoction that was all the rage, the same stuff that Mum used in her coffee-and-walnut cakes. 'That's good, sir,' I said.

'Acquired from our American cousins, my dear fellow.'

I nodded as a new friend, Bourbon, kicked in. Hales dribbled some Carnation cream from a tin into my mug. What in our meagre ration packs would tempt the Yanks to trade proper coffee with us? Plum duff, maybe?

After carefully measuring another slug of the hard stuff, he quickly screwed the tiny silver top tight. 'Enough of the foreplay, Meadows. Let's get down to business.'

The major gave me a heads-up on our plans and asked me to remain discreet because his full briefing would occur in the morning. Another product of Sandhurst, he spoke quickly and was frighteningly enthusiastic. The quality these commissioned officers had in spades was invincibility and confidence; with absolutely no experience but tremendous self-belief, their manner helped calm the nerves of mere mortals like us.

He explained that the Americans were moving around from the west and our objective was to link up with them in the Normandy town of Vire. The heavy aerial bombing had flattened much of the region and Vire, understood to be a German stronghold supporting much of its communications network, had not been spared. Our mission was to check out this intelligence.

It felt good to have the major's confidence; so far, the vibes around my promotion were encouraging. After a little more post-coital chit-chat – his words, not mine – he asked me to attend an O-group meeting at 06.30 hours the following day.

'I suggest we find your tank and its crew, trooper.' He winked, presumably a tease regarding my forthcoming promotion, and stood up abruptly. Like Foster earlier, that signalled the end of our meeting.

We searched through a maze of vehicles and military paraphernalia before finding the crew asleep underneath my new tank. Introductions could wait; rather than disturb them, I laid my bed roll out behind my new office, the turret.

Despite the feral snorts permeating from below, the residual engine warmth made it wonderfully toasty. While the Ford engine cooled down from its exertions, I came down from mine. With a gutful of coffee and a generous quantity of bourbon inside me, I lit up my last cigarette and inhaled deeply. It felt good to chill for a while and to reflect on another crazy day.

'Sergeant Meadows, that was completely nuts,' I told myself. That first bit sounded good, but the last few hours had been traumatic and my hands started to tremble again. I had just killed three men, for fuck's sake – torn them to shreds.

Some innate self-preservation instinct kicked in that stopped me from dwelling too much on that thought. It had been them or me, and this time I had won. But surely remorse should have overridden that sentiment? I had none, and sleep came quickly.

In terms of contribution, my first O-meeting was a non-event. Being the new boy in our group and three other keen tank commanders looking to impress, I thought it best to listen and learn.

We were Troop 2 in B Squadron; our tanks were unimaginatively allocated numbers rather than names. I commanded Tank 2 and would lead the group for our trip to Le Beny Bocage. Our destination was only twenty miles away, but due to the rugged terrain it would take about ten hours of travelling time.

My old muckers in the recce team reported small pockets of German resistance concealed in the usual hiding places; it was always easier for them to defend from the bocage than for us to flush out the buggers. The Recce group also informed us that the hills were steeper nearer to Vire, and the fields were tighter than those we were accustomed to.

'Hopefully a pleasant introduction for our new tank commander,' concluded Major Hales, having just imparted the news about my tank leading off proceedings.

I returned from the meeting to find my new crew mates seated in a tight row on the back of our tank. They looked nervous and

112

more than a little angst-ridden. I guessed what they might be thinking and reverted to a strategy I'd used in my old life when meeting new sales teams. A quick observation confirmed two things: firstly, and valuable to see, there were no old-timers in the mix. They could be awkward buggers who like to throw curve balls. Secondly, they were all bigger than me; I was the smallest person on our crew. Back to my father's height phobia! Would they see me as the little guy with a chip on his shoulder, or just one of them?

Whatever their response, this would be a new experience for me.

'Good morning, my name is Peter Meadows.' They straightened up; that was nice to see. 'Tell me who you are and how you're feeling.'

This was a time to be on the front foot and show confidence; they didn't know me from a bar of carbolic soap. The first to introduce himself was Trooper Ian Taylor, my driver; I liked him immediately, probably because he came from Norwich and I'm shallow.

I went round the other three in turn. They all seemed keen and 'talked a good talk', but they were raw, which worried me. My big concern was being first out of the starting blocks supported by an inexperienced crew who had not seen action. They told me their last stop had been at Worthing camp near Brighton just two days earlier. It crossed my mind that the grown-ups knew this and that we were expendable, chosen to lead this mission as decoy fodder. After our demise, the Fireflies would mosey in and finish off those targets we'd softened up.

That is paranoid, Calum. I dismissed the fear immediately.

'Okay, listen up. These are my ground rules.' I explained what was expected from the team. 'One hundred per cent focus, ignore the rule book and listen to me.' Pausing for effect, I added. 'Lastly, look after each other.'

'Yes, sir.' They nodded in unison.

In tanks more than elsewhere on the battlefield, survival depended on this. And then I remembered Buff and replicated his final briefing order, which was always the same. 'Finally, chaps, respond immediately to my orders and ask questions later. Do you have any questions now?'

'What do you do for a piss, mate?'

Apart from Brummie, a Geordie accent is probably the most annoying. This one belonged to my new gunner, Sidney Cartwright. He smirked at the others, which I noted they didn't reciprocate. I also noticed that he worked hard to avoid eye contact with me.

'If it's safe, Sidney, piss outside the tank.' I looked at the others. 'If not, there's always an empty shell casing.'

They laughed, he didn't, and nothing came back to me in response. I couldn't leave it at that. 'If that doesn't work, piss your fucking pants.'

The man irritated me; if his attitude was typical of the crew, there was work to do. His smirk annoyed me, too. 'And finally, *mate*, call me sergeant.'

Apart from that initial spat, the crew got our tank ready in textbook fashion. Our loader, Charlie Downs, and bow gunner, Chris from Diss, another Norfolk lad, made up the team. Both seemed anxious, so I spent time with them as they completed their preparations.

In my limited experience, tankies lived in a bubble and were generally a very insular group of men. I think that was why Pop was suited to that environment: being a loner was good. At the time of his death, you could name his true friends – including those in the family he liked – on one hand!

Since the start of my current situation, I had been surrounded by men just like me; all that mattered was 'the bubble' and the people inside it. Everything is about survival in an adrenalin and emotionally charged environment; to achieve this, we looked out for each other.

It was gratifying to see how quickly the boys worked together, including, to be fair, Knobhead Cartwright; it was a good sign and the crew impressed me.

Tanks always needed routine maintenance, and having recently become a driver-mechanic, I checked in with Taylor to see how he was doing. His focus was on hydraulics and suspension in the track system, supplemented by the joy of walloping various parts with a sledgehammer.

Taylor was a squat, powerful man with arms like tree trunks and hands like shovels. He reminded me of Mac Beanland and my adolescent farming days.

'It's just like a tractor in many ways, sir.' His broad Norfolk, 'Hev yew gotta loight boy?' dialect made me feel good. He gave one of the bogie wheels another almighty thump and I watched dried mud and stone explode from the track above it.

Mac was the first to show me how to use a grease gun; when Taylor picked up his and pushed the head onto a grease nipple, I chuckled at the memory of my first time using one. 'Gentle son, like it's your mam's tit,' said Mac in his soft Derbyshire accent. That was pretty rude for the ears of an innocent, hormone-fuelled teenager. 'Squeeze the trigger until you see grease gunge out somewhere, and then find another teat, son.'

I was good at using the grease gun, and it soon became a regular job on Mac's two tractors, baler and the colossal combine he leased at harvest time.

'You know much about them?' I asked Taylor hopefully. 'Tractors, I mean?'

'Yep. Farmer's son born and bred.'

I wished I had taken that path in my youth. Good at biology and chemistry, and with some farm experience, agricultural college and animal conservation would have ticked all my career aspirations. Sadly, my vocational guidance teacher had other ideas. His advice was to drop my two strong subjects, take my weaker ones (mathematics and physics), and join the merchant navy. The navy? Why?

It was utterly ridiculous, but my father also liked this crackpot idea. I didn't and I loathed the urgent call he made to the personnel department at Shell UK in London to get me an interview. Up we went by train. Thankfully, it didn't go well, and my chance to join the oil tanker fleet sank, along with my father's aspirations.

I failed most of my exams and the opportunities I dreamt about as a kid disappeared. I wasn't bitter, just annoyed that life-changing decisions had to be made at thirteen years of age.

'Guess what I have found, sarge.'

I shrugged and waited while Taylor gently rummaged inside a khaki-coloured kitbag. Eventually, a small round tin appeared, and he carefully flipped the lid open. Nestled in some straw were six brown eggs. After tenderly brushing them with a finger, he closed the cover and offered them to me like some sacred offering.

The image of a raid on a chicken shed in Norfolk made me laugh. He read my mind and shook his head. 'Got them from a Froggie farm yesterday.'

I liked him even more and imagined the taste of these beauties in a full English. I made a note to myself to get hold of some bacon.

We had a couple of hours to kill before leaving the laager. Mobile shower units had arrived again, a luxury we probably wouldn't see for a while. The major had already tipped me off about its arrival time, so I was at the front of a fast-growing queue. Armed with my shaving kit, a wooden toothbrush with pig-hair bristles and a round tin of Colgate tooth powder, I waited for the shower block to open.

I remembered the Gibbs brand from when I was a boy. All you did was dip a dampened toothbrush into the minty green powder, load it and brush away. Toothpaste technology was in its infancy; the alternatives were a red-striped paste in a tube or powder. Pop didn't like either, so he used salt!

The distinct disinfectant smell of carbolic soap greeted me as I walked into the cubicle. It was surprising how hot the water was and how much muck came from unmentionable parts of my body. Not since my trip to Kilimanjaro in 2013 had so many unknown orifices made themselves known to me! It had been over two months since my last proper wash and the simple pleasure of a hot sluice-down felt great.

Allocated ten minutes, I forgot to shave and shut my eyes as warm water jets went to work. This was a moment to savour.

'What the f…?' What I saw on my left forearm shocked me. The tattoo – why hadn't I noticed it before? My old man was among the minority of dads with tattoos, which impressed me and my friends. They were not as common as in my modern-day life, and they certainly weren't considered fine artworks; they were vulgar and worn only by ex-military men and hairy bikers. However, Pop's explanation seemed heroic as my gang of admirers gathered around his arm.

'A badge of honour, boys. We were about to go to war.' We waited for more. 'It was a bond.'

'Ugly fucker looks like my sister,' quipped Ricky.

'Prettier than mine,' countered another mate, Alun.

My arm had been itching and I'd put this down to a mosquito bite, but it soon became apparent behind the soap bubbles that my body-art acquisition was new. It also felt raw and the emblem, a skull at the centre, looked gruesome and familiar. Stabbed through its left eye, a black-handled dagger with a wide blade appeared underneath a cracked jawbone. I had never noticed but it dripped blood, or were they tears?

Zig-zagging across the angry face swirled a banner boldly exclaiming *Death, Before Dishonour.* The other surprise was its high definition and bright colours; they had faded badly by the time I was a kid.

My college mate Nigel and I nearly succumbed to the temptation of arm art during a summer job in 1976. We pontificated for hours over our designs and tried to get clever with the words for our motif. Ultimately, we didn't have the money or the balls to go through with it.

Interestingly, what happened next was another form of art that cost more than £20 and was far more frightening: I had my hair permed. It was arguably braver than having a tattoo, and there was soon a different type of agony. It wasn't the pain of chemically infused hair wrapped around granny-sized curlers, or the cotton-wool strips twisted around my head and over my ears. Neither was the Star Wars array of light radiation a problem as I waited for things to bake, rise and curl. No, this pain was about humiliation, caused not only by my college chums watching through the salon windows like agitated baboons but also my dear old dad.

'I've inherited a son – I think it's a son but I'm not sure – who now looks like a bleeding Swan Vesta match.' An erupting Mount Vesuvius would have looked more benign.

Admittedly I was a skinny youth, and I liked to think I was a strawberry blonde not a ginger, but he did have a valid point. I think it's fair to say my father was utterly freaked out by the apparent demise of his son and his 'gay hairdo', as he put it.

117

'That's it, Shirley Temple! You look like Shirley, bloody Temple!' He called me that from then on and refused to talk to me for weeks. Had Esther Rantzen's Child Line been up and running, she might well have received a call.

As for Mum? Well, she loved it! 'I think it looks very nice, dear,' she said, smoothing her hands over my new creation as only women can do. That didn't help things at all.

'God al-effing-mighty,' Pop erupted again.

I felt sorry for the dog. Having returned from a five-mile route march with my father, he was promptly dragged out for another one!

There was an interesting footnote to this tale of woe: Nigel, most of my mates and Great Britain soon followed suit and had their hair permed. I blame Kevin Keegan.

'Come on, mate, time's up,' a curt reminder came from the other side of the shower door.

Agreed: it was time to get out and give someone else a chance. I gathered my stuff and went out into the morning sunshine to dry off, secretly admiring the new accessory on my forearm. I remembered one of our more creative motif ideas: *Always keep your chin up* bannered through a French guillotine. That amused me on my jog back to the others.

A few days later, we were heading south from Le Beny Bocage. It was miserable and drizzling with rain, but I felt like the king of the road; sitting on top of a Sherman made you realise how powerful these monsters were. It also reminded me how vulnerable the commander's position was.

But something was bugging me about this tank and why it differed from others in the battalion: it was the turret hatch or, to be correct, the door. This tank only had one, unlike the newer M4s with two: one for the loader and the other for the gunner and commander. Trust them to give me an old tank. I didn't care, but my loader might because in an emergency evacuation, he would have to climb over me to get out.

In terms of size, M4s were significantly taller than every other tank on the battlefield, including those of the enemy. Size is not always essential, and height is definitely not an advantage when hull-down in the bocage or trying to reduce silhouettes on the horizon.

On this day we were leading 2 Troop 'heads-up', and so far the terrain had been as predicted by the major. 'A piece of cake, old boy,' had been his assurance.

Although I liked my new boss Hales, he had been aloof after his initial welcome, and he'd recently made me forfeit three days' pay, which didn't help his cause much either. 'Due to your neglect of duty,' was how he'd framed it.

On a recent reconnaissance trip, I'd forgotten to ask my driver to complete the customary route back-up cards, which had led to my misdemeanour charge. It was tough at the top. To conclude my disciplinary meeting, Hales said, 'My dear fellow, the devil is always in the details.'

That was the friendliest bollocking ever, but he'd still docked my pay by six shillings, which in 2019 equated to around twelve pounds. On the plus side, he had promised me five days' leave once the Vire mission ended.

My initial thought was that we'd wait and see on that one because I didn't believe his promise for one minute. However, every cloud has a silver lining and the grapevine had recently told us that a patched-up Major Foster was back in command of C Squadron.

The terrain got more challenging as we eased our way around the edge of a steep slope between the dead carcasses of our rotting bovine friends. We were accustomed to this by now, and the odious whiff that went with them.

As yet another field presented itself, we crashed through a clutch of young conifer trees into an area of harvested corn. The straw lay in straight rows ready to be baled and the scene looked serene, enhanced by the sunshine breaking through. Sunshine always lifted the mood of a tank crew.

Only an intermittent radio crackle interrupted a feeling of relative calm inside our thirty tons of lumbering hulk. I flipped the frequency onto intercom mode. 'How are my happy campers, then?'

'We are doing okay, sergeant,' replied my new driver friend.

Cartwright gave me a thumbs-up, and Charlie, who was sitting beside him, did the same. I noted that his acknowledgement was more half-hearted.

'What about you, Chris?' Chris Smith was our lap gunner and he seemed to be the most nervous member of our crew. At eighteen he was also the youngest, the son of a WW1 veteran who had driven one of the first Mark 4 tanks in the Somme.

'Pretty fucking scared, if I'm honest, sir.'

'We're all scared, Chris.' My pounding heartbeat and parched tongue were a testament to that. I wondered whether he'd felt obliged to volunteer for the tank corps like his father.

Crouching like a crab behind Cartwright, I rested my binoculars on his shoulders. Situations like this had become familiar to us and made me especially wary. How depressing that such a gentle scene would forever be scored in my mind with a threat of danger.

These bins were heavier than my modern-day plastic ones but also seemed more powerful, which was helpful. Anything nasty lurking in the bushes had to be spotted quickly, and because we were the leading tank the pressure was on us to clear the way forward.

I looked behind me. Like some Roman general, the major was sitting astride his Firefly, doing the same thing as me. With his field glasses fixed firmly onto mine, he signalled us to move down to the left and onto what looked like a narrow farm track that ran directly parallel to us. 'Did you get that, Meadows?' he asked.

'Yes, sir. Are you following, or are we on our own?'

'On your own, son. Follow the track and see what you can find. We'll see you in the next field.'

I gave Taylor the order and immediately felt our tank slide down the steep slope to our left. Glancing down my route map, I noted that the next field was about one mile away. As we slid slowly down the track, I wondered whether anyone had ever rolled a Sherman M4.

'Close down, please, chaps.' As the driver's hatches clunked shut, I sank into my seat behind Cartwright and did the same thing. Around the inside rim of the cupola were six small windows, all I had to see through plus a periscope to give me another, albeit restricted, perspective.

We were on a heavily rutted farm track between two rows of spruce trees. 'Slow it down, Taylor. Eyes peeled, everyone.'

We lunged forward about a hundred yards before the welcome we feared most greeted us. A screaming blast of molten metal came from my left and hit the ground in front of Taylor.

A moment of stillness followed. We all knew what was coming next, and it came with an almighty boom. The tank shook violently as muddy bits of farm track lifted like a carpet before crashing back down to earth in huge lumps.

Like swifts in a feeding frenzy, two more missiles shrieked overhead. One landed beside us and the other thumped onto the road behind the tank. Both erupted in dustbin-sized chunks against our hull, which acted like a giant amplifier.

'Give it some welly, Taylor. Get the fuck out of here,' I ordered.

Our escape was going to be bumpy. I could hear the crashing sound of utensils and empty shell casings smashing around the driver's section below.

This strike had come from a six-barrelled field mortar known as a 'Moaning Mini'; their technical name was Nebelwerfers. Sinister weapons with types of cluster bombs, the Yanks liked to call them 'Screaming Mimis' because sirens fixed onto their tail fins howled for up to three miles before exploding amongst their traumatised victims.

I noticed that the bocage was denser to our left. My gut feeling was that the offending mortar was concealed somewhere there. 'Gunner, traverse ninety degrees left. Prepare to fire when I say.'

We had a high explosive in the spout and the coaxial machine gun was primed and ready to go as always. I desperately looked for clues as to where the enemy lay and soon found one. Farmers, in my experience, always liked neat hedgerows and I hoped the French were the same. A rough opening had been created about fifty yards ahead of us behind a wooden fence.

I gave Cartwright the heads-up and he manually set the elevation of the big gun as best he could, given our lurching forward movement.

We heard another screech and felt a jarring thump as the next shell fell just short amongst the trees to our port side. Birds exploded out of the bracken, which fizzed in tall flames. A cluster of young fir trees turned to charcoal in seconds.

'Driver. Stop now,' I instructed.

Shermans, as well as being fast, could stop quickly. We shuddered to a halt and I waited for the big gun to stabilise before I gave the next command, 'Fire and repeat. Fast as you can, gunner.'

Cartwright and Charlie worked well together, and I saw the hillside to our left burst into an orange glow of fire and smoke. High-explosive rockets and more machine-gun rounds battered the trees, hopefully terminating anything behind them.

After a few more tracer rounds, a German soldier appeared in the bullet-mown, smoke-filled clearing. He was in flames. Sid launched another rocket, and we watched an explosion of fire and black debris catapult him into the air like a spinning doll.

As a surge of adrenalin coursed through my veins, I felt euphoric. 'Go, driver. NOW.'

The farm track ended abruptly with the customary iron gate, so as standard practice we crashed through it and found ourselves in an open cornfield. This one hadn't been cut and we had no track marks to follow. I looked back to see the result of our work. 'Great job, boys.'

'Did you see that fucker fly?' It was Cartwright, and I knew he was getting off on the same irrational high as me. Perversely, I made a mental note to think about this later, but for now I would settle on the fine line between fear and battlefield exhilaration. We had survived.

The others said nothing. Smoke and flame stretched into the sky, accompanied by the gratifying noise of exploding ammunition. This was no time to dawdle, so I asked Taylor to put his foot down. The boys stayed quiet, apart from Chris from Diss who was singing.

I could see that my loader's hands were shaking uncontrollably as I reported to Major Hales, who seemed typically relaxed about our situation. Was it just a game to these guys? They were indeed a breed apart, and I admired their coolness.

'Saw the smoke from your little kerfuffle,' Hales said. 'Damned nuisance.'

How irritating for him. I smiled and calculated our meeting time to be approximately thirty minutes. The troop had pushed on fast and our orders were to catch up quickly.

'Guys, that was a near miss but a job well done.' No one said anything. 'Talk to me, boys. Are you okay?'

Cartwright was the first. 'Yes, sir, just a bit shook up.'

Charlie gave me a shaky thumbs-up and nodded vigorously, but he was clearly not okay.

'Let's get clear of this, then we'll stop for a brew.' I had no intention of doing so, but the crew were wiped out and needed a break. None of them had seen anything remotely like this before, nor presumably had Charlie or Sid ever killed anyone. The last few minutes had been brutal and as hardcore as it got, like everything I'd seen so far in this war.

We crossed the field and headed for a road that would take us straight to Major Hales and the rest of 2 Troop. I again gave the heads-up order because the field was open and it seemed we were not under threat. There was another more pressing reason for my decision: human shit! The uniquely awful smell of it filled our tank.

'Someone's crapped themselves,' announced Cartwright as he proudly hit his own eureka moment. The subtle Geordie was right; a pitstop would be a relief for everyone, not just Charlie who had seemingly loaded his pants as well as the big gun.

My retort could have been 'he who smelt it dealt it', but the Geordie bastard was correct; a despairing Charlie was sitting with his head in his hands.

The sky was a gorgeous powder blue, and it made me think back to a summer afternoon when my dad and I rode horses across a ripening cornfield just like this one.

The ride was about moral indignation and shameless retribution. The unfortunate victim of this wilful act was a local farmer who had mistakenly assumed he held the moral high ground when he had shouted abuse at us a few days earlier.

It was our daily hack and we were always careful not to trample on any crop wherever we rode. As we calmly skirted the threshold of this particular wheat field, a maniac driver in a battered green Land Rover suddenly appeared. To paraphrase the raging sentiments of this lunatic, 'our horses were making love to his crop, and we were nothing but female genitalia!'

'Perhaps you shouldn't have ploughed over the bridleway in the first place?' countered Pop calmly. He had done his research.

'Bridleways are for horses, and this one goes directly across this field.'

'There is, is there?'

'Yes, indeed there is.'

Pop suggested that going around the field was perhaps more sensible, but if the farmer didn't like that option we would ride across it instead. God, I felt so proud of him.

'Well, I'd like to see you try,' the farmer retorted. That was wrong on every level, and an incorrect response to a man who was probably the most stubborn person I knew. In an attempt to spin his Land Rover around by flooring it, the farmer stalled instead.

'I know an excellent driving instructor, mate,' was Pop's sarcastic comeback. He emphasised the word 'mate', a term he rarely used.

We continued our trek in contemplative silence. I noticed that we strayed slightly more than usual into the ripening crop.

Two days later, it got even better as we waded through the middle of our favourite person's land. I imagined that I was Clint Eastwood heading into town for another showdown. Spaghetti westerns were all the rage then, and though I was too young to watch them legally Pop had described them brilliantly to me. Our horses were also enjoying their yomp as they carved two fresh paths, precise and true, straight through the middle of the field. Pop was 'walking the talk' and getting off on it.

Then there he was, Mister Angry himself. Our fat farmer friend propped up on a walking stick, leaning against the side of his battered old Landy. Curled up at his feet was a scruffy black Labrador with a grey beard and one eye missing. I noticed that both the dog and farmer were now panting hard.

Thinking back on it now, the scene was more like something from the film *Deliverance* because, to complete the picture, his halfwit son, Brian, was perched on the bonnet of his clapped-out vehicle. All we needed now was a banjo and a squealing pig. My mind raced ahead. No threat here: Pop would take fatty and I'd go for the village idiot.

Not quite Lee Van Cleef: our foe was more like Captain Mainwaring. Instead of a cheroot, he was chewing on a piece of straw while his dog scratched a flea-ridden ear with its hind leg.

As we slowly rode our trusty steeds, Muggins and Tricky, towards our greeting party, they watched with noticeable unease. A complete silence followed as the standoff between our two gangs began.

I can't imagine how much less than intimidating we must have looked. Muggins, my Welsh mountain pony, was at least three hands shorter than Tricky, and my feet almost touched the ground on either side of him. Instead of a Stetson, I was wearing a bashed-up brown-velvet riding hat, and Pop wore white breeches that flared out at the side like gigantic ears.

'Do not say a thing, Calum,' he instructed as I watched him tuck his riding crop between his left thigh and saddle. Mine was already out and held ready like a Winchester rifle.

I waited for the tumbleweed to bounce across in front of me and strained hard to hear the distant clanging of a single church bell. Neither was evident.

An occasional clink from our horse's chinking bridles broke through the tense atmosphere and the heat of the late afternoon sun. Someone had to make a move.

'Leave this to me, son. I'll do the talking.' Relief.

The four of us looked at each other; nothing was said, no one went for their gun, nor was a dagger spun into someone's chest. Instead, the sound of a loud and long runny fart came from the rear end of Muggins as he unloaded a pile of poo onto the cornfield behind him.

I knew we had won when Captain Mainwaring and his sidekick Pike began to shift uneasily. Just like the Man with No Name, my father spoke in a quiet voice. 'Excuse me, gentlemen. You're blocking the bridleway.' A couple of furtive glances flicked between our adversaries. 'I have maps in my saddlebags.'

It was as easy as that. The farmer muttered something incomprehensible to his son and, shaking his head, clambered back into the Land Rover. Their dog had already given up and was on the passenger seat, licking his balls. Retard, as my mates and I cruelly called Brian, flipped his tartan baseball hat back to front and tried desperately hard to look cool. Even at twelve, I knew the Bay City Rollers weren't anywhere near cool.

'Just be careful when you go round the field in future, then.' Defeated, that was the farmer's best shot.

'Yeah, be very careful,' said idiot boy. This supplementary comment made us laugh out loud.

The Landy didn't stall this time, but it took ages for the grinding gearbox to engage correctly. Eventually the lynch party lurched off into their sunset and we rode into our memorable high noon.

How to resolve Charlie's predicament was on my mind now. He had filled his pants, and he – *we* – needed an escape from the situation. The tank reeked of shit and the rest of us were getting near to gagging point. Horse dung is OK, cow shit is bearable and pig shit is unpleasant. As for human shit? It has to be on another scale.

We had almost reached the end of the field and, by my calculations, were only about fifteen minutes away from the rest of our troop. The gate was open, leading onto a narrow, freshly concreted road. 'Okay,' I said. 'Pull up, driver. I need air.'

It could have been more subtle, but everyone got it. We came to a halt and I climbed out first, followed quickly by the others. Charlie was last out; gingerly, he eased himself out of the cupola and dropped down onto the other side of the tank. With that tricky manoeuvre carefully completed, he made a rapid dash into the bushes. Taylor followed, a noticeably safe distance from our compromised loader.

While the others took an opportunity to relieve themselves against the gate post, I took a swig of water from a canteen strapped to my bedroll. Hats off to the boys: their banter was carefully structured to put Charlie at ease.

Balancing his dignity with our safety, I knew this unplanned stop was against orders and potentially dangerous. Camouflaged in dense bocage, tanks were tricky to see despite their enormity. Anyone who has experienced an elephant safari in Africa would confirm the similarity. These magnificent beasts can be silently tucked away in the trees less than ten feet from you, and no one would know. That thought immediately made me uneasy; we had to leave this place fast.

We were relieved to see Charlie return; however, there was no sign of our driver.

'Present and correct, sir,' still embarrassed, Charlie seemed more buoyant now. 'Sorry about that.'

'You won't be the last. Seen Taylor?'

'Nope, he went the other way, boss.'

'Taylor, time to go,' I called out not too loudly.

There was no response, only the rustle of leaves in the breeze and some sporadic birdsong that I worked out came from a blackbird. I felt comforted by the sound; although a trillion light years away from my 'real life', birdsong seemed to normalise things.

'Don't be a prick, driver. It's time to move out.' Slightly agitated now, I wondered where he was in the scrub. I gave the others a look and slowly reached for my Luger in its chest holster. Something felt wrong. 'Charlie, Chris, mount up. Sidney, come with me.'

I waited while Chris got into the driver's seat and Charlie wedged himself into the gunner's position vacated by my Geordie friend who was standing beside me. We had one high explosive in the breech and the main gun pointed over our heads into the bocage. If Cartwright and I weren't back in ten minutes, both remaining crew members knew the drill to kick things off. If the Krauts hadn't got to us by then, the HE or coaxial machine gun fired from our tank certainly would.

'Sidney.'

'Guv?'

'You might want to bring a gun, mate.'

Was I surprised? Not sure. The idiot was unarmed, and I waited patiently while our temporary gunner carefully passed down his Sten gun. Their training and the battlefield grapevine would have emphasised how sensitive these unreliable weapons were; I was pleased that at least this knowledge had sunk in.

'Sorry, boss,' Sidney said. 'Ready now.' Although he wore that smirk again, he seemed genuinely embarrassed.

My irritation would have to be parked because something was telling me that this war was about to become real again. I diverted my attention back to the curtain of foliage and the spot where my driver had disappeared. 'Taylor, where the fuck are you?'

I gestured to Sidney and he went the opposite way to me. I tucked the Luger into my belt and edged forward. It took both hands to tug back the drapes of overhanging thicket. Although dense, thankfully the undergrowth wasn't choked with brambles.

It was all too surreal now; with my Schmeisser slung over my shoulder, I could easily have been Rambo. I quickly ignored that thought; this was serious. It was time to enter into a deadly combat scenario.

As far as I could make out there were no traces of the enemy. Holding my breath, I worried about exhaling and giving away my position. Concentrating and making as little noise as possible were paramount, though every step I made seemed to explode with noise. It reminded me of creeping up the creaky stairs in the dark after a boozy night out with the lads. If only that were the case here.

We had to find Taylor quickly and it was Sid who did it. 'Guv. Over here.' He was leaning over Taylor, desperately trying to stem the blood flowing from a deep gouge in his neck. It was thick, bright red, and pumping in squirts between Sid's fingers.

I looked down at Taylor; he was quiet, but his eyes were bright as he stared back at me. 'Cover my back, Sid,' I said.

He was desperate as he tried to position his hands over the gaping wound. 'I can't stop it, sir.'

'I repeat, cover my back and pass me a morphine shot.' I coaxed him away and took over.

Syrettes were like tiny tubes of toothpaste, the sort you find in hotel amenity packs. Instead of a fresh minty gel, they were filled with liquid morphine and used for front-line injuries like this. A vital part of every first-aid kit, every soldier carried one and hoped they would never need to use it.

Taylor had fallen onto his pack, so Sidney handed me his own syrette and I jabbed it straight into Taylor's neck. The pressure of his blood pulsed against the palm of my hand, slimy and warm, and I pressed down harder. When the tube was empty, I considered my next move.

This was alien to me – all I'd ever done was basic CPR training at the village hall – but a force had taken control as the mortally wounded man beneath me gurgled out froths of foam and phlegm.

'Pass me the first-aid kit.' I smothered the wound with sulphur powder and applied all the dressings we had available. I seemed to be on autopilot and knew exactly what to do next. How could that be?

'How is he, boss?'

'He's doing okay, Sid. Just keep a look out in case.'

My first-aid training must have been good because the morphine hit on Taylor was almost immediate. Gradually he stopped squirming and I felt his body relax. We could all relax because the running repairs seemed to be holding up for now.

Taylor mumbled, 'Can't a guy have a crap in peace?'

'You're doing fine, mate,' I lied and looked around for signs of what had happened. It was simple enough to work out: someone had grabbed him from behind and slit his throat, though not very well because he was still alive. To keep him that way, he needed some proper medical assistance – and fast.

I nodded at Sid, giving him a signal to lift at the same time. 'Time to get you home, son.'

Taylor was heavy, but speed was more important than delicate handling as we lugged him back to the tank. Despite his weight, it only took us a couple of adrenalin-assisted minutes, and when we got there the others took over. Their look said everything as they began padding the wound with more bandages.

After another shot of morphine, Taylor got the shakes and began to fit badly. 'What's happening, boys? I've got a tank to drive.' His skin had turned marble white, and it was then that we knew he wouldn't make it. Whatever the training, there were no answers to this.

'Please can I have the padre? We need him now.' My call on the RHQ frequency gave them our position as requested, and a couple of minutes passed with no response. The boys huddled around Taylor, jesting and joking with him, but we all knew he was a lost cause. I tried again. 'Come on. We need medical help NOW. And we need a padre. PLEASE.'

'Load him onto the tank and get back here,' replied an indifferent voice. 'This is the padre, and I'm not going anywhere. It's far too dangerous.'

It took a couple of seconds for me to reply. 'Well, you're a fucking coward.' My response was spontaneous. Some might describe it as understandable in the heat of battle, though the authorities didn't see it that way. But I'd said it, and it was something I would live to regret. The regimental padre was Captain Phillip Huggins, and no one called a captain a coward.

Ian Taylor died on our short trip to the rendezvous point. Our welcoming party included Major Hales accompanied by a puce-faced and agitated regimental padre. They watched intently as we gently slid our friend off the blood-pooled deck of our tank onto a waiting stretcher.

The medics were unemotional as they calmly eased us out of the way. A crimson-coloured blanket was placed over Ian before they lifted his body and slowly moved him away. Red, for fuck's sake! I wondered whether crimson was a regulation army-issue colour for a mortuary blanket.

We watched as they loaded him into the back of my friend Trooper Robertson's ambulance. My crew looked devastated.

I glanced at the two senior officers who were now glaring at me. Major Hales' swagger stick tapped impatiently against the side of his knee-length right boot. The padre was smiling, so I decided to pre-empt the inevitable. 'Can I have five minutes with the boys, sir?'

'You can have two,' replied Hales.

Huggins continued to smile, and I wanted to call him a cunt. I had nothing to lose. They both turned and walked away briskly.

From Peter Meadows' memoirs

Shortly after I was promoted to sergeant tank commander, my name was put forward for a 'commission in the field'. Then, in the midst of battle, my driver was mortally wounded and over the radio I'd asked the padre to come up and observe the last rites, which he refused to do. He held the rank of captain, so after I told him what I thought of him I was rightly charged with a serious offence against an officer. It was probably the stupidest thing I ever did in my whole life. However, from then on I was occasionally invited to drink in the officers' mess.

That swine lost me a well-deserved rest from the ravages of war. It was about this time that I realised this battle could not be won without me, which was probably why I was allowed to survive the war, look forward to my eventual 'demob' and move on with my life.

Falaise

What followed was predictable. After I was marched into the major's tent by an upright and officious RSM, Major Hales promptly informed me that my promotion to the rank of sergeant commander had not been ratified. 'And so, therefore, Meadows, luckily for you' – this was the good bit, apparently – 'repercussions from your tardy show of disrespect towards a superior officer will be minimal.'

It was a painful message but equally a remarkable result. He punctuated his statement with coughs and splutters for effect. 'No one needs to hear about this, Meadows.'

'No sir, but...'

'No buts.' With that, he stood up abruptly. 'You are now dismissed.'

That was it: docked three days' pay and a swift demotion back to the lowly rank of trooper. Until notified otherwise, my orders were to remain as a temporary driver replacement for Ian Taylor.

Seeing my shell-shocked state, the crew were welcoming; even our new commander appreciated my circumstances. 'If it helps, Peter, I've got no time for that smug bastard either.' Word got around fast.

To be fair to Padre Huggins, he gave me a wide berth; even he appreciated that losing a man under your command is painful. Knowing that Pop and I had short fuses, and that any repeat would be severely punished, it would be prudent to keep my head down. The right time would come and revenge would be sweet when it did. I was looking forward to it already, though I had to park that thought for now.

Being brave and obedient seemed the only way to get promoted, and avoiding a bullet measured your performance. This was a slightly different method from the one an old sales manager used with his skill-set cards – his bible – housed in a black plastic company binder. Starting in a column on the left, a slide to the right was good and put you onto the pathway to success and maybe promotion. When all the cards reached the other side, his job was yours! Ducking a bullet and staying alive versus hitting targets for selling cheese? I know which method of measuring I preferred.

Thankfully nothing else occurred in Vire and we were eventually loaded onto tank transporters and returned to Caen on August 12, 1944. As we rolled off the ramps, some excellent news was there to greet me: my immediate orders were to report to Major Teddy Foster and C Squadron.

I was sad to say goodbye to my new chums, but after an emotional farewell I wandered the camp to seek out familiar faces. Our time together seemed like five minutes in the grand scheme of things, but it was enough to squeeze in a lifetime of emotion that would bond us forever.

A scrap of paper told me to find Troop 3 and that my glorious leader was Captain Freddie Smythe, he with the Bob Hoskins' voice. This was promising stuff, and it lifted my spirits as I thought about my old muckers, Big Nige and Tony Auden, whom I'd last seen grumbling their way towards Smythe's tank a week or so earlier.

Our camp was in the apple orchard (minus apples), and it was late afternoon. An aroma of something tasty and meaty drifted over from the busy cook's kitchen where an excited queue had already snaked its way to the serving tables. That was always a good sign and chicken stew, the dish of the day, was the reason why. I wondered whether 'smash and grab' birds had been abducted from local farmers, or if they had been clicked and collected from a local supermarket. How the world was going to change!

British-built Mulberry Harbours were the chickens' more likely route to the cook's tent. Two floating pontoons, towed across the British Channel in segments, were a concept of sheer genius. Constructed from 1.5 million tons of concrete, and forming ten miles of floating roadway, they protruded into the sea from Gold and Omaha beaches. Like veins, they pumped the lifeblood of cargo, men and army provisions onto the invasion beaches of Normandy.

Theoretically they also meant that our supply ships, which were anchored off the coast, were out of reach from enemy artillery. However, Mulberry 'A' on Omaha, a supply route for the Americans, was destroyed during the autumn storms of 1944.

Port Winston, a conduit for the British at Arromanches, was battered by the seas of time but is still in place seventy-five years later. If epic engineering feats like this were considered art, those pontoon bridges were a masterpiece.

Hearing the guys and their childish banter was relaxing and allowed me to reflect. I thought of Taylor and his family in Norfolk who knew nothing of his demise, and that made me sad. And what of my wife, Tess, and the boys? What were they thinking in that distant other world of mine right now? Was I a missing person or just some lost soul in this so-called time warp, as Pop had put it?

I scrunched the scribbled notepaper and threw it on the ground before realising that there was another bollocking right there. Quickly picking up the ball of potentially valuable information, I stuffed it into a pocket and looked around. No one had noticed, but my action irritated me because such a security breach could have been catastrophic.

It was time to calm down with a ciggy. I rummaged around in my fag pocket, found an American crush pack and lit one. I'd had too much thinking time, but Pop must have spent time thinking about his wife and son. That was not a good track to follow; mind games were dangerous out here; they could only weaken my resolve and would ultimately destroy me. The only thinking game to play was how to survive.

'Meadows, you old tosser.' Tony's voice was unmistakable as a familiar gangling figure wearing a black beret back to front wandered towards me holding a billycan overflowing with chicken stew, and with a half-smoked, ash-laden fag drooping from the corner of his mouth.

After my Laurel-and-Hardy double take, I noticed a small Hitler-style moustache sprouting from his top lip. Tony read me beautifully. 'Oliver Hardy, actually.'

'Yep, of course. Thanks, mate.' I made a grab for his food but he swerved exaggeratedly out of the way.

'Off you fucking well go, sunshine. We're over there.' He nodded to where Nigel Morton was pontificating over his favourite pastime: making a brew. It was great to see that some things stayed the same.

'You sure, Tony?' I asked. 'Am I really with you boys?'

'Yes, mate. We need a crap driver and heard you were back in town.'

'Ha bloody ha. And our commander?'

'Over there is Sergeant Bollock-Brain Caddick.'

Auden led me to Morton, who was all man hugs and back slaps. It was a bit like being greeted by a slobbering Saint Bernard on heat.

Next I went over to the new boss. 'Heard a lot about you, trooper,' was his opening line, and that worried me. Any recent appraisal would be harsh, so I gave the 'all good, I hope, sir' routine a miss.

Sergeant Valentine Caddick was much older than the rest of us, probably around fifty, and he was rotund. Flicking away his cigarette stub, he ran his fingers through a thinning mop of silvery-grey hair.

'All good, I hope, sir.' In the end I couldn't resist it. 'And how are your shares in Brylcreem?' was what I wanted to say.

'Heard you like to drive fast.' Caddick covered his mouth when he spoke, which was strange, and he had a familiar Essex accent. 'I need you to get us the fuck out of trouble when asked.'

'I can do that, sarge.'

'It is "sergeant", trooper. We'll see, won't we?' He turned on his heels and strode briskly towards the mess kitchen.

'Oops.' I looked at Tony, who shrugged and mimed 'bollock brain' again. Valentine Caddick was abrupt, with an unusual name and a weird habit. My first impressions of him were somewhat discouraging.

'Better get some grub, Speedy,' mimicked Morton, putting two hands over his mouth. That was funny.

'I'm going back for extras. Can I get you some?' Tony's unusual goodwill gesture surprised me. I accepted his kind offer and began to sort out my bedroll for the night.

'Don't make yourself too comfortable, fella.' I recognised that annoying Geordie whine immediately. Sidney Cartwright poked his ginger-topped head out of the turret; I had no idea he'd been transferred to my tank. He lobbed out an empty shell casing, making me dance away as it bounced around my feet.

'And why is that, you old git?' I asked.

'Because Betsy is on guard duty tonight.'

Our resting lump of killing machine – and my new home – was called Betsy. What was it with these names? And guard duty was always bad news because it meant two hours maximum kip at any time. Apparently most of the enemy in the vicinity had been flushed out, so our shift was expected to be quiet – quiet, apart from the usual rumble of distant artillery that followed us everywhere.

'What's your job, Sid?' I asked. I knew Morton was an excellent gunner and so was Cartwright. Everyone in a tank crew had interchangeable jobs, but Sidney was exceptional and the top brass had noticed.

'I'm gunner. Old Fussy-Bollocks down there is my bitch loader now.' He said it loud enough for Nige to hear, who gave him the middle finger.

'Correction,' Nige returned. 'They wanted to give Junior up there a chance to catch up.'

'Agree with that, Nige.' I winked at Cartwright, who ducked back into the gunner's seat.

'Oh, and I'm the same rank as you now, matey!' His voice echoed out from inside the turret chamber. That was undoubtedly true – touché and ouch!

The next few days were uneventful and much of our time was spent carrying out tank maintenance while we waited for our next orders. We finally got them on August 15th and, together with the Canadian 1st Army, headed south towards Falaise. The Germans were trapped there and our job was to squeeze them into what would later be called the Falaise Pocket. The United States 1st and 3rd Armies, led by General Patton, were to push up from the south and act as the second prong in a classic military pincer movement.

A crucial part of the pincer plan was to close the gap between the towns of Falaise and Argentan; the middle ground would then become our main target area.

What I knew – and what the others didn't – was that the Falaise Gap initiative worked horrendously well. I also knew that the centre area became a killing field and mass graveyard for a soon-to-be-decimated German army. All of this was true – but I still had to survive the battle ahead.

Our job in the 44th was to mop up, or 'de-louse' as Caddick put it. After one of his O-group soirées, he soberly informed us that several pockets of resistance existed from about 5,000 Seventh Army fighters led by Field Marshal Gunther von Kluge.

Kluge had correctly predicted the Allies' movements and urged Hitler to withdraw. The Führer had not listened; as with many of his decisions, he ignored his generals and this specific request was denied. Later Kluge committed suicide having been implicated in an assassination attempt on his leader.

Another problem for us still fresh in my mind was the Schutzstaffel, otherwise known as the SS. Formerly a paramilitary organisation in Nazi Germany, it was also Hitler's personal protection squad. The SS gathered in Falaise consisted of the 12th SS Panzer division led by Commander Kurt Meyer, who would later be tried for war crimes. The 101st Heavy Tank Battalion were also there, commanded by the infamous tank killer, Michael Wittmann. Both groups had fearsome reputations and wouldn't be easy to roll over.

Thank goodness I couldn't tell the boys about Wittmann's eventual standing. His reputation was building at that point in the war, and his most famous exploit was the battle of Villers-Bocage. Legend has it that his Tiger tank ambushed and systematically destroyed more than twenty tanks from the British 7th Armoured Division, the infamous Desert Rats. It was a chilling statistic and, for a tank driver who could face him one day, something not to mull over for too long.

During our final briefing session, we were told that the ultimate objective of this mission was to form a ring of steel around what was hoped to be a shell-shocked and defeated enemy. The not-so-good news was that a fresh and hungry 89th Wehrmacht Army would also face us. These soldiers were still high following their victory in Norway.

A gruesome overture got things going. Rockets launched from British Typhoons, supplemented by an unprecedented bombardment from our ground artillery, pulverised swathes of land and anything moving on it. Words cannot begin to describe the noise and light show above us.

At around 22:30 hours, we set off in convoys on an overnight march that included 600 tanks. Above us, an armada of Flying

Fortress bombers and hundreds of Typhoons and Thunderbolts filled the night sky. Carpets of bombs fell, 5,000 tons in total; all we could do was watch, wait and hope. The magnitude of these payloads annihilated everything on the ground, including many Allies who were obliterated by so-called friendly fire.

As we thundered towards Falaise, the scene around us was horrific. The sky was a sci-fi purple, and we choked on the dust and debris thrown up by each passing regiment.

In every direction the decimated terrain looked like a blanched, lifeless moonscape with one perverse addition: trees. Skeletal fingers pushing up from the earth, they were petrified and dead. Among them were buildings blitzed to rubble; they steamed like mini-volcanic mountains as we slowly trundled a weaving pattern between them. Unparalleled for anyone in this war so far, the mental impact caused by this devastation would last forever.

'Chaps, try to concentrate.' An order broke the silence. 'Just do your jobs.'

The dead, animal and human, lay twisted in unidentifiable, undignified lumps. My strict orders not to deviate around them had tested me severely. Beasts, hundreds of them mainly horses, were now boulder-sized charcoal shards and shattered into pieces as we ploughed our way through them.

As the trauma built up, the stink of death seeped through our tank's skin into ours. It was impossible to put the scene into words, but General Eisenhower, Allied Supreme Commander, had a good try. He later said, 'Scenes that could only be described by Dante. It was literally possible to walk for hundreds of yards at a time, stepping over nothing but dead and decaying flesh.'

Although it was still daylight, we needed lights. We followed each other in fast-moving columns, and on this part of the trip the usual crackle of radio noise was almost non-existent.

An occasional flare spun into the sky, breaking the monotony. Orange signalled friend, and our orange response meant 'understood' or 'okay'.

'Meadows, watch those tail lights. DO NOT dilly-dally.'

We rumbled on towards Pierrefitte, our proposed laager for the night. Dilly-dally? I'd not heard that for years!

A Sherman tank had its escape hatch on the floor behind the bow-gunner's seat. Ours had somehow been ripped out during the march, making comfort levels worse because muck was pouring in through the opening.

As we rucked over yet another bump and bounced into a dip, a German helmet appeared. Tony saw it first. I heard his yelp and made the same noise when a bloodied head rolled onto the floor behind it. Like a giant cheese slicer, the torn edge of our escape hatch had probably severed the head from the body as our weight compressed the soldier into the ground.

'Holy Jesus. Shit. What's that?' We knew exactly what it was.

Tony stated the obvious. 'There's someone's head in here.'

What did Caddick say? 'Keep driving and ignore it. Has he got blue eyes?'

I heard the black helmet scrape against the side of the hull, followed by a squelching, thumping sound as the German's head rolled over. Concentrating on my driving, I welcomed the order. Tony didn't have that luxury and curled his arms over his head. Surely we had seen everything now?

We were last into camp at dusk. I let the engine idle before closing down. Morton, our newly appointed loader, broke the radio silence first. 'Pass pretty boy up, then.'

Only an experienced front-liner or an idiot could make light of such a macabre incident, though Adolph was not looking good. Detached from the rest of his body, his head was now at least two feet away from the bloodied helmet that had once protected it. To my relief, his face was facing the other way and pressed against the bulkhead, but we could see his black hair, cropped short and surprisingly clean. What a weird observation to make; it struck me then that this war was doing things to my mind. Another strange thing was the lack of blood; he had been dead for a while.

Or is he still alive like a worm, the rest of him hidden somewhere? I refused to pursue that line of thought.

Morton passed down a towel and Tony, who had been motionless, suddenly spun around in his seat and grabbed our new friend; the towel-covered head wobbled against the transmission box to my right. Fumbling badly, he bound the package up and thrust it into our loader's waiting hands like pass-the-parcel in reverse. 'Take the fucker, quick!'

Impressed at his speed, I was relieved that Nigel's hands held firm. 'Thank you, darling.' He grabbed the package and pretended to spill it.

Auden ducked back, thumping his head hard on the white bulkhead. 'Go to hell, you bastard.'

'Gentlemen, gentlemen, please.' Valentine Caddick's placating tones drifted into the newly created guillotine chamber, an apt new name for our driver's compartment. 'Tidy up. We're on the move in one hour.'

It sounded like he'd asked us to spring clean our bedrooms rather than wash out an abattoir. Hats off to Tony; he did most of the work.

After the exit hatch repair, we completed some other much-needed mechanical checks, and then it was time to wait for our next set of orders.

Squeezing through the driver's hatch, I noticed that most other tank crews, like me, were taking the air. The banter around camp was less animated than usual because there was still work to be done. It was heartening to see this focus and our battle-hardened regiment quickly becoming a formidable and experienced battle group.

After a brew and five cigarettes, I returned to my driver's seat. We had twenty tanks and twenty crews in our troop, but I knew little about them because we rarely left our bubble. The only time we mixed was at the cook's kitchen, bath time or, if lucky, an impromptu social event. The latter was rare – then I remembered Major Hales' half-hearted invitation to the officers' mess after firing me as a sergeant tank commander.

Caddick briefed us in his laconic style: lazy Essex, not quite Cockney. I noticed yet another mouth-inflicted quirk: he talked from its corner like he was trying to keep a secret. The man was indeed extraordinary.

We listened intently and became slightly agitated when it dawned on us that part of our night mission would be carried out on foot in darkness. That was new to us. Sidney Cartwright, usually quiet at these meetings, asked a few questions but the rest of us said nothing. Foot patrol? This was something the infantry boys did, so why us? Everyone was wondering the same, but no one dared ask.

We set off at 20:45 hours, and C Squadron soon found itself in familiar bocage territory. It was half-light, and the only way to navigate visually was to tailgate your buddy's lights in front. Using our spotlight would give us away. What about night vision? This invention had not been introduced yet; even if I could have told them about it, they would have laughed me out of the tank.

Second out, behind troop leader Freddie Smythe, all the crews were in their favoured heads-up position. The combination of warm summer air, swirling dust and the acrid smell of exhaust smoke didn't depress us; actually it did the opposite. It was intoxicating and gave us all a massive shot of adrenalin.

It didn't take long for the fireworks party to start again, and the inky-black sky, previously filled with Christmas-card twinkling stars, soon became a rainbow-coloured light show. However, our tried and tested warm-up strategy in Normandy had one missing element: there was no aerial bombardment to start proceedings. To soften Jerry up, heavy artillery rockets sent from the infantry lads behind us boomed over our heads into the darkness instead. The ground rocked as wave after wave of heavy-duty explosives did their work.

Our turn came next. As our choreographed approach led us towards yet another hedgerow, relentless bursts of firepower obliterated anyone foolish enough to get close to it. Our machine-gun rounds and high explosives screamed into these natural barricades, paving the way for swarms of ground troops to finish things off. Any subsequent machine-gun fire told us survivors had been repelled and terminated. There were no night-time prisoners.

The stage-managed dance of metal and flesh continued field after field for about an hour. Caught up in the brutality, I soon realised this was solely about destroying the enemy before they could get to us. I confess it gave me a massive buzz.

'Those little fuckers need us now, don't they?' Caddick's voice came down the intercom. 'Fucking spongers.' He was referring to our infantry colleagues.

'Yeah, better us here than them there,' Auden and I said simultaneously, and it lightened the moment.

Tony wedged his feet against the bulkhead and fired off another round from his bow gun. 'Not for long, boys. We'll be joining them soon.'

'What was that?' Our reply was once again simultaneous.

Then, to our right, I saw one of our Rhino tanks with a hedge-cutter device welded onto the front of its hull. A spontaneous invention by the Yanks following manoeuvrability problems in the bocage, life had become much easier since they had started slicing corridors through the hedgerows and trees. They contributed massively towards our progress through the fields of Normandy.

Plans often hit a snag, especially when something big and serious returned fire. Bocage-secreted Panthers or occasionally – even worse – Tiger tanks did this often. If the unmistakable whistle passed overhead, it was an AP and usually good news because they had missed. We would wait for the distinctive *krummpp* sound, signifying someone else had got the sharp end instead. Our response had to be instantaneous, and we prayed our gunner was on form and more accurate than theirs!

As if to make a point about returning fire, I saw our Firefly in 2 Troop, the so-called big hitter, get one right on the nose. Although these tanks had decent guns to match the Germans, they flashed like a firecracker when they were let loose – a weakness and a fatal giveaway, which is probably why the Americans didn't adapt their tanks like us.

The Firefly's main gun buckled in two and, after a pause, seemed to bulge and explode into a massive ball of orange flame and sparks. Her name was Moto. Did the clever buggers who named her know it meant fire in Swahili?

'Meadows, keep going. Don't even think about slowing down,' came the blunt order from above.

You don't say? I jammed my foot hard onto the floor. About fifty yards away, the Firefly roared like a furnace. I couldn't look as we left her incinerated crew behind.

'Down to our last ten HEs.' It was not a welcome message you wanted to hear from your loader. Betsy rocked up and down as another one left the spout.

'Okay, we'll hold up and wait for instructions,' Caddick paused. 'As it happens, chaps, we are almost where we need to be.' He flashed the tank's spotlight on and off to help me stay on track. He also tried to contact the infantry but their radio 18 sets still didn't synchronise with our regiment's 19s! 'How fucking useful is that?' Caddick grumbled.

I remembered my book research, but now was not the right time to soothe his frustration. Later in the war this problem would improve, but that was in the future and I couldn't tell him about it right now.

After our rampage through the bocage, we could still hear sporadic machine-gun fire and it prompted those infantry boys who were still clinging on to investigate.

Our next job would be in the other direction and on foot; our orders were to recce a bridge that crossed a link road between Falaise and Saint Marc d'Ouelly. Caddick explained that this would be perfect ambush fodder for us. 'Piece of piss, boys.' He said it repeatedly, trying to convince himself. We had figured it out already; this perfect spot was also good for a trapped German army to repel us.

'Nice one, boss. I'll stay here and make us a lovely cup of tea.' Morton seemed more flustered than usual.

'I'll help you,' said Tony.

Crouching down on a grassy meadow beside the tank exposed us, but we had parked below the ridge to avoid creating a silhouette. Caddick gave us a brief heads-up and told us that each tank would remain with its gunner. 'The five Ps. Does anyone know what they are?'

Silence. I did – it was clichéd, and I had often used it as a sales manager in my other life. 'Perfect Planning Prevents Poor Performance, sir.' I always added a P to make it 'Piss-Poor Performance'.

'Excellent, Meadows. And unless you want your fucking head shot off, put out the fag, Meadows.'

'Add another P, sir, for Prick.' It was Tony.

Caddick shook his head in mock desperation, and we headed into the darkness. A glowing cigarette made a perfect target and I should have known better. I stubbed it out with my thumb, then wished I hadn't.

It was 22:00 hours and a heavy dew coated the grass making things slippery underfoot. We skirted the edge of the field and for the first time in this war I felt vulnerable. Yes, we lived in a tomb, but at least we had metal walls around us. This was like Billy Crake's paintball game with the fear and pain factor ramped up a thousand times.

Stumbling down the hill behind the group, I held my breath again. 'Breathe, you idiot,' I told myself, but my lips were stuck together and my tongue glued to the roof of my mouth.

Caddick had placed me at the back while he led at point; Big Nige was huffing and puffing his way in front of me. But where was our mate?

'Auden, sir, we've lost him.' Caddick didn't hear my strained whisper, so I called out again, 'Tony's gone.'

Caddick raised his hand immediately; it was almost like a scene from *Dad's Army* as Big Nige, followed by me, blundered into the back of him. 'Where the fuck is he?'

We lifted our guns and flicked off their safety catches. I did the same with my Schmeisser, which felt snug in my hands and seemed to be leading me like a dog.

We didn't have to wait long. I heard a rustle and turned round when Tony appeared from behind a bush. 'I needed a piss, boys.' No one said a thing. 'A man has to do what a man has to do.'

Caddick glared at my bow gunner and simultaneously raised a tightly clenched fist in front of his nose. After mouthing something primitive, he waved us forward again. We dropped back into line and continued down the hill in silence. Soon something loomed up through the gloom and, on another signal, we settled onto our stomachs.

The narrow farm bridge, probably used as a cattle crossing, was made of red brick and wood. Caddick put his field glasses away and gave a thumbs-up all clear. Able to breathe again, I felt my heart smashing impatiently against the inside of my rib cage.

On his next signal, we edged forward.

Behind me, the red afterglow from our riot through the bocage was dimming and even the distant crack of gunfire had ceased. Everything seemed normal for a warm summer's evening except for one thing: the cool night air seemed unusually fragrant. We all caught the pleasant aroma at the same time as it drifted towards us from somewhere on the other side of the bridge. First it was sweetness and then came the unmistakable whiff of its source, tobacco. It took me a while to identify the type until I finally got it: Gauloises, the famous French cigarette brand.

'Is that a fag?' sniffed Morton. Distinctly pungent, the rich smoke also had a running partner. 'And that, my friend, is perfume?'

I couldn't believe it. We knew the Yanks wore cheap aftershave, but this was too good for them.

'That gentleman is odour de Hun,' said Caddick.

As he ran a finger across his lips, the urgent 'zip up' sign prompted my heart into sledgehammer mode again. Always expect the unexpected, and this duly came with his next order: I was to accompany him while the others stayed put.

Wondering what misdemeanour deserved this honour, I was soon on all fours literally following his arse with my nose. The mystery scent led us over a dry, rutted farm track, eventually bringing us to a steep-sided stone wall.

Anyone who has strolled over a pretty narrow bridge over a river always stops to look down. This bridge spanned a road, and what I saw next tripped my heart into palpitations. Below us, almost within touching distance, the outline of a colossal Tiger tank reared up. As it sat astride the road, half on and half off, its 88mm cannon was pointing skywards towards me.

'It's been terminated,' whispered Caddick. 'Don't panic.'

Imposing and formidable as they were, only 200 were ever sent to Normandy. I asked myself again why we had to meet one head-on. Despite its apparent incapacity, it still looked magnificent; only a gaping black hole gouged into its side destroyed the image.

'No obvious signs of life.' The boss made another positive observation, which was good for my ticker.

We eased our way down the grassy slope to where she loomed over us like some Jurassic monster. I ran my hands over her crinkled skin, a two-tone, dark-brown-and-grey camouflage. I knew this surface was designed to repel magnetic mines, which was ironic in that the Allies generally didn't have magnetic ones in their weaponry. Not so good for us, though; our smooth armour worked wonders for the enemy who did have them.

Although I didn't see it immediately, I could hear the trickle of water from a nearby stream. Trying to remain calm and not panic, the whiff of Gauloises cigarettes and aftershave didn't help much. It was alarmingly strong and it came from that direction.

'Dammed buggers, where are they?' Caddick shrugged his shoulders.

And then we found them. 'Jesus.' There were two men huddled closely together, both motionless with their hands already in the air. My first thought was, 'Why didn't they shoot us?' My second: 'Where are the others?'

Quickly scanning the area, my inability to breathe and the heart failure problems of the last hour returned. 'Where are their guns, boss?'

His reply surprised me. 'I guess they were captured earlier. They'll be taken away tomorrow.'

Why didn't I think of that? German PoWs were often left on the roadside to be picked up later. It was common practice on the battlefields where there were so many men to deal with. In Falaise especially, PoWs numbered around 10,000 and Allied units had few backup resources to keep them together. Simply put, the enemy was defeated, and we had nowhere to put them. Interestingly, the plan to deal with us backfired spectacularly because, ironically, German PoWs found themselves in compounds built to house our PoWs!

'*Gibt es noch jemanden*?' Carrick asked. That was as much a surprise to me as to the guys who were facing us. He may have looked out of place in an army uniform, but the talented Valentine Caddick had some linguistic skills that would soon prove beneficial.

'*Nein,*' the one on the left replied. '*Tot.*'

Even I could work that one out: the others were dead. The other man stared ahead and then pointed to his right without looking there. Under a tree alongside the stream were two freshly dug graves, a German helmet plonked on each one.

The stream was close and ran off the hill. I noticed some washing paraphernalia on the bank beside it and soon found what I was looking for: a small bottle of elaborately labelled cologne sitting against a wooden-stemmed razor. It was a brand called Muelhens, apparently a German favourite.

'What of Old Spice?' I wondered if the distinctive white porcelain bottle with its grey stopper was familiar to the

Germans. Always my dad's aftershave of choice, it was launched in the British shaving market in 1938. I had a bottle in my kitbag. Sadly there was no sign of Henry Cooper's 'Splash it All Over' Brut, which was a shame because that and Hai Karate were the scents from my teens.

'You like?' said the friendliest-looking German.

He was no more than a boy, and I questioned his need to shave. I had to check myself on that one; in my other life, I'd been one of those hairy adolescents who started his shaving career early. Ignoring the fledgling sideburns gently sprouting from either side of my face, the flat Wilkinson blade would sweep down; it met little bristle resistance. Over time, and as part of a carefully crafted shaving regime, the downy strips of 'bum fluff', as Pop called them, soon cultivated themselves into wiry Noddy Holder-like sideburns. These manicured ginger fluff handles were not as unkempt and unattractive as my father said because they showed off my innate masculinity that girls found alluring. Well, that's what I believed. But thinking back to the sideburns, my gay perm and bull-worker device, for the first time I began to ask myself some serious questions about my formative years.

'You like?' he asked again.

'Too sweet, Kaiser dick,' I replied. He looked genuinely hurt, and I regretted saying it.

'You want? *Mochtest du*?' he prompted me.

'Never trust a Kraut,' snapped Caddick.

'Don't you mean the French?' If I'd elaborated, he wouldn't have understood.

'Are you sure? *Danke*, my friend.' I was overcompensating for my dick insult, a gesture made out of guilt more than a need for cologne.

I could hear the jibes from the boys. Sitting before us were two unarmed, unguarded prisoners looking for a lift; at the same time, they looked like regular guys getting ready for a night out – they even had time for aftershave. The situation was as surreal as it got, but something worried me. Two alive and two dead; where was man number five?

'Meadows, get up here.'

Glancing up, I saw Sergeant Caddick peering down between his legs into the black hole of the Tiger's turret. Its blown hatch cover lay like a giant bottle top near my feet.

'*Nein*. Please.' It was my new German friend. He and his companion moved to get up.

'Calm down, Fritz, or you'll get this.' Caddick waved his Sten gun. 'Back up. *Bitte.*'

They did. Caddick was unfit, and how he managed to mount this beast as quickly as he did impressed me. My new and diminutive 5' 4" struggled, and I was half his age.

A narrow torchlight beam guided my gaze into the black abyss below. All I could see was darkness.

Caddick waved the torch and ordered me inside. With more than a bit of apprehension, I dropped onto a metal deck and immediately noticed how much space they had compared to us. Brew-ups were the same, though; theirs had left nothing except a blackened, completely hollow cave, devoid of odour or anything animate. I was in a sanitised black hole.

The driver's section was interesting because it was completely separate from the bow-gunner's area and must have been hugely claustrophobic. Then the beam of light probed further into the tank's guts. 'What's that, Meadows?'

'Looks like a steering wheel.'

It was large, and the recent inferno had blackened its rim. It was impressive and so very German to think of this; all we had were levers to steer with.

The skeletal remains of the driver made me freeze. Sitting upright, this hideous creature stripped of flesh was still wearing a helmet; he was gripping the steering wheel with bleached white fingers, making the scene around me look like a fairground.

'Fuck, it's a ghost train,' laughed Caddick.

If the man's skull had turned 360 degrees right, I would at least have known this was all a bad dream!

Hung around the skeleton's neck was a dog tag. Caddick had seen it, too. Obliged by law to retrieve these tags, I correctly guessed my next instruction. 'Go and fetch it, my son.'

'You're having a laugh, sir.' My last brush with seniority had not gone well, so to push the matter would be foolish. 'It could be booby-trapped, sir.' That was a long shot.

'It could be, trooper, but it's not.'

I didn't ask the obvious question.

Tugging gently at first, the dog tag resisted. I gave the silver chain another firm yank, and something gave. The tag melded into a splintered shard of the collarbone, came away with a strange plopping sound. As a clump of bone and tin swung up against the hull with a metallic clunk, I felt the familiar rise of nausea from my guts.

Like a diver clambering for air, it seemed to take me hours to reach the surface. Valentine Caddick, with the body of a space hopper and the apparent fitness of a hare, was already off the tank when I crawled out.

In mental preparation, I had already decided to take the demotion should my three-striped senior ask me to do anything else. I jumped onto the ground beside the two watching German soldiers who were waiting for my next move. Interestingly, so was the sergeant.

'I am so sorry.' That was all I could say as I carefully placed the tag at their feet and turned away.

Caddick's stare said it all. He shook his head and told the Germans to wait for their lift. It might have been a nod of acknowledgement from my German friend, but Caddick was still shaking his head as I followed him up the hill and back to the others who were playing cards.

The following day was clear and the weather forecast was good as we prepared to leave at 05:30 hours. The sight that greeted us at the bottom of the hill was extraordinary. The same valley, apparently devoid of enemy soldiers the previous day, was alive with them. Closer still, and directly below our bridge, was a group of German soldiers busy laying out necklaces of land mines across the road. They were only a quarter of a mile away but hadn't clocked us yet; maybe the ribbon of fine mist draping across the middle of the valley was doing us a favour.

'Fuck my old boots, Meadows. They've been reprieved,' the sergeant's voice drawled down the intercom.

Hardly surprising if you tell them to wait for a lift. That was one of my thoughts. *They may regret that*, was another.

I guessed what would happen next and looked towards the other side of the valley. A faint wisp of morning mist clung to that side of the hill, and I made out a row of about twenty tanks from A Squadron lined up facing us. Their thoughts on 'friendly fire' and self-preservation were no doubt the same as mine.

C Squadron, who had joined us during the night, had spread out to our port side in a row. There was no sound, no roar of tank engines, just silence. A massive weight of expectation hung in the atmosphere.

Our radio was tuned into the squadron frequency when Teddy's unmistakable voice announced loudly, 'Freddie, old boy, can you please ask your boys to do the necessary?'

Confirmation of this polite request came down from our tank commander. Our radio frequency flipped back to the tank's intercom system, allowing Caddick to give Cartwright a few directional coordinates. It was pretty simple: aim at the bridge where the Krauts were still planting gifts and destroy the fuckers. His order was to use high explosives with tracers, and our troop would do the business.

When it started, as usual all I had to do was watch. After a short but noisy bombardment, most of the bridge had been deconstructed. Wooden bits and human matter flickered and burned around it. It took less than five minutes, and when the smoke cleared those Germans who could run were picked off by the infantry secreted around them. Any who were still crawling would suffer until they died.

'Much less messy that way,' said Caddick ironically.

It was Morton who asked the question about PoWs.

Tony got out the playing cards while we waited for our next orders. It had been catastrophic for the Germans, but I felt nothing for them. Such emotion had long gone; our enemy had been extinguished and their memories would only live on with those who loved them. Job well done.

I couldn't imagine my father being so callous in his thinking but maybe secretly he was. On the outside he appeared compassionate, especially towards those less fortunate than himself, quick to donate to charities or provide hands-on help for struggling people. I remember him making up food parcels for the elderly during our 'winter of discontent' in 1978. But this was war and so far, for me, compassion had no place. It wasn't good for your health.

The next few days were spent doing the usual: we stayed put and carried out ongoing tank maintenance. Like painting the Forth Road Bridge, there was always something to do. Never a practical person, I was surprised at how proficient I became in using tools and sorting out mechanical problems.

Pop was very different to me in this aspect and gave everything a go. Whilst not a craftsman, he was a practical man. The tree house he built was the envy of all my mates and soon became the meeting point for our boyhood adventures and misdemeanours. However, his bizarre irrigation system that displaced rainwater from our garden into others could have been received better by the neighbours!

We were bored, so the occasional trip along the ridge was a welcome interruption. Firing down onto pockets of enemy resistance as they dashed into the gap 'would keep our eye in', they told us. It was too easy, and it was gruesome.

The missile traffic wasn't always one way, though, and we lost a couple of tanks when a few Jerries fired back with anti-tank guns and mortars. This show of defiance was always short-lived; a short, sharp tank barrage followed by a Typhoon air strike quickly sorted things out.

'That's put paid to those cheeky blighters,' was a typically understated response from Teddy Foster.

August 19th saw us harboured on the high ground overlooking the Falaise to Futanges road. We were outside a village called Ronai, and a chilly dawn had just cracked open another new day.

During a brief reconnaissance trip into the town, we found several abandoned vehicles and numerous PoWs wandering the streets waiting to be picked up. After corralling a few, we pulled back onto the hillside that overlooked the only exit route available for the scampering Germans. We didn't have to search for them – they were in their hundreds. Like a burning ants' nest, what was left of the Seventh Army had scattered around the valley basin. More and more men flooded into the gap, flushed from the Falaise pocket by a marauding American army that was chasing them from the West.

'Boys, you are witnessing the end,' announced Caddick proudly.

Typhoons seemed to confirm this as they screeched overhead and unleashed their loads into the valley. Nothing much came our way; desperate to escape, the souls below us didn't have time to fight.

There were lulls in the chaos unfolding on the killing grounds less than a mile away. In their final death throes men pleaded for their mothers and we heard their screams echo up from the valley floor.

It began to rain heavily as the bombardment continued.

'Down to the last twenty, sir.'

There was no reply from the boss man, just an open-hand signal, which required another high explosive. A clenched fist meant AP.

I saw our most recent missile plough into a column of marching soldiers. Why were they marching and not setting sprint records? It was all far too easy, but then I remembered Buff and my other dead companions. No, today had been our day.

More ammunition arrived from the supply echelon as I continued to watch the mayhem below. I saw men on bicycles going the wrong way up the road, and lots of horses, frantic and wild as they bucked and galloped away from danger. My pity was for them; it would always be for horses over the doomed men who scrabbled about in the mud, blood and gore.

'Come on, you beauty.' I picked out individual horses in my binoculars and urge them to safety as if they were on the racetrack at Fakenham.

Pop preferred animals to humans, and I remember our back garden being a sanctuary for injured birds and hedgehogs. On one occasion, even a squashed frog, inadvertently trodden on by my mortified mum, found its way into our A&E.

'Peter, Peter, I heard it pop,' Mum shrieked.

Our car often screeched to a jarring halt on country back lanes. Like Superman, Pop would leap out to rescue another pigeon or rabbit (fingers crossed it was myxomatosis-free). They were transported back home in the wooden crate that was always ready for this purpose.

Mum and I would look on as Pop carefully transferred the patient into a cardboard box lined with one of her best fluffy towels. Bread soaked in milk was apparently the elixir of life;

151

after being mushed into a liquid paste, usually in one of Mum's Royal Doulton cereal bowls, Pop would gently place the concoction underneath the beak or mouth of its desperate recipient. 'This is the same as us having a saline drip,' he would say proudly.

It probably did more harm than good, but it's what we did in those days. Looking at the quicksand of milk and white bread, I was more worried about the poor creatures drowning; I didn't recall seeing any of them eat the stuff.

The three of us waited on tenterhooks. Sometimes they lived, but mostly they didn't. It was always sad at the burial when a cross made out of lolly sticks was ceremoniously stuck into the small mound of earth carefully piled over the deceased. All of them had names.

One of the only times I saw Pop cry was when the vet put down Prince, our black Labrador. Before the fatal injection, Pop sat and talked to him for hours; when the time came, he gently held Prince's paw and watched his best friend's life slowly ebb away. On reflection, neither his father nor mother got the same emotional response on the days that they passed.

The rain continued to slant down. It was heavier now but nowhere near enough to douse the fires and black smoke that funnelled skywards. As Typhoons continued to roar overhead, the ground resembled a badly stained carpet of man, metal and beast.

'Take a look at that.' Like several other commanders, Caddick had just clocked a Panther bombing down the road at well over 30mph with at least thirty men clinging onto it. That was until several gunners, including ours, focused their sights on what would be a perfect prize.

We watched as the men were wiped from this earth a few moments later. 'Bingo,' Sid and Big Nige celebrated enthusiastically.

'Okay. Ceasefire and await further instructions.' Our commander's matter-of-fact voice boomed loudly over the intercom. I seemed to be the only relieved person in our tank; the others wanted more, confirmed by the disappointed whines that acknowledged this order. It depressed me; I imagined what it must have felt like to be one of those boys desperately clinging to life, euphoric at the scent of freedom and the faint hope that they might survive.

The rainfall grew heavier. After the misery of resting under a mud-caked tank that channelled torrents of water onto us, we spent the next day trying to get dry inside it. There were no further orders to move and it was my most miserable time. The others quickly came down from their 'highs', and we sat silently in our crew positions.

Caddick was the only one who moved anywhere, hopping in and out to attend various briefings. Apart from pee breaks, we all stayed where we were.

Thank God for tommy stoves. All five of ours were on the go, keeping us warm and fuelled with tea. Although the tank stank like a wet dog, it was our home and it was almost cosy inside. Tony had a pair of socks drying over the barrel of his Sten gun, and Morton's boots were dangling by their straps just above my head. Every time I leant back, they thumped into the back of my head, and water continually dripped down my back.

Over the gear stick hung a pair of my underpants. I really did want to stuff them into Morton's horrible, dribbly mouth. 'Move those fucking boots, knobhead.'

'The missus is fucking pregnant again,' Auden said, his feet up on the bulkhead. It was a casual mention as he flicked over the pages of another handwritten letter.

'Who's the father, then?'

'Fuck off, Meadows. At least I get letters.'

Touché. He was correct. Whilst the others received regular correspondence, nothing came my way. My father – now me – was separated from his wife, so that was to be expected. But what about *my* wife, Tess, and the lads? They were somewhere in another world... I couldn't dwell on that for too long. And what about my grandparents, Percy and Gladys? Absolutely nothing from them yet.

I had always thought it strange that Pop seemed to be a black sheep of the Meadows dynasty. He had four siblings, including a twin brother, but none of them were close. Pop always seemed to be at the bottom of the family pecking order, an underachiever and, to be cruel, the runt of the family. Maybe there was a simple answer to this: for huge chunks of his life, he had been away in foreign lands. But then again, so had his siblings!

As a child, I remember our trips to Norwich for an audience with my grandparents. These were God-awful occasions, except when it was home time and my pockets bulged with Mintoes and chocolate eclairs, and Grandpa surreptitiously pressed a half-crown coin into my hand. He always did this with a knowing wink.

To be blunt, the rest of our visit was an ordeal. This family was from a 'children should be seen and not heard' generation. I remember my angst at dressing in what Mum called Sunday best, which became incredibly tedious as I got older and more Kevin-like.

The biggest humiliation was the customary parade around Granny's show-ring lounge when all the elders sat in comfy chairs and scrutinised me like a rescue pet. The only thing missing was a thumbs-up (or down) and a lead. I'm sure the dogs at Crufts would have found this performance more distressing.

'Do you think you need to put a brace on him?' Nana asked my parents one day. Being quite a shy, goofy kid, this was as embarrassing as hell. The grown-ups huddled together to discuss this and any other concerns about the subject of interest in front of them.

'Remember to speak only when spoken to,' my mother whispered every time we went to Norwich, giving my arm a reassuring squeeze. This was especially the case when we went for Sunday lunch. This was an event where all the adults swooned over Granny's apple-pie pastry, whether shortcrust or puff, and the excellent choice of Percy's table wine. It was 'van ordinaries' every time.

I reflected on Tony's comment; he did at least get letters. 'You're not wrong, Tony. My wife has just left me, mate.'

He said nothing and continued thumbing through his wife's letter before folding it neatly into his kitbag. It was strange saying that, because I knew Tess was still there in my other life. I hoped she was safe and okay.

Tony threw me a cigarette and lit one himself. 'That's a bummer, mate.' I waited for another piss-take follow-up but it didn't come. 'I've heard that where we're going the birds are right up for it.'

What a comforting thought. He was referring to the wholesome reputation Dutch and Belgian girls enjoyed at home in England. Indeed, the German Fraulein had an excellent reputation, too, and they were all called Helga. What he didn't know was that many of the, shall we say, flirtatious ones would also have had their heads shaved when we got to the Motherland. We had seen some evidence of this in France already. Fraternising with the enemy was forbidden, and it went both ways.

August 21st arrived, and with it came more wet weather. 'Who switched the sun off?' moaned Morton.

'Liquid sunshine, mate,' I joked. No one said anything. This was an expression I'd picked up on holiday in Antigua. Did anyone in 1945 know about the Caribbean, its constant sunshine and rum punches?

We had gone from summer light to a grey autumn shade with depressing cold rain. After a few miserable days of inactivity, we received orders to move again, a welcome relief from the collective morose mood.

'Right, you horrible lot. Let's be having you.' It was the boss and his sudden instruction made me jump. The last time I'd heard 'Let's be having you' was Delia Smith's legendary half-time rallying call. Norwich City were playing Manchester City in 2005, and it felt like a 'where were you when John Lennon died?' moment. I was at Carrow Road with the Canary hordes, and the score was balanced at two each. Like all the stunned fans on both sides, we were shocked at what slowly emerged from the players' tunnel at half-time. There she was, our illustrious chairwoman and goddess to the faithful: Delia.

She stumbled across the boggy February pitch and zig-zagged towards the centre circle in her muddy-soled, no doubt Christian Louboutin shoes. A cross between Dick Emery and Larry Grayson, and possibly lubricated by a glass of Merlot or two, she started to wail. 'A message to the best football supporters in the world: we need a twelfth man here,' she slurred.

It was a bit like hearing your granny fart. Everyone was embarrassed and shocked at the same time. With a Sky Sports microphone snatched from a bemused reporter, the TV cameras lunged at her like hungry hyenas, but she continued her Churchillian speech. 'Where are you? Where are you? Let's be having you!'

The rest is history.

I used this event as the basis for a speech at a conference once. Don't ask me why; the response was much the same. And were they Louboutins? I still find it amazing that we didn't see Delia prostrate and the famous red soles of her shoes to confirm that they were. We went on to lose 3–2!

And so the rain continued. We were eventually called forward into what can only be described as a smouldering fire pit of death. Our orders were to terminate anything in a German uniform, but the order should have been 'any sad bastard wanting to fight' because they were everywhere.

As we eased our way between thousands of beaten men, they marched alongside us across the battlefields of Guepress, Villedieu-l'es-Bailleul and Tournai. The sheer numbers overwhelmed the liaison officers sent out from brigade HQ to martial the situation. They resembled agitated school prefects, all clipboards and newfound authority, rather than Army officers supposedly in charge.

And then there was the death and destruction that confronted us and always silenced the banter inside our tank and across the airwaves. As far as the eye could see, walls of fetid humanity lay piled up in heaps or mashed between war machines, decimated by days of Allied air strikes and artillery bombardment.

We found a relatively clear bit of road to rest from this visual onslaught. Our next orders were imminent, so we enjoyed our nicotine hits and waited. The Canadians from the north and General Patton's Yanks in the south were due to meet us on August 21st.

'What the hell is that?' Caddick asked suddenly.

The answer was apparent. 'It's a horse, sir,' I said. 'Permission to catch it?'

'This should be fun. Have a go then, son.'

By the time I hit the ground, I had an audience. Together with my crew and a few other interested parties from our troop, I noticed Colonel Hopkinson sitting in a staff Jeep nearby. An

156

absolute giant of a man, he was observing me intently through thick, black-rimmed glasses. His driver, crushed alongside him, made me smile.

'Make it look good, Meadows,' I told myself.

The horse was fully tacked and very distressed. We had seen many dead on the battlefield, usually with their hides stripped bare, but this one was very much alive. His giant head swooped up and down like a Status Quo headbanger as he came to a faltering and snorting halt in front of me. His chestnut-coloured coat made him look similar to Tricky, my dad's thoroughbred Exmoor cross from my youth.

Tricky could be feisty. I remembered Tess calling me the 'horse whisperer' because these beautiful creatures seemed to respond to me. It was time to test my skills again. This animal was agitated and needed time to calm down, so I held out both hands to make peace. 'Come on, big boy. I won't hurt you.'

His broad black nostrils flared, and from six feet away I felt his hot breath hit my face, sweet and moist. He noisily gnawed the shiny chrome bit clamped into his mouth. White globules of froth splattered down his chest and onto the ground.

'Someone get me some water, please.' I was conscious that I sounded like a surgeon requesting a scalpel.

It was Sidney Cartwright who responded first. He crept up behind me as if being shielded from a lion and carefully passed me a billycan filled with water. 'I was thinking more of a bucket, mate,' I said, before I offered it to my new four-legged friend. 'Come on, big boy. I won't hurt you,' I said again.

The horse began to rise and his ears flattened across the top of his mane. My calm offensive took time to work, but I felt strangely empowered. 'Show him who's boss' was Pop's mantra when dealing with spirited horses. 'And never show them you're scared.'

The silence behind me was deafening; all attention was on me, and I could feel numerous eyes drilling into the back of my head. This was not the time to back down.

'Come on, Boris.' I'd already named him. Was it his unkempt, cream-coloured mane? Probably.

I could see the fear in his eyes as they stared directly at me. I stared back and, moving forward slowly, placed the water near his front feet.

Horses, like elephants, are intelligent and emotional creatures. Some people think they are telepathic, and I certainly experienced that during my early riding days. Boris was magnificent, but knowing I was frightened and I was his new friend, the breakthrough came when he gave up the macho stuff and hesitantly nosed his way forward, one step at a time.

With restored confidence, he dropped his head and guzzled up the water.

'You're a beauty, aren't you?' Rather than grab his harness, I waited to see his next move.

With hardly enough water inside it to quench a mouse's thirst, Boris dismissed the billycan with a nudge and slowly lifted his head to look at me. 'I'll get you some more, big boy.' I beckoned to Cartwright again.

A quick nuzzle and prod of my chest from Boris's velvety nose came next. Patting him firmly on the side of his muscled neck, I found his smell intoxicating: sweaty and damp, but with a wonderful earthy aroma oozing from his pores. As we stood together, getting to know each other, he nuzzled my pockets in search of treats. It didn't take him long to find the barley sugar I'd tucked away; I offered it to him on the palm of my hand, and he crunched it down in one loud chomp.

'Okay, now for the next bit. Don't show me up.'

I hadn't ridden properly since my teens and, given that I was now my father, the next part of the show could be interesting. Pop had informed me on more than one occasion that, from a young age, he was an extremely proficient horseman. It was time to test his boast.

My charge was huge, much larger than anything I had ridden before. Gripping the reins and saddle pommel in my left hand, I slipped the toe of my left boot into a shiny brass stirrup. Trying to remember the order of things, I faced towards the back of the horse and heaved myself up and round onto the seat. So far, so good; he didn't move, which was excellent news.

'Don't bolt now, my friend. Time to make some minor adjustments.'

The stirrups needed to be shorter for the new me; a buckle adjusted the leather straps under my legs. At the same time, I took the opportunity to check out the guys behind me, who were already beginning to show signs of disinterest. But while there was any chance of this highly energised horse dispatching me, they wouldn't give up entirely.

'Trooper, what is your name?' the colonel asked. It was not exactly the voice I wanted to hear at that moment.

'Meadows, sir.'

'There's a farm over there, Meadows.' He pointed towards the hill behind us. 'Take him there. I'm sure the farmer will be grateful.'

It struck me that Boris might not belong to the military as I'd first thought; he may well have come from the farm. He seemed to know my thinking and lifted his head with his long ears pointing forward. When you're on the back of a giant beast like that, it is better to see their ears forward than back, which reassured me.

'Yes, sir.'

Tony gave me his customary wanker sign and Valentine Caddick offered a cheerful thumbs-up.

'Commander, take your tank along with Meadows and do some recce work while you're at it,' the colonel ordered.

Caddick's face was laughable. He glared at me and followed up with a wanker sign that was much more animated than Tony's. The colonel's Jeep fired up with a splutter and roared off down the road, leaving a cloud of dust and black smoke behind it.

He was in the iconic Ford 'Willys' Jeep, and I was struck by how tiny they were and the narrowness of their wheels. I guessed that in my other life of Chelsea tractors and other off-road imitators, everything was bigger than in WW2.

After a tentative tap and no response, I gave Boris a sharp jab with my heels and off we went. We started with a slow walk that quickly became a rising trot. It reminded me of Pop, who was a stickler for trotting correctly. American riders sit firmly in their armchair-like saddles when they trot, but the Brits bob up and down – quite a sight, especially when their breeches flare like sails.

The other thing Pop always watched out for was boot heels: they must always point downwards. 'And squeeze your knees, son. You won't fall off.'

Easier said than done. He used to drop behind me on Tricky to look for gaps of daylight between my knees and the saddle. Muggins and I would wait to see if we had passed the test.

With newfound confidence, I looked over my shoulder and saw the guys reluctantly clamber into their rearranged crew positions. Auden was now at the helm in my driver's seat. Wearing dark sunglasses, Caddick waved his arm forward like a cavalry officer; of course, he was one of those who considered tanks to be motorised cavalry that had replaced horses. 'Follow Roy Rogers,' was his joke to the others.

I sensed a disappointment amongst my mates that their brave comrade had not been de-saddled and flung into a distant field, though there was still time for that.

I looked behind and smiled as Boris eased into an extended, lunging canter. We even took the opportunity to jump over a few obstacles, including a couple of low wooden fences. This was all new to me but a skill my father had mastered early in his riding career. Pop's experience got us over the jumps safely!

After his initial surprise, the old farmer who greeted us produced a bottle of Calvados followed by two large hunks of dried meat on a wooden tray. Feet out of stirrups first, I slid off Boris and landed impressively on the ground on his left side. Well-remembered, Calum. Americans keep their holding foot in place when they dismount.

The farmer's wife, equally astonished at the arrival of her new house guests, presented us with a large brown hen. Morton eagerly retrieved the flapping bird from her. '*Danke! Danke!*' What an idiot – we were in France. Holding the bird like a puppy, he cuddled it under his floppy pink chin and whispered something.

This immediately set off alarm bells. As I attempted to explain to the couple that Boris was a gift, I heard the fowl's final cluck and then a loud crack as the heavy hands of our loader twisted its scraggy neck.

'Jesus, Nige!' The old folk looked horrified, especially the poor woman. '*Pardonnez- moi, madame,*' I apologised.

160

Having whispered the bird's last rites and wrung its neck, Morton was already starting the plucking process.

'*Allemande.*' Ignoring the commotion of flapping wings and flying feathers behind him, the old farmer pointed to Boris. '*Le cheval appartient aux porcs allemands.*' He lifted a crooked walking stick and pointed towards the fighting zones of the last few days.

'Boris belongs to "those German pigs",' translated Caddick.

That surprised me because the saddle didn't look military. Perhaps the Germans had acquired him from another farm? I didn't know how to say that, but I was more worried about the old lady, who seemed to be convulsing.

Then, it really kicked off. Cordiality and all the initial *bon humour* went out of the window when Caddick aggressively ran a flat hand along the underside of his throat.

I think it was the sawing motion and the recent 'hen genocide' that finally did it for the couple. Misinterpreting this gesture, the old boy dropped to his knees and desperately began to claw at my feet, whilst his wife screamed beside him. The Globe Theatre would have appreciated this dramatic Anglo-French Shakespearian scene.

'*Non, non, s'il vous plait.*' He pleaded with me.

'*Monsieur, monsieur, non blessez.*' That was my surprising response. I didn't speak French, but Dad did a little; he had always been heroic when he gave foreign languages a go. I immediately remembered the embarrassing time he tried to ask for a toothpick in Italian. The clumsy combination of jabbing a pointing finger into his open mouth and using rustic Italian stunned the poor waitress serving us.

'*Pompino, pompino,*' he gestured repeatedly. The restaurant served great food, and the service had been genuinely excellent, but quite understandably she wouldn't give him a blow job as well!

'*Pour que vous ayez des œufs!*' screamed the farmer's wife.

'Yes, it was for eggs, you blithering idiot,' confirmed Caddick.

Peace and relative tranquillity eventually returned, helped by a realisation that we would only be garrotting their gift of an egg-producing pet chicken. I brushed the farmer down while the boys fretted over the stricken woman.

'Tea and biscuits, tea and biscuits,' fussed Morton. With that offer reluctantly accepted, and a fragile *entente cordiale* restored, we opted to say our goodbyes to the dazed couple rather than overstay our welcome. Boris munched through a bucket of carrots and didn't look up as our tank slowly backed up the muddy farm track.

'Bye. *Au revoir. Guten tag,*' yelled Tony. 'We'll be back.'

The old folks clung to each other and returned a crazed farewell wave. Finally, Boris looked up and gave me a swooping nod as only horses can do, though probably more from carrot pleasure than acknowledgement. Then, he sank his head back into something far more important.

I didn't hold a grudge; however, I did worry that his new owners might get their own back and eat him. The French had a penchant for horse meat – and this one also belonged to those German pigs over the hill!

Some of our troop were waiting when we returned an hour later. We had guests, too; a couple of American platoons and a handful of Canadian tank crews were now part of the welcoming party. The Yanks were as predictable as always: all chewing gum, bluff, bluster and shiny new kit. The Canadians were grimy and dirty like us.

'Boys, you'll be pleased – we're not staying. Put your foot down, Meadows, we are outta here.' Caddick said the last bit in a poorly imitated American accent.

I swear I saw Auden middle-finger the Yanks as we roared off to meet with the rest of our regiment and towards the next part of our adventure: crossing the Seine.

Historians and military observers grimly described the battle of Falaise as a 'duck shoot'. They also claimed that our sustained air attacks had such a psychological effect on the enemy that the traumatised German army destroyed more of its armour than the Allied bombing.

From Peter Meadows' memoirs

The valley was alive with movement – men marching, running with columns of horse-drawn transport and with cavalry horses running loose. It was quite an unbelievable sight, and one that will never be repeated. Roads and lanes were choked with vehicles, carts, dead horses and men. At one point, the whole lot being overtaken by a Panther tank crowded with Germans doing well over 30mph gave us some amusement. Prisoners were also a source of embarrassment; thousands wandered about, waiting to give themselves up to somebody. We alone collected more than 3,000, together with innumerable tanks, guns and vehicles.

Later on, while in tank laager formation, I caught a fully equipped cavalry horse, erected some suitable jumps and enjoyed my favourite pastime. I was to discover that this did not pass unnoticed by my commanding officer, Colonel Hopkinson, who later rose to the rank of major-general with CB, DSO, OBE, and MC. So ended the Falaise battle, and we prepared for the swan through France, Belgium and Holland.

Our Swan through France

'Swanning about' was an expression used by tankies when battalions such as the Desert Rats made rapid advances in the battles of North Africa.

After the excitement of Falaise, the next few days bordered on dull as we swanned our way through France towards Belgium. The Germans were in full retreat and our main task on this trip was to push them back and move fast. Not for the first time avoiding numerous booby traps made this objective difficult; land mines had to be navigated as always, but more sinister and devious contraptions began to appear, too.

We already had one casualty: a tank commander from A Squadron who had garrotted himself. A tripwire wound around his neck connected to a tree-mounted Panzerfaust had obliterated his Sherman and the crew inside. The commander escaped incineration but was left dangling like a highwayman on an eighteenth-century gibbet. We heard that no one survived.

We crossed from the west bank of the Seine a week later, having first enjoyed the fungal delights on its riverbank. There were brown mushrooms everywhere, the non-hallucinogenic kind but still magic, and they more than supplemented the cook's breakfast that day. The unmistakable aroma of bacon, eggs and now mushrooms was a gift from heaven compared to the heady smell of rotting flesh that had enveloped our battalion on its journey towards the Seine.

On the 29th of August, we crossed the river using one of the last bridges standing and spread out. Finally moving freely on open ground and feeling unleashed was liberating. Our tanks seemed to feel the same release and charged along at 25mph. Everything felt easier, especially with the steering controls and the responsiveness of my accelerator pedal. The best I reached, according to the speedometer, was a magnificent 28mph; it was exhilarating as the cobwebs shrouding my anxiety and doubts were blown away.

'Okey dokey, Meadows, ease her down.' It was Caddick who broke my thoughtful but happy silence.

'Problem, sir?'

'No, son. We have a job to do.'

The mood changed immediately. Our private thoughts snuffed out, it was back into work mode as we flicked those internal switches back on again.

Auden dropped his feet from the bulkhead, lit two fags and inhaled noisily. 'Thanks, big boy.' I took one gratefully from him, keeping my eyes on the road.

We crept along at half speed. The rest of our troop continued ahead, with C Squadron and Teddy Foster in the lead. The other two squadrons were about a mile on either side, and RHQ, with the Echelon support groups, were backing us up at the rear.

'We've been asked to investigate those vehicles.'

We could see them in a gulley to our left, three in a line and all stationary. Grey smoke puffed out of one, which I quickly identified as German.

We had seen hundreds of abandoned vehicles during our trip, including a few Tiger tanks plus the biggest of all, a fantastic 77-ton King Tiger. The spectacle below us was surreal as we ran alongside the leading car. An officer was sitting bolt upright beside his driver as if they were waiting at a set of traffic lights; both were dead. If there were degrees of dead, the guys in the vehicles behind them were even more dead, their bodies roasted into pieces of twisted charcoal.

As we towered over the leading car, our sergeant dropped onto its long black bonnet to investigate. 'It's a Mercedes. And it looks like he shot his driver, then himself.'

I saw the pistol in the officer's gloved hand and noticed that each corpse had a small red hole in the temple. Surprisingly, there was little mess and virtually no blood. Sad fuckers – but the fewer of them on this planet the better, and the quicker we could get this war over.

'Don't get any ideas, sarge. You really don't need us down there.' Morton was remembering our old commander and the mannequin men, but did our sergeant know about our escapade in the dunes?

Evidently he did. 'Lighter on my feet than some.' Caddick winked at me and dropped heavily to the ground. Private relief all round. This could be one big trap. He wandered off towards the car's boot and opened it.

'Something nice?' Sid asked.

The smile on Caddick's face put us at ease. 'If you call a boot full of liquor nice, then yes, Sid.' There were three cases of six green bottles; he reached in and lobbed a bottle up to Cartwright. 'Jägermeister?' Caddick frowned and passed a case to me.

'This will blow your socks off, guv,' I said. The memory of Jäger bombs and past-life corporate events sprang to mind. It was incredible that, seventy-five years later, this strong alcoholic drink would reinvent itself as a trendy shot mixed with a famous energy drink. The Germans, inventive as always, had also utilised Jägermeister as an anaesthetic and disinfectant in WW2. What a waste!

We had Caddick covered; I hoped all our guns had their safety catches switched on, especially the Stens. He rummaged for a few more minutes before giving us the thumbs-up and returning to take his commander's position. 'We'll let the stiffs in RHQ do the tidying up here.'

'Looks like someone burnt the sausages,' added Auden referring to the human barbeque below.

On receiving the order to move, we lurched back into motion. The engine roared approvingly as we headed back on course towards our comrades who were now thirty minutes ahead. 'Meadows, DO NOT let the fuckers get there first,' Caddick ordered. RHQ was just a little behind us so, like big kids, we had to get home before them.

Nothing much happened for the next two days. It was August 31st and stormy as we slowly eased our way through the streets of Villers-Vermont. The town had been cleared of enemy resistance and our infantry comrades were rounding up hordes of PoWs. A small group of them were huddled together on the side of the road with a muddy pool of water at their feet. I was tempted to drive through it but gently eased the right stick back instead to avoid giving them even more misery.

They looked up, and I caught one young soldier's eyes on the edge of the pack. I didn't recall seeing any living creature look as pathetic and hopeless as he did. His eyes, vacant and devoid of life, were fixed firmly onto mine. I pointed at my cigarette and then at him. 'For you. *Fur dich.*'

We drove past at no more than a slow walking pace, and there was a flicker of recognition as I flicked it at him. My aim was good; the glowing cigarette missed the puddle and landed on his lap. I noticed the toes of his feet were peeking through the worn-out ends of his boots. God, my boots were barely broken in.

I noted the foresight of having leather straps to bind my tankie boots tight around my ankles. There were no laces to snag anything, which was especially important in an emergency evacuation. In my wing mirror, still amazingly intact after weeks of battle, I saw the German soldier fumble for the cigarette, and then that was it: he disappeared out of sight and out of my mind.

At around 17.30 hours, we were ordered to support B Squadron, led by my old acquaintance Major Hales. They were absorbed in a tricky skirmish on the outskirts of a small town called Poix. We let off some fireworks to assist them, most of which landed on a Jerry transport division, which we later found out was predominantly horse-drawn. I felt sick as Boris and his bucket of carrots came to mind, but luckily we weren't asked to clear up.

We captured more PoWs; nearly a thousand had been rounded up by the end of a pretty miserable day. It was made worse by the news that we had to hold our position whilst the rest of our battalion headed into Poix to laager down for the night.

Caddick was genuinely upset. 'I don't know what we've done to deserve this, lads, but we're not going.' We remained silent as the information slowly sank in.

'Nay bother. We have booze, bacon and a field full of lady sheep to play with.' Sidney Cartwright's Geordie attempt to ease our collective pain broke the deadlock.

'And let's not forget Henrietta, our hen,' came Morton's inevitable – but still surprising – contribution.

None of us knew where the flow of this conversation would take us but someone had more to add. 'Been there, done that,' said Auden. 'When I was a chef.' Full house – but really?

We were truly pissed off. Being billeted in a liberated town usually meant comfortable beds, decent grub and, for the more romantically inclined, a shag. Pop had never spoken about the latter but must have been tempted to dabble, though evidently not yet. I wondered how he – I – would respond if and when the opportunity arose.

Whilst the rest of our squadron awoke from its slumbers on September 1st with sore heads (and some with sore other parts), we were on the road at 06.15 hours. We eventually found a suitable sapper-repaired bridge to take us over the Somme River.

It was a dark place; we spent most of the day in subdued reflection and wrote letters home. I bucked the trend and wrote a poem instead.

Run boy run.
Bodies foul, grotesquely warped like mannequins
Falling, smouldering and melting down.
Death is jet black; it clings like Lucifer's cloak,
Run boy run.
Stench trench, sheer fear, rotten and forgotten tears
Throat-burning smoke, acid heat, choking.
Blood pools from weeping limbs, flies flit, please save me,
Run boy run.
Finally, death smells sweet,
The end is determined
The end is complete
Run boy run.

My old friend Padre Huggins held a short remembrance service for those who had fallen in the Great War. He was the archetypal clergyman, all teeth, waving arms and no chin, but I always felt a tad of respect for the guy after this gesture. At the same time, I hadn't forgotten that Captain Nigel Huggins, padre extraordinaire, was the prick who had got me demoted.

Apart from the niggling interference from a Panther, which was promptly dispatched by one of our Fireflies, C Squadron led our battalion march towards Berneuil. This became a charge that continued through the night for more than one hundred miles guided by bright moonlight.

In their various guises Shermans correctly took criticism during and after the war, but if nothing else they were fast and reliable; this one purred like a cat. So far she had not let us down.

We pushed on at 05:00 hours after a short pitstop. It was the 2nd of September; we were tired, and our tank was showing signs of strain, especially in the steering. Fortunately, our deployment was at a crossroads, while the rest of our battalion continued towards the village, which had a population of around 500 people. Warnings from the Maquis had told us that German soldiers were hiding there, and subsequent reports of snipers and tank movements confirmed this as the morning wore on.

We were quiet; A and B Squadrons enjoyed most of the action, which included capturing two high-ranking officers. They also captured two hundred ordinary ranks and shot up a column of German staff cars as it entered Berneuil from the south. More stressfully, friendly fire fell onto one of our patrols in the village from tanks belonging to a group of our 7th Armed Division. No one was hurt, but one wayward missile roared over our heads before smashing into a rickety old cattle shed behind us.

'Steak and chips all around, then,' was Sid's reaction. He was busy dismantling the coaxial Browning machine gun at the time. The rest of us nodded approval and continued our daily chores before a conversation about 'your last meal on earth' started.

'Steak and kidney pudding, mashed spuds and gravy,' drooled Tony.

'Ham, egg and chips,' came from Caddick.

Cartwright declared steak and then added eloquently, 'Just wipe its backside. I want it rare!'

'Sherry trifle for me,' chipped in Morton.

'Poof. That's not a meal.' Predictably unpredictable as always, Big Nige's input was met with howls of derision.

'What about you, Meadows?'

Pop's favourite meal was always roast beef, followed by apple pie and custard, Bird's, of course, so my answer was that. I didn't have the heart or, conveniently, the ability to say McDonald's filet-o-fish, followed by a Big Mac and fries, topped off with a Strawberry McFlurry and coffee. How I could demolish that lot now? I often used to. And how great it would have been to educate the boys on fast food and the culinary landscapes ahead.

We were advised to stay put for forty-eight hours due to petrol shortages; it would take that long until the next delivery. Despite being sitting ducks, it gave us a break and the regimental engineers an opportunity to complete more intensive surgery on our tanks, including mine.

The 3rd of September 1945 was a quiet day and provided another period of reflection. It had been five years since the start of the war, and most of the guys in our brigade had not been home. Even though we had our enemy running, the mood was muted, and banter was minimal as everyone got on with their tasks.

'I'm going for some beauty treatment.' Making my grand announcement to the crew, I grabbed my wash kit and wandered down to the mobile unit, which was 'in town' again. It seemed quiet, and one of the stark wooden cubicles was free as I went inside to shave.

I hadn't inspected myself recently. Pop's army photograph greeted me in the small round mirror, startling me and then making me laugh as I remembered watching him shave as a kid. The forehead in front of me sloped back more than mine and the complexion was dark and swarthy. 'You weren't quite the sex god you made yourself out to be, Pops.'

The mug looking back at me was not the face I remembered, but this one was only twenty years old and not the forty-plus I had grown up with. The hair was the same, though: black and combed back; it did thin out and go grey in later life. Then there was the moustache, which was something to behold. A tiny strip of brown hair lay across my top lip like a small garden slug. 'That's coming off first.' And it did.

I put away my razor, congratulating myself that I'd only nicked myself once. The flat blade that did the business was famous for this, especially if it was blunt. Pop often came into the kitchen after his 'morning ablutions', as he put it, with tiny bits of loo paper dabbed onto cuts on his chin and neck.

'Time to change the blade,' he would mutter.

Like blotting paper, the red spots of blood grew until they looked like the result of some horrendous plague. Sometimes, he forgot to peel them off until Mum reminded him as he approached the front door for work.

'Come on, you cunt. My turn.' The voice came from outside and didn't sound much like a jape.

'I'm not finished yet. Use another shower, mate.'

'But I want this one.'

As I prised the door ajar, I recognised the face but couldn't place it. Who was this prat giving me a hard time? 'And I said I'm not finished....'

Before I could continue, the numbskull, who was six inches taller and a yard wider, barged inside my cubicle to grab me. We stumbled into the open, each grappling for a decent hold.

My first thought was, 'Thank God I'm not naked!' He had me by the throat and his nails were digging into my skin, which hurt; the moron also looked as if he were winding up to launch a massive left-hander.

Pop was a fighter and I knew that I wasn't. With little time to work out the repercussions, my right fist, a ball of rock down by my knee, swung up and smashed into the guy's jaw above me. My tight left hook follow-up caught him firmly in the groin. The violence of this action and the result of these blows were astounding. Two things happened: first a searing pain like an electric charge flashed through my hand up to my elbow, and second, the talons attempting to strangle me turned to rubber and fell away.

'*Tim-fucking-ber*!' I couldn't resist as the human lump in front of me folded and crumpled like a felled redwood.

Were there any other assailants, and more importantly, did anyone witness this unprovoked attack? No to both questions. I could see my crew perched like monkeys on top of the turret further up the hillside. Their chatter was just audible but how much they'd seen, I couldn't tell.

'What the fuck is wrong with you, mate?' I demanded. The victim of my impressive two-shot combination punch did not answer me; he couldn't – he was out cold.

I noticed Caddick, whose amble down the hill towards us had turned into a gallop.

Holding onto his balls, Desperate Dan was also coming around. I couldn't back down; keeping the initiative before my boss interrupted things was vital. 'Don't ever try that again, you prick.' I resisted the urge to give him a boot. Instead, and more worryingly, I said, 'Or you won't see another Christmas.'

Christmas. How naff was that? As puzzled as me, he looked up and spat out a gob full of blood.

'Okay, Meadows, back off, boy.' Caddick pushed me to one side and stooped down over my aggressor. It was then that I saw his stripe. This was not a good situation.

The groggy lance corporal at my feet with sore balls and a swelling jaw glared up at me and said nothing.

'Boss, he started it.' It was essential to get in quickly. 'It was self-defence.' There was no CCTV to back up my plea.

'Shut up, Meadows.'

With Caddick's overly attentive help, the lump sat up gingerly. He held his head and rubbed his jaw, and all I could imagine now was another almighty bollocking or worse.

'Is that true, lance corporal?' Caddick demanded.

My opponent didn't say a word; instead, he spat globs of bloody phlegm onto the ground between his legs. Then a miracle happened: he nodded his head slowly.

'On your feet, man.' Caddick's empathy for my assailant quickly evaporated.

My wrist, the perpetrator of this situation, was throbbing like hell. I gripped it tightly as the sergeant looked at me. 'Go and sort yourself out, Meadows. I'll get this chap to a medic.'

I returned to the shower block to run cold water over my swollen right hand. Out of the corner of my eye I saw our crew dramatically re-enacting their interpretation of my haymaker punch on top of the tank.

Although I had boxed under Dad's supervision, my playground scrap with Ralph Green was my only real fight in anger. There were lots of air shots, grunting and bluster before Mr Mann waded in to break things up. That same heroic teacher slammed Dwayne Corcoran against the blackboard for being disruptive, which, at the time, was a perfect vigilante act against a school bully. Ralph and I did detention together, shared our sandwiches and, in the end, packed up our satchels and went home. What would Sergeant Caddick's punishment be?

Pop, on the other hand, was experienced; he had won boxing medals at school and enjoyed a good scrap. With boxing well behind him, he liked to keep fit. Karate made a late appearance; I remembered those dark, winter training nights when he went running barefoot on the road. He was not a sadomasochist but seemed to thrive on the discomfort of keeping fit and everything that came with this particular martial art.

His dojo in Braintree practised a full-contact style of karate and, much to Mum's distress, Pop often came home with broken toes and fingers. 'Stop fussing; it will heal with time, my dear.'

If he was hardcore, then I was very much soft porn.

I also remembered the Muhammad Ali fights of the 1970s. Pop and I both worshipped this genius of a man. Pop would set the wind-up alarm clock for 01:00, and we would huddle around the wireless with cups of cocoa and toast, listening to Harry Carpenter who let us into this world with his brilliant commentary.

There was another noteworthy commentator at the time, too: James Alexander Gordon gave us the 5pm Saturday footy results. As he read them out, Pop would check the pool's coupon, and our game was to guess the second team's score. 'Tottenham Hotspur ... 1,' then it was our turn, 'Arsenal ... 3.' It became surprisingly easy to get the second score right based on the tone and inflection of JAG's voice.

Although impressed with the execution and devastating impact of my newfound boxing talent, I was surprised at how easily this fighting instinct had been triggered. Pop did not have a temper as such and, importantly, he was never a mean man, but he got angry with injustice, whether directed towards himself or others. Perhaps the shower cubicle spat with Desperate Dan was an example of that. Or was it just a justifiable excuse to give someone a good 'whupping', as Muhammad Ali would have said?

Occasionally I got a whupping, but only rarely and in the conventional, old-fashioned parental sense. They were memorable though, and one such event sprang to mind. The late 1960s and 1970s was an era infamous for television programme catchphrases: 'Stupid boy,' from *Dad's Army* and 'I'm free,' from *Are You Being Served?* were two classics. 'You dirty old man,' from *Steptoe and Son* was another that my father particularly enjoyed, but it was Alf Garnett's 'You silly old moo' that landed me in big trouble. It came from the controversial sitcom *Till Death Us Do Part*, which is still funny and relevant even in the politically correct shenanigans of the 2020's.

I was about eight years old at the time. My mates and I were hanging onto the inside of our playground mesh fence like demented apes waiting for the bell to go for class when some grinning old dear shuffled up from nowhere towards us. She was all beige Mackintosh, smudged lipstick and hairy chin moles. As I mimicked those four memorable words, 'you silly old moo' to her smiling face, her Zimmer-frame-cum-shopping-trolley started to run away with her.

Like the famous toy of the nineties, the old biddy transformed. 'You cheeky little monkey,' she squeaked.

This aggressive reaction only prompted ape-like impersonations from my pals and me. Her blotchy old face was now contorted into what looked like a dried walnut as she attempted to impale me onto the end of her walking stick. 'Take that, you little bugger.'

'Oooh, she swore, she swore!' bleated Ricky, who was now hanging upside down with his tongue out. D'Artagnan would have been impressed as she repeatedly attempted to stab us through the caged fence.

'Just wait until … your father hears about this.' She choked midway through her short but alarm-bell ringing pronouncement, and I immediately began to worry. My fellow baboons laughed hysterically when she finally retracted her stick from our cage and trundled off like Quasimodo on wheels.

Slowly, very slowly, the enormity of this disastrous event set in. With it was a sense of imminent doom: mine.

The punishment was swift and severe. Belt off, trousers down and then whack at least half a dozen times. Pop was too strong for my wriggling resistance and the pain was immense. Afterwards Mum pretended not to fuss, though she did. Pop remained very quiet, and I firmly believe it hurt him more than it did me. He admitted later in life that he hated dishing out 'corporal punishment', as he put it 'but it was necessary for good discipline'.

'It never did me any harm,' he used to say in clichéd justification. Really? His father used a heavy walking stick to beat him.

My boys got a scaled-down version of his treatment but I used my palm on their backsides, which really *did* hurt me more than them! I wonder how they feel about it now?

Then I remembered the Caister Hotel poached-egg incident when Pop hurt me again, though not physically. I asked him what poached eggs were, and foolishly, rather than accept his explanation, I asked the waiter, too. For some reason Pop was incensed by this and sent me to my room. The emotional pain was worse than any smack because I had only wanted to participate in a grown-up conversation like the adults.

I meandered up to our tank to delay what I thought would be the inevitable. My wrist was severely swollen, but it didn't feel seriously damaged.

'Here comes the "brown bomber".' Auden, who made the Joe Louis comment, ducked as I faked a left jab.

As he went into a prolonged Norman Wisdom-like fall, Caddick stood patiently with hands on hips. 'Trooper, ease up, son.' 'Trooper' sounded bad – Peter would have been better – but 'son' softened things. Confusing.

'Sir?'

'That was Lance Corporal Davidson from Sergeant Moxton's troop that you decked.' His face was expressionless. 'You'll be pleased to know he has admitted to his ungentlemanly conduct.'

'Ungentlemanly conduct? The guy's an idiot, sir.'

'Maybe so. But his father has just been killed.' *So fucking what?* Is what I wanted to say. 'V1 bomb did it. Fucking Jerries.'

'Yes, sir.'

'I think we'll leave it at that, don't you?' Caddick looked for my acknowledgement and I nodded.

Although hugely reassured by this turn of events, something else gnawed into my gut. 'From Moxton's troop? That Nazi killer on the beach.'

'Absolutely right. Best leave it there, then.'

I desperately hoped the feeling would be mutual.

From Peter Meadows' memoirs

Before this, we had lost many tanks and lives but the enemy lost considerably more, quite apart from thousands of prisoners that were taken. I felt no hatred towards these German soldiers for they were not to be compared with the SS troops nor the Gestapo, and in general they were better soldiers than most of our allies.

Belgium, Scraps and Cats

Famous Belgians? We laughed then, and I did now. On a business trip, our tour around the country's renowned brewery would conclude with a beer tasting in its portrait gallery of famous Belgians. This puzzled us on two fronts: Poirot was the only name we could come up with – and he was fictitious – and why would anyone be interested anyway?

As it happens, the Italians and French were. As we entered the small room, Poirot's face greeted us, together with a few sports stars and one other notable addition: Tintin.

We crossed into Belgium on September 6th 1944. It was pelting down again; in a 'heads-up' position, I could feel the cold fingers of rainwater trickle down the crevice of my back. Our battalion's orders were to form a line from Ingooigem to Wortegem, a stretch of around six miles. Squadron A was on the left, B on the right, and our boys from C were located in the town of Anzegem plum in the middle.

Our drive there was short and uncomfortable and my self-bandaged wrist made it worse. If I tried to operate my right steering lever with an open hand, an electric pain instantly charged up my arm. However, with a pull or push of my clenched fist and some adapted wrist action, the pain became more bearable. *Mastered by his fists*. The thought made me smile.

'What the fuck do you call that, trooper?' Valentine Caddick's perspective was not the same as mine. He was right; having missed another telegraph pole squonked forty-five degrees over the road, there were more issues ahead.

My wrist remained in its sorry state mainly because I wanted to avoid interfering questions from nosey medics. Selfish, maybe, but this was about self-preservation. Hats off to Caddick; he hadn't forced me to go for a check-up, which he should have done.

I squeezed my wrist, hoping to master this new driving technique quickly.

'It's wanker's cramp, sir.' Auden decided to raise our level of conversation, which wasn't difficult. Of course, the rest chipped in. Creatively is one word to describe their observational skills on the decline in my driving skills; crass is another.

'I have to use both hands, sir,' clucked Morton.

'I prefer someone doing it for me,' added Geordie Boy. 'Preferably on two knees.'

'Okay, girls, SHUT it.' Our sergeant concluded the verbal ping-pong then added, 'Boys, you wouldn't know how to even if Mae fucking West was sitting on your lap.'

I smiled at the thought, then it was time to re-focus on my immediate challenge: how to steer a giant lump of metal as it tacked and jived down the road. At least the topography of this Flemish landscape was pancake flat, and the narrow tarmac roads were relatively straight. This was different from Normandy; the engine loved it as we belted along at nearly 30mph.

We advanced into Anzegem, a small town where the narrow cobbled streets were utterly deserted. No flags were flying this time, which was the usual welcome for liberating Allies. That was a strong indication that the locals were scared.

'I smell Kraut,' confirmed Caddick.

The high buildings made it perfect sniper territory, so we closed down and moved towards the railway track where enemy infantry had been reported. The rest of our squadron moved north towards Kruisem to help the 15th Scottish reconnaissance unit that had run into a 'spot of bother'.

It was noon and the weather had cleared into a bright autumnal day; for once we were drenched in warm sunshine rather than rain. The command to halt came through as we approached a tunnel underneath a railway bridge. We had been leading 2 Troop at that point but our troop commander in his Firefly swerved past and into the tunnel in a cloud of dust. He reached the end and began to exit left when his brake lights came on. They flickered once or twice then extinguished themselves. The closest thing to a tank-wheel spin occurred next as the driver slammed his vehicle into reverse and hurled back towards us.

'Tiger! Back off. BACK OFF!'

At the same time, a platoon of 2/60 KRRC infantry boys slid down the muddy embankment to our left and others emerged from the tunnel ahead of the fast-retreating Firefly. In quick time our troop leader's tank was alongside ours. Both crews watched as a colossal Tiger tank appeared through the swirling dust.

Slowly it trundled in our direction. Panic changed to intrigue as we noticed something hugely important in our favour: their crew, who were concentrating on urgent matters in front of them, had not clocked us yet. Although the grey monster was heading our way, it was travelling in reverse with its mighty cannon pointing in the wrong direction!

'Nice soft arse,' leered Tony Auden.

'And with a juicy weak spot,' replied our sergeant.

When the Germans eventually noticed us, their initial excitement at seeing two tommy cookers must have turned into horror when they saw two big guns primed, sighted and locked onto their rear end. I imagined the total mayhem that must have kicked off inside the normally invincible iron box. The grim inevitability of insufficient time or room inside the tunnel to rotate would be a killer.

A cloud of black smoke choked out of the Tiger's exhaust pipes as its driver belatedly tried to engage a forward gear. It was too late.

'Enjoy this moment, Cartwright. It'll probably never happen again.' Caddick's voice was almost euphoric as he gave the order to fire. 'Machine guns first.'

Auden and Morton let loose with their respective machine guns. Bits of shredded bedding and canvas tarpaulin flew off the back of the stricken tank before it shuddered to a halt; one man's attempt to escape was short lived as he disintegrated into a mushy pulp in front of us. I shut my eyes and hoped that none of our infantry boys was on the other side as an AP from the Firefly and high explosives from our gun slammed into the tank's hull. A couple of early rounds couldn't penetrate and exploded on the outside instead.

'Come on, this is meant to be their weak spot,' yelled Cartwright.

As a general rule, the diameter of a fired missile can penetrate the same thickness of armour plating that it hits. The following two rounds speared their way through and soon the awesome beast, wallowing in a sea of flame and smoke, slumped down and died. There was no match to be had on this day; like a big-game trophy hunt, this had been one-sided and cruel.

Later that afternoon, we found ourselves at a crossroads near Tiegem. Intelligence reports indicated that a significant enemy force, around 200 soldiers, had gathered there. The force comprised foot soldiers on transporters, horses towing self-propelled anti-tank guns, and a few armoured vehicles. What sort and how many, we were not told.

At our final briefing, A and C Squadrons were told to 'meet and greet' while our infantry boys, helped by B Squadron, were tasked with flushing 'this shower of shit' down the road towards us. Our immediate order was to harbour at strategic picket points and wait for Jerry to arrive.

Predictably, there were some nervous chuckles as Colonel Hopkinson, the leading man, held the briefing. He explained in his deep Bristolian voice that we would deploy a hedgehog defensive formation. This was new for me and nearly everyone in C Squadron; even Major Foster appeared to scratch his head at this military term.

Hopkinson was a big man who wore a black cape loosely draped over his broad, square shoulders. This quirky addition to a regular army uniform made him appear schoolmasterly; he reminded me of my head teacher at Alec Hunter High School who had sent shivers of fear through everyone including his staff, especially on his corridor patrols when he hunted down and later punished classroom-dismissed misbehavers. I nearly got caught once, but on that occasion his attention was diverted to someone else, giving me time to escape through the girls' changing rooms. Poor busty Rosa Karron in her blue gym knickers and infamous 'lift and separate' bra! It was a front loader, too; I had more than enough time to note that!

The colonel explained that we would set our defences deep and position ourselves in a series of spaced-out 'strong points'. I smiled at the connotation and quickly noted that no one else had got it; maybe it was too early for recreational drug references in 1944.

In our particular case, we learned that our troop would be about half a mile north of the road junction to Tiegem. The picket set-up was simple enough: two tanks faced forward and two back. The plan was also easy to understand. As our attackers advanced through strategic gaps left between our tank clusters, their forward momentum would be stifled by strikes from our Sherman M4s and the infantry boys. These 'strong points' would focus on pulverising the rear end of our ambushed enemy as they passed through on their attempt to advance. As a backup, the 2/60 KRRCs had to broadly flank us and deal with any enemy who hadn't read the script. As a grand finale, should it be needed, positioned on the road junction about a mile behind us was a blockade of four Fireflies and a bank of Howitzers. Indeed, there would be an impressive farewell to any German soldier with the tenacity or luck to get that far.

'What could possibly go wrong?' Others, not just me, muttered similar half-hearted sentiments.

The day was fast turning into night in a golden autumn twilight. Most crews, including ours, were silent as they deliberated over a hot brew. Most also slopped shots of hard stuff into their drinks. Our magnum-sized bottle of medicinal-only Calvados made its pre-battle appearance at times like this and was tucked safely beside a box of celebratory cigars recently bummed off the Yanks. They were for something special – and what a party that would be. We also enjoyed the delights of gooey milk chocolate traded for six chicken eggs; it was okay, but everything they ate seemed sweet; even their bacon – or ham, as they called it – was cured in maple syrup.

As for things sugary and trans-Atlantic, their aftershave was sickly-sweet stuff. My father once said that the Brits always knew when the Yanks were around because you could smell them a mile off. In military terms alone, this must have been a concern for the top brass.

'Scrapper Meadows,' Caddick said.

'Yes, sir?'

'Auden will drive us today. Your delicate little wrist is giving us a problem.'

This order was not unexpected and it meant I got to sit in the passenger seat for a change. It also meant firing a machine gun again. Not so good.

Auden read my mind. 'Proper job now, sunshine.'

'I bet your driving kills more Jerries than my gun.'

We laughed and shook hands. It was warm and spontaneous, a genuine gesture of comradeship. 'I hope so. And the more the fucking merrier,' he said.

Tony straightened his beret and buttoned up the top of his overalls. We always had a deep mutual respect for each other's jobs in our tank crew. No one wanted to be there, but every part we played was crucial to our survival. I'd quickly learned that a tank crew was the ultimate team and that 'life and death' was not a token cliché; our lives really did depend on each other.

Our group's usual pre-battle atmosphere intensified, but this time it was different. So far in this war much of our fighting had been reactive, but this time according to our sergeant, 'we held all the trump cards'. His confidence didn't make it any easier, though; it was worse because it gave us time to think, which was not good. Before a battle we all experienced flashbacks, and reminiscing about our past lives made it difficult. According to the quacks, it was customary for this to happen in the same way it was normal to chuck up the contents of your stomach as it went into overdrive.

My flashbacks were always chaotic and incredibly disorientating. The added complexity of my other life, tangled with being dropped into a historical period of my father's past, made it ultra-confusing. And to make things even worse, it was also a lonely, violent and insanely frightening part of his life.

Thankfully, as more orders came down the line they broke up the tension and adrenalin quickly got to work. We weren't going anywhere this time, but all tank crews were instructed to mount up, which we did in silence. As I slowly sank into the bow-gunner seat, Auden dropped into mine like a sack of coal.

'Jesus, mate, how short are your legs?' He asked.

'Short legs and big feet. You know what they say.'

It was all I could muster to match his usual sarcasm. He fretted about adjusting the seat height while I checked over my new toy, the Browning 30mm. 'Where's the ammo?' I asked.

Auden pointed to the canisters on the shelf to my right and those around my feet. Inside a driver's compartment, which we ironically called 'our happy place', it was always tight for space. This mission was even more cramped than usual. Extra munitions, mainly high explosives and dozens of hand grenades, had found homes wedged into every crevice the tank offered.

'Meadows, it kicks down to the right, so you must force it up a bit.' This was welcome advice for someone who hadn't fired a fixed gun like this before. 'The tracers will make it easier to line up on those cabbage-munching fuckers.' Tony sensed my nerves, and I was grateful for his subtle reference to pickled sauerkraut; it made me smile.

A black-and-white photograph of his wife caught my eye as it curled off the side of the bulkhead above me. She was blonde and pretty. Next to her picture was a wooden crucifix and a message that said: *Someone is always there to protect you, my darling.*

I wondered whether to pass the cross over to Tony but I didn't, thinking, 'It can effing well protect me instead!'

Not usually one to sweat, I felt a clammy dampness spread over my body and drip down my face even though the tank was cold inside. There were two pieces of news to digest next and both were bad: first, our troop was at the front end of our so-called 'hedgehog', and second, we were only one hundred yards from the road, close enough to smell the enemy coming.

'We're in a carefully chosen dip,' muttered our sergeant unconvincingly. He had read our mood. Our position was precarious and he knew it; not only would we be first to entertain our friends head-on, but we were directly in line for a homegrown round of fire up the arse!

From my new vantage point all I could see was a steep slope of earth in front of the tank. It was also dusk, so how would I determine friend or foe when they charged over the horizon? Caddick pre-empted my question. 'Shoot *anything* that comes your way, Meadows,'

The sound of boots clambering on the back of our tank unnerved me and indicated that things were about to get lively. Then the intercom buzzed as Valentine Caddick's voice crackled into radio life. 'Okay, lads, we'll see the scum in about thirty minutes. There are lots of the slippery little fuckers and our job is to hit them with everything we have. Some of the bastards will get by but don't worry, – they'll get taken out later on down the line. And let's not forget, chaps, we have the infantry girls with us, so just be glad you are in here and not out there.'

There it was, Caddick's inspirational battle speech; if nothing else it was succinct, but his voice was gloomier than usual. I took away two things from this new enlightenment: the only scum I could reference were supporters of Ipswich Town football club (apologies to them). And yes, being inside a mobile metal coffin was possibly better than being out there, but the comparison was marginal.

'And check your firearms. We may have to bail out.' That was the most chilling order so far. Bailing out into bullet-strewn darkness probably meant that we had been hit and, next up, the six-inch rounds from a Spandau machine gun would probably mean curtains. If we survived all that – and it was a big if – it was every man for himself.

Tony and I swapped guns, me being overly careful with his Sten. My Webley and Luger pistols were easily accessible, both tucked snugly into a newly adapted shoulder holster underneath my overalls.

At around 21:00 hours we heard them before we saw them: a low, grumbling groan at first, punctuated by the unmistakable metallic clanking sound of bogie wheels and tracks. Their grinding, clanking rumble always sounded worse at night. It grew louder and I immediately felt the usual gut-wrenching hit of nausea and an urgent need to shit. We all did. Always.

'Wait for my order and not before,' Caddick said.

I still couldn't see anything through my periscope except the top edge of the muddy bank facing me. However, Morton reported that he could see German infantry, 'Crawling everywhere like fucking ants.'

Then two things happened: Caddick instructed Tony to start up and move us forward out of the dip, and almost simultaneously a couple of huge spotlights burst into life and slowly lifted their beams our way. Initially blinded by their piercing light, we saw the outline of foot soldiers; they were swarming everywhere.

About two hundred yards away, I saw a couple of half-tracks and several teams of horses shackled to self-propelled cannons – but there were no tanks. The shock of eyeing each other on both sides of the narrowing divide froze the moment; although we temporarily held the initiative, our commander's order to let loose could not come fast enough.

Although our movement forward exposed us, it also improved visibility. For this group of Wehrmacht to see a troop of M4s loom out of the mud must have scared the crap out of them. Unprepared, their only response was submachine gun fire and rifle bullets. We heard their rounds ping off our front armour in cluster bursts. This early part of the hedgehog plan was critical. Anything remotely German-looking had to be blitzed in our blender before they could mortar us and point their more heavy-duty weaponry our way.

'Rats. They are more like rats than ants,' I thought. I had last shot at rats with that trusty old air rifle, Diana. Mike was my wingman again, and this time he supported me as we zoned in on a stack of rotting straw and potatoes. Looking like a demented maniac, he slammed round after round from his pump-action beanie gun towards the unperturbed rodents.

I was a more calculating sniper, slowly aiming, firing and then methodically reloading from a tin of pellets in front of me. His strategy was more scattergun but I didn't have the heart to wind him up. His feeble gun didn't have the power to reach, let alone kill, these foot-long rodents as they scattered over the broken bales and mashed potatoes.

Whether it was our firepower's accuracy or our infantry boys letting loose in support, nothing significant came from the Krauts. Some did pass through, however, and it was cold sweat time. I hadn't expected to have difficulty holding my gun but I did. A stab of pain from my wrist startled me at first and it meant an instant flip to left-handed firing; this stalled me.

A reprimand came down the line in a rage. 'Have we got a fucking bow gunner?'

One German got too close to my side and I shut my eyes as my Browning eventually swung towards him. He was a small man, and I think he was trying to escape. His grey helmet fell off as he desperately slithered to one side revealing gelled black hair and a neat parting down the middle. Funny what you noticed.

Now under my complete control, my Browning clamped onto a rotating metal ball and, held in place by a squeaky steel spring, did its thing. When I looked up again, the man was in bits and dead.

'Pay attention, gunner. Nicely mashed up, my son.'

I enjoyed killing the farm rats, which were useless, disease-ridden things. They were the only animals I had ever killed. As for German human life, that was different; killing a man was the vilest thing, but I wouldn't hesitate in doing it again.

Another victim jumped into view and I pulled the trigger. *It's him or me, it's me or him.* That became my constant reminder as one corpse after another twisted into the blood-soaked mud. It helped if I imagined they were rats.

The thousand-dollar question – was it my bullet or someone else's? – was cold comfort.

The battle raged on for what seemed like an hour. Although our screams synchronised, they were drowned out by the intensive din around us. But it was so easy; in the obscurity of evening light, the black skittle-like objects were systematically taken out one by one, group by group.

Our strikes always had the same horrific outcome. After the initial impact, sometimes two or more of us hit the same target, and a convulsive contortion twisted the victims into two. Occasionally an almost comedic-like wobble followed. Drenched by flumes of their blood, and often dragging their seeping entrails behind them, the lucky ones were already dead when they fell.

It was as easy as my rat-sniper days, but with half my ammo used up I began to worry. Big Nige reported the same thing. 'What if they keep on coming when I run out?'

Caddick urged Tony forward again and we ventured onto the road to unload a couple of AP shells down the track; presumably because of an order from above, this was something new in our repertoire. We watched as they bounced off the tarmac and ricocheted towards an enemy half-track, that still wanted to fight. Something out of the manual? I doubted it, and we never saw that bouncing-bomb trick again.

A few minutes later we got the order to hold our positions and cease fire, but only after our machine guns finished off a few more rats as they scuttled away in a futile attempt to escape.

The acrid smell of cordite, swirling smoke, and adrenalin-driven sweat brought us back to earth. Our adapted bunker on wheels groaned eerily as the strain on her joints eased and everything slowly cooled down. That included us in our hate-filled, testosterone-charged lair. Defence of the hedgehog and deconstructing a half-track were our parts in the battle of Audenarde on September 6th, 1944.

'You had to really hate to survive,' Pop said in one of our chats. It was only now that I truly understood what he had meant.

'Only fire if you see one,' was our next order.

The mêlée behind us continued as the rear-facing tanks blasted the enemy's backsides into a catastrophic end; then, to our relief, the furore began to diminish.

I noticed soldiers from 2/60 KRRC slowly prowling from left to right. Following the mayhem of battle, an eerie stillness clung to the air and at first I couldn't determine what they were doing. Then it dawned on me that they were snuffing out the leftovers with their bayonets probing the ground, followed by the occasional blast of machine gun fire or the single crack of a rifle. It was gruesome confirmation that the wounded were being dealt with – humanely, perhaps?

I also saw the burnt-out M4 belonging to Freddie Smythe. We were told later that an AP shell hit them and that his top half was catapulted out by the blast. The rest of his body stayed with the crew, who died with him. It was sombre news. That night, as we toasted our captain with a bottle of Calvados, I remembered my dad's words about hate.

The officers' mess was for commissioned officers only; even on the front line they were often set up in our laagers. Pigs really do fly because my invitation to the officers' mess, promised by Major Hales, finally arrived – much to the dismay of my irritated crew mates.

'Ooh … who's the special one then?' Geordie Boy instigated the tirade of abuse that came my way.

I ignored him; my main concern was what to wear. When I asked Caddick that question, I ensured we were well out of earshot.

'Battle dress with tie,' he confirmed. 'The best I can hope for is the sergeants' mess. Well done, my son.' He seemed genuinely pleased for me.

It was September 8th and we were on the outskirts of Termonde village. It was also Friday, which usually meant payday. The guys had snaffled up their Belgian francs and were making lusty preparations for our regiment stop in Saint Nicholas the next day. While they were hoping to sample a deluge of sensual delights in what was going to be a sex-starved town, Tony described where he would be: 'Knacker deep in fanny fat.'

'Eloquently put, Tony.' Admittedly, my response showed a touch of envy. A possibility is all it was, though; our collective record in that particular arena of enjoyment had not been impressive to date. The only body fluids likely to be dispensed from me were the ones coming out of my backside as I crapped myself in the austere surroundings of an officers' mess drinks party.

The mess was a gazebo-style erection made from a canvas tarpaulin attached to Colonel Hopkinson's command tank. I slicked back my hair and straightened my perfectly straight tie before pulling the entry flap aside and shouldering my way into the unknown. The first impressions were not great; it was the smell that hit me most, a musty, damp-canvas aroma mixed with body odour and smoke. It smelled of men and made me think of my mates and the mucky fun they would probably not have.

'Meadows. Come in and make yourself at home.' Teddy Foster broke the ice and I was grateful. He was sitting at a table constructed from what looked like someone's front door balanced on two petrol drums. Sitting next to him was Major Hales, and both were shrouded in clouds of smoke as they puffed and re-lit their pipes repeatedly.

I noticed a packet of American Lucky Strike cigarettes in the middle of the table. Seeing I'd clocked them, Foster picked up the pack and offered me one. 'Fresh in today, along with some of the hard stuff.' He nodded towards another table with several liquor bottles and glasses scattered on it. The first bottle of note, a Glen Grant 1936, was impressive; as a serious malt-whisky drinker, I reckoned it would fetch at least £4,000 in modern-day money.

'Before you think about that, Meadows, you have to do something first.' Colonel Hopkinson laid this one on me.

'To do, sir?'

'Yes, indeed.'

The CO hadn't even looked up from his deckchair beside the spluttering campfire between the mess tent and his tank. Alarm bells rang; this was an initiation ceremony – or worse.

'I'll explain, son.' It was Major Hales this time. 'Any ordinary rank invited into our mess has to do a party trick.'

That was it: schoolboy games. There was always a catch. I waited for an explanation, but no explanation was given; there was just silence. Party trick? I wondered if this was a set-up and whether these guys were being pricks, but the weight of expectation and all their eyes were focused on me now, including the piggy-red set belonging to Padre Huggins, my old tormentor, who had just entered the tent.

He smirked broadly as he recognised what was about to happen. 'Well, well.' He plonked himself into a chair, mock interest registering on his face.

Although I had come to terms with the fact that my body was an outer shell of my father and that I was in control of it, something else took over momentarily. I dragged a small wooden box from under Huggins' feet and stepped onto it. He didn't like that much. Nice.

'Mind the carpet, trooper,' joked Teddy.

'Trooper 7952180 would like to recite a poem, sir.'

'Get on with it, Meadows.' The colonel stood up to listen, glass tumbler filled with whisky. His impatient prompt was alarming enough; even more so, Major Hales was sitting in the corner reloading his Webley 38.

'Oh, you who sleep in Flanders Fields,
Sleep sweet, to rise anew
We caught the torch you threw
And holding high, we keep the faith
With all who died
We cherish, too, the poppy red
That grows on fields where valour led;
It seems to signal to the skies

That blood of heroes never dies
But lends a lustre to the red,
Of the flower that blooms above the dead
In Flanders fields
And now the torch and poppy red
We wear in honour of our dead.
Fear not that ye have died for nought
We'll teach the lesson that ye wrought
In Flanders Fields.'

It was stunning, as was my delivery: no pauses or hesitation, pitch-perfect and, by the look of it, they liked it too. But I had heard the poem before on my father's eighty-fifth birthday. Without any explanation, he had surprised a small lunch gathering when suddenly he pushed back his chair and stood to attention. After calling out his army number, he recited the words as perfectly as I did. Later, my unusually emotional father explained that he was invited into the officers' mess during the war and was asked to address those present with this poem.

'We Shall Keep the Faith' was written by Moina Michael in 1918 in response to John McCrae's famous poem, 'In Flanders Fields'. Some sixty years later, Pop had somehow reached deep into his memory banks to retrieve it. I was sure the open-mouthed family assembled around him on that day were truly enthralled and would never forget it.

'Good stuff, Meadows. Help yourself to a drink.' Colonel Hopkinson seemed impressed, Hales and Foster likewise, but Huggins looked disappointed. He grunted something, grabbed a bottle of whisky (thankfully not the 1936) and sat alone in a corner. Room dynamics told me he was not well-liked, which pleased me.

I noticed a bottle of German white wine next to various liquors, including a collection of bourbons. Tall, slender and green, I guessed it was a Mosel. How did I know that? The selection of wines available to the great British public in the 1970s was limited. Pop, who was not a great drinker, enjoyed the odd glass of wine, though, and he had two preferences.

'Brown bottle and therefore a Hock,' he would proudly proclaim. That would be Niersteiner Gutes Domtal, then; not a fine wine by today's palate. 'A green bottle means Mosel,' he concluded somewhat smugly. Green bottle, maybe, but the classic and corrosive Liebfraumilch Blue Nun bleaching its way through your Paris goblet could not be classed as fine wine either. Beloved lady's milk, indeed!

Those who bothered to listen to his short, familiar lectures on wine didn't give a monkey's. Uncle Paul, Pop's twin brother who had a taste for fine wines, would get visibly irritated. All he wanted to do was to tip the stuff away. 'No, Peter, really, that's quite enough,' he would say politely, covering his glass. He preferred reds, but my father insisted that nothing was better than a 'good white wine' or perhaps 'a nice Mateus Rose'. That said it all.

I picked up the bottle of Glen Grant and furtively splashed some into the bottom of a cut-glass tumbler, careful not to overdo it; perhaps their assessment of me was not quite over. I needn't have worried because Major Hales urged me to be more generous and Teddy Foster nodded his approval. 'Bally well make it worth your while, Meadows.' Was this a subtle hint that the invitation was a one-off?

Aside from classy German wines, Pop's idea of a bender was a glass of Cinzano and lemonade, sometimes Dubonnet if he felt reckless; he never understood the concept of drinking beer in volume.

'I drink water when I'm thirsty,' he said, watching me nurse a hangover one morning. It made our first foray into a pub together fascinating.

'Two small glasses of beer, please, my good man.'

'Lager or real ale, sir.'

'Real, of course.' He laughed; the barman didn't. 'Only the best for me. Don't like getting short-changed.'

That made it worse. Two half-pint pots with handles appeared; their contents looked like frothy piss, and I immediately knew where this was going. 'No, no, young man, proper small glasses.' No answer. 'And what in heaven's name is this?' Pop took a tentative sup. 'It's bloody warm.'

Occasionally he suggested a Sunday lunchtime visit to the Fox at Finchingfield; this only ever happened when we had family over. My cousin Lisa and I loved to sit in the back of the car while the grown-ups indulged in pre-lunch drinks and Twiglets. It was an excellent time because we each got a Coke bottle, loaded with the customary red-and-white striped paper straw, and crisps, the sort that had a twisted blue wrap of salt hidden in the packet.

These goodies were shoved through the car window, accompanied by a waft of cigarette smoke and real ale from the pub doorway. It felt naughtily exotic; kids were not allowed into pubs in those days and we didn't care. We just hoped the elders' boozy session would be lengthy.

'Excuse me, please, trooper.' It was the padre again.

His reference to 'trooper' rather than Meadows was designed to irritate me, so I just smiled, stepped back and ignored him. He reached down towards a plate of what pretended to be canapés, if you could describe slimy Spam slices layered onto thin pieces of toasted white bread as canapés.

'Help yourself, trooper.' There was definitely an emphasis on 'trooper'. 'How did you damage your wrist?'

This question concerned me as I didn't know if Huggins already knew. How could he? All eyes latched onto me again. This could be an honesty check, and I couldn't take the chance, so I decided to give them the truth. Sort of. 'An altercation, sir. Not serious, all sorted now, sir.'

The padre was about to say something when Teddy Foster jumped in to rescue me. 'Good man, Meadows. We have enough problems with bally Jerry. Good that it's sorted.' He knew.

I did not enjoy my time there, and the chilling howl of Nebelwerfers outside did nothing to improve the overall ambience. Ironic as it sounds, this was good news because it gave me the perfect cue to bow out. The question now was how? Did I bid farewell or did I need an invitation to leave?

Major Foster rescued me again when he grabbed a bottle of rum from the table and passed it to me. My permission to escape had just been granted, it seemed. 'Consider this your rum ration, Meadows.'

'Thank you, sir.'

'It's Time for us to wrap this party up, I think.' He nodded to the colonel, who bowed his head in agreement.

A small provision of rum or gin was often issued to crews; with us, it was usually before – and occasionally after – a battle. My crew mates would be pleased.

Another high-pitched scream, followed by several loud crumping explosions, shook the ground. This time, they were virtually on top of us.

'Thank you for your generous hospitality.' I made a crisp salute to the senior ranks and retreated from the officers' mess much faster than I had entered it. The others saluted back; they didn't have to, and Huggins didn't bother.

I hadn't noticed the fat tabby cat lying near the Colonel's feet by the fire. In synchronicity with the last mortar strike, he shot up and shrieked out of the tent between my legs.

I remembered Suku. He began life as a conventional, cuddly kitten; Pop got him from a farmer friend who 'had enough bleeding cats to fill a zoo'. There should have been a clue in the word 'zoo'. Suku, which I think means 'night' in Cha Lapa Lapa, soon morphed into a giant black tomcat who enjoyed nothing better than a scrap with the wimpier cats in his territory. A V-shaped tear in his raggedy left ear gave him a notable badge of honour as he slunk like a panther around the boundaries of our garden, his manor.

In addition to carrying out noisy and regular muggings of other cats, he had a disturbing habit of squirting foul-smelling scent trails everywhere he went. 'Peter, get the Dettol. He's done it again,' was a familiar refrain from my poor old mum, and a fragrance not dissimilar to that left by a skunk was ingrained forever.

He also liked to hunt; I'm sure Suku was related to the two leopard skin hides hanging on our hall wall. These were not trophies but big cats shot by my father to protect livestock on his farm in Africa. Much to the upset of our prissy CEO at work, the skins were draped over the chaise longue in my office many years later.

Mum's shriek from the kitchen signalled that Suku's kitchen door was open for business as another day's catch lay bloodied and steaming on the cream lino floor. Other than mice and small rodents shoved through what we amusingly called the 'pussy flap', his victims were often bigger than this and very much alive.

I can't forget the poor bunny that spent its last twitching moments underneath Suku's teasing claws between the teeth of a proud 'look what I've got' cat. I'm sure the neighbours never forgot either, as my mother's frantic screech went up at least two octaves, from an operatic soprano to a spine-chilling death-throe gurgle.

Sadly, Suku went AWOL one day and was eventually found dead beside a country lane near our house. We all felt sorry for the poor driver's car: it must have been a write-off.

Most of the remaining tankies who were not enjoying the town's 'enchantments' had dug themselves in underneath their tanks. The rogue mortar stonking continued to irritate us; whilst moaning minis' warnings frightened us, there was no signal when a bog-standard Granatwerfer 34 mortar landed.

I watched a platoon of foot soldiers trudge out of the camp in search of these silent and deadly assassins. Weighed down by bulky cameras, giant telescopes resembling PIAT bazookas and dressed in camouflage, the birdwatching Gestapo from Cley marshes would have blended in well.

'Time to hide, Meadows,' I instructed myself.

I rolled into the newly scraped hollow beneath our Sherman and waited for these guys to do their business. Although I was alone while our boys were out having fun, having time to myself was a relief. Their predictable officers-mess autopsy would now be delayed; equally, the gory details of their messy and exaggerated encounters with the fair maidens of Saint Nicholas could also be postponed.

Another direct hit into the middle of our compound exploded in a shower of earth and flying flint. A couple of guys cried out. Unsure if it was from shock or they had been hit, I waited for the next blast to arrive, kept my head down and thought about the last twenty-four hours.

What a day it had been. It started so well when we'd crossed over a slate-grey river by way of a rickety, wooden bridge. This took time because it was a single-tank crossing and none of us fancied the drop into what looked like a deep and ice-cold river Scheldt.

We entered Saint Nicholas like returning heroes at around 11am on September 9th 1944. Flowers, fruit and bottles of hooch were thrown onto our tanks as we edged our way towards the town hall.

When we eventually arrived, Colonel Hopkinson was welcomed by the mayor and given the freedom of the city. He lapped it up and, as their liberators, the townsfolk welcomed us too.

Then, of course, there were girls – lots of them. Young ones chalked welcome messages onto the sides of our vehicles, and confident older girls clambered up onto our tanks to kiss us in jubilation. Some courageous ones were up for it and indulged us in longer, more passionate embraces; this ticked almost all the boxes.

'I've still got it,' gasped Auden, coming up for air. He was in his element, and admittedly I also enjoyed the attention but had the added distraction of trying to avoid flocks of gorgeous felines spread out in front of us! Most were blonde, very pretty and undoubtedly called Helga, I surmised. Granted, we'd been away from home for too long, and the war had probably given us beer goggles, but feeling this outpouring of unconditional love was flattering.

Being right in their line of fire was the most accessible place on a tank for these eager ladies to reach us. 'Perk of the job,' I replied when the man above asked why he had been neglected.

'Too ugly, boss,' commented Tony.

'Lids down,' came his response. We ignored it.

The fantastic welcome continued for a couple of hours as we positioned ourselves at various entry points around the town. It was surreal because random gunfire from enemy snipers could be heard over the party's hullabaloo. These shooters were considered a mere irritation and were taken out systematically by our infantry as they cleaned up the streets around us.

Then something bizarre happened mid-afternoon. The sound came first, and then the sight of a Panzer Mark IV as it trundled slowly up the road towards B Squadron. This time, instead of creating terror, it was comical and more akin to a gatecrasher at a party. Like the Red Sea parting, the swarming crowd calmly moved to one side and watched as the 'uninvited imposter' was duly terminated.

A short barrage of intense gunfire interrupted my thoughts, followed by a muffled explosion. As I shuffled up towards the edge of our shallow-cut trench, clouds of black smoke rose from the hillside behind our colonel's tank. The infantry lads had completed their task well, but not before a final Nebelwerfer stonking demolished the officers' tent about a hundred yards away.

Through my binoculars I could see that the command tank was undamaged, but the remains of the officers' mess tent were smouldering and steaming in front of it. I could also see the ginger tabby cat stretched out and very dead on the scorched drinks table doing the same thing.

From Peter Meadows' memoirs

When we entered the town of St. Nicholas, we received a fantastic welcome amidst great jubilation on the part of the citizens. Colonel Hopkinson was swept onto the steps of the town hall and given the freedom of the city. I remember sitting on the turret of my tank, signing scraps of paper with a blue map pencil. About this time, suddenly, a German tank rumbled down the road and with great difficulty, the crowd was removed so that we could knock it out to thunderous applause.

2. Peter Meadows 7 from left at the back. Note the Pixie suits

3. British Stuart 6 tank, Peter 2nd from left in goggles

JEAN PETERSON

4. My mum, Jean Peterson

5. Tank C Squadron

6. Cool dudes? Peter and chum to his right

7. Trooper 7952180

8. Hold your breath? Percy and sons L-R Val, John, our hero & Paul

9. Leaning against our turretless Stuart 6. St Nicholas 11th November 1944

The Secret

We stayed in Saint Nicholas until 12th September and then moved to Heist-op-den-Berg for a five-day rest and recuperation. As always with these high-command promises, we could never gauge when the curtain would come down. Orders to re-join the battle would inevitably cut short our moments of peace; we all knew that, just not when. But until that time, maintaining our tanks and ourselves was the game.

Our swan out of France into Belgium and soon Holland had been Blitzkrieg-like. On the Belgian leg we witnessed fewer scorched-earth tactics, and there were undoubtedly fewer land mines to contend with than in France. Travel was much more manageable, too; although dull and dreary, the Flemish landscape was flat and allowed our tanks to pick up speed.

My problem was concentration: keeping thirty-four tons of rocking iron jammed full of explosives moving at nearly 30mph was challenging. This feat was made even trickier by the narrow roads that rose high above the plains around us. 'It's like walking a tightrope, son,' commented Caddick. Little did I know that the approaching winter would render these same roads virtual ice-skating rinks.

On September 16th an order finally came for us to move, and at 07:30 hours we were called forward. This was on the eve of Operation Market Garden, often called 'the Battle for the Bridges'. It also focused on Germany's V2 launch sites; the V2s were causing problems for the Allied supply routes into Antwerp and for British citizens in London, another prize target.

Seven key bridges were involved, and the 44th RTR was to come under the temporary command of the 101st US Airborne Division, known as the 'Screaming Eagles'. Along with the 82nd Airborne, the ill-fated plan was to drop into pre-determined zones and secure bridge crossings along a sixty-mile stretch between Eindhoven and Nijmegen.

Of course no one in our battalion knew anything about this except me because I knew how this situation worked out. As I moved through the war, more facts slowly dropped into my consciousness; it was like being intravenously fed. WW2 research refreshed my memory as history became a reality.

'So that's it, that is how it works.' Revelation time: Archimedes would have been pleased with my eureka moment. Each day triggered more information in my brain, facts about what would happen in the future. And so, it went on.

Thinking about our imminent introduction to our American colleagues, I recalled Steven Spielberg's excellent 2001 series *Band of Brothers*. Pop enjoyed it because of his war connection, but, as with most American war films, he found it frustrating due to what he considered to be their overt bias. And, as with most of his generation, he was fiercely nationalistic for a good reason. 'Typical Yanks taking all the glory. The British were there too, you know!' he used to exclaim.

Due to my roots, I've never had the same passion for my adopted country; I saw myself as more African. Depressingly, I have often felt embarrassed to be British, especially when on holiday abroad – though not ashamed, which is a subtle difference. I'm proud of Great Britain's history and long-standing contribution to the world, warts and all, but why do we let ourselves down so much? Loud, boorish and entitled seems to be the name of the game. Is it a hangover from the years of our colonial past? And how did a nation of blinged-up, hungover, pork-bellied idiots engraved with Banksy-on-speed body art achieve what she did?

I thought of my early youth when life was less complicated. For starters, it didn't have twenty-four-hour rolling news to depress the grown-ups, nor social media, fake news and phoney 'influencers' to confuse us all. Kids were free to grow up and childhood was innocent and unrushed. We walked to school, read books and climbed trees. We were allowed to taste danger, eat sugar (sometimes on toast) and play with fireworks. Guess what? People felt safer. Policemen existed, authority was respected, and we knew there would be consequences for our actions.

Obesity was scarce, schools had playing fields and allergies were rare. Boys had cocks and went to Cubs; girls didn't and went to Brownies. Birthday parties took place at home with real food and homemade cakes. We scoffed jelly, ate ice cream and played games rather than babysat adults who took over and got pissed.

Rip-off high-street chains serving shit food for lazy parents didn't proliferate in every town. Dogs were proper dogs, not children pushed around in prams and carried in baby harnesses. Families consisted of two parents: Dad did the gardening, and Mum cooked dinner. Our expectations weren't high, and we managed them better at a time when people felt contented with less money.

Finally, people were happier—and guess what? My mum and dad said the same about their youth when they had nothing except a sense of community and deep respect for their country and each other. This cancelled out the nightmare of wars, rationing, and real hardship.

What an upside-down world my other life was now. It was truly mystifying. Pop would turn in his grave; God bless him.

Even if I wanted to, I couldn't communicate any of these thoughts to the others and, more importantly, I couldn't tell them what was about to happen. 'In the future' things were about to get lively. Message to myself: 'Keep your head down, son.'

'Tony, you're a much better driver than Meadows,' teased Big Nige. I could imagine his fat face wobbling like a kid's party jelly above me.

Every village has an idiot, and we've got one in here, too. Another private thought, so I decided to say nothing.

'Aye, less wanking and this thing might go straight,' was Geordie Boy's unoriginal contribution.

Tony chose to stay quiet for a change; he smirked instead and slowly nodded his head in extravagant approval.

'Meadows?' Caddick barked.

'Yes, sir.' Now what?

'If you put us in a ditch, I'll break your other fucking arm.' Our boss was not in one of his more convivial moods. I ignored him because my wrist felt better and I had regained my rightful place, the driver's seat. I accelerated and gave the steering levers a little left and right wiggle.

'Oy, Meadows! Don't be silly.'

Spirits were up as our dysfunctional family roared through the cobbled streets of yet another Flemish hamlet without a name.

Women and children lined the pavements and waved flags to greet our liberating army. So far the Belgian locals had been very welcoming and were in much better shape than the crushed people of Normandy.

On September 19th, we were called forward and crossed the border into the Netherlands. There I saw my first Allied paratroopers in action – and there were lots of them. As they streamed out of C-47 Dakotas in their hundreds, there was a pause before a splash of white exploded across the sky like a flock of wintering knots on Blakeney Point. I estimated their landing zone to be about ten miles ahead of us, just north of Eindhoven.

'Here comes the cavalry,' chimed Auden. 'Sooner them than us.' I wondered about that.

This glorious sight should have lifted my spirits but it didn't; it disturbed me and I knew why. A postbag had arrived early that morning and the experience had been bittersweet as I'd opened the only letter addressed to me. Getting it was excellent but its contents troubled me profoundly.

As I looked up, a multitude of white-silk parachutes billowed open and spiralled earthwards. They belonged to the Airborne Infantry, or Paras as they were more glamorously known. There was little glamour in what faced them, and I thought about the men's emotions as they circled in the sky and glided toward an unknown landscape.

'Poor fuckers.' For once, I agreed with Morton. Some Paras would feel euphoric; they had passed the first test by exiting a Dakota with heads and limbs intact. Those surviving Normandy would be anxious about what lay in wait on the ground. In Normandy the Germans had flooded fields and set booby traps and mines to slow their advance. What did Eindhoven, Nijmegen and Arnhem hold for them? Many would be dead already, blasted into oblivion by enemy ground fire.

'I'd piss on the fuckers as I came down,' said Auden.

No one responded as we looked at the weirdly beautiful sight unfolding before us. Soon we would support these airborne troops. The thought kept us silent and dampened the mood.

I noticed darker-coloured chutes and their bulky loads swirling between the others, the operational supplies for the onward part of their mission. Some larger canopies bullied through the others; these carried Jeeps and other huge lumps of military hardware. The picture evolving in front of us was extraordinary, almost like a Jackson Pollock, as an array of fantastic shapes and spectacularly coloured blobs splattered across a big canvas-like sky.

'Like confetti at a wedding,' suggested the poetic Geordie.

Utrinque paratus, 'Ready for anything', is the motto of the Parachute Regiment. While exploring his story, I uncovered a shocking secret about my father. In October 1942, whilst undergoing his training in the Royal Armoured Corps, Pop applied successfully for a transfer to the Parachute Regiment. That was ironic: he could have been spinning down from the heavens right then had he survived their inaugural campaign in Normandy when nearly 3,000 Paras died. And it could have been worse; given my current circumstances, it could have been me up there.

I was a curious boy, and Pop's gruesome tattoo and the stories behind it intrigued me, as I urged him to tell me more about his adventures. Occasionally he did, but usually he didn't. Catching him off guard one day, he recovered to underplay one of the three jumps he'd made in the army. I sat in awe; this was impressive stuff.

I immediately grabbed hold of my Action Man, who was sitting in his plastic desert Jeep, and attached a hastily made parachute constructed from a large white handkerchief knotted at each corner with kitchen string.

'That is your father's, dear,' Mum said when I snatched it off her wooden ironing board. Ironing board? Handkerchief? Mums ironed everything in those days.

Ready for Clint's next daring mission, I rushed upstairs, slammed the dormer window open and slung him into the abyss. It didn't go to plan; I watched in horror as the tightly folded canopy stayed neatly folded and poor old Clint dived head first onto the lawn. Mum was blamed for his catastrophic parachute failure; her neat and crisp ironing was just too good.

Even at that age, connecting Pop's jumps with the Royal Tank Regiment was a struggle until I learned the truth. I knew for sure that he hated heights – diving boards, for example, were off-limits. I remembered his story about climbing to the top board of an open-air swimming pool in Great Yarmouth when he was only about ten years old. At the top, he realised his plight. To climb down in front of his contemporaries would be a show of weakness, so he jumped.

I felt the same about diving boards, though climbing the Scottish mountains was never a problem. Pop, enthusiastic to hear about my Munro-bagging adventures, used to shake his head in disbelief. 'You mad fool,' he would say. 'Not even in my reckless youth could I have done that.' So why the Paras?

He joined the 8th (Midlands) Parachute Battalion, part of the 3rd Parachute Brigade, in the autumn of 1942. The umbrella organisation was the 6th Airborne Division and they were training for D-Day and Operation Tonga. The 6th sounded impressive, but actually, only two divisions existed, the other being the 1st Airborne, to confuse the spying ears and eyes of Adolph Hitler!

Later this group would be involved in the post-Falaise Seine advance and the Ardennes counter-offensive known as the Battle of the Bulge. And it didn't end there: Operation Varsity was an Anglo-Canadian-American assault on crossing the Northern Rhine into Germany, involving more than 16,000 paratroopers. Under the command of General Montgomery, who was licking his wounds from Arnhem, Varsity was completed in one day and proved to be the largest airborne operation in history.

However, the British army implemented airborne infantry quite late in the war. The Russians led the way, followed by Hitler's Fallschirmjager, and then came the United States Airborne divisions. Churchill realised that an airborne elite army was imperative to our military success and the ultimate goal of liberating north-west Europe. Comprised of 5,000 soldiers, the Army Air Corps and its Parachute Regiment were born on June 20th 1940. Eight months later, No.2 Commando, re-designated as the 11th Special Air Services carried out the first British Airborne mission. Operation Colossus.

Why did my father volunteer for the Royal Armoured Corps and then ask for a transfer to the Paras? There are reasons other than a pay rise and promotion. He was an extremely fit man, a fighter in every sense of the word, and someone who liked to be alone. Perhaps he figured out that controlling his destiny would be easier in the Parachute Regiment than in tanks.

I can only surmise, but on deeper reflection I believe that was it. Money and status were not motivations; put simply, he craved space, including his own, and he had few close friends. There is a paradox here because he was also extrovert and noisy, the life and soul of any party or family get-together. Maybe it was superficial to disguise the real person underneath.

It was Sergeant Caddick who broke into my thoughts. He ordered me to slow down and halt behind the rest of our troop while the C Squadron gathered itself to wait for further orders. A pitstop was welcome, so I pulled off onto a grass verge and let the engine idle before shutting her down. Sounding like a twenty-fags-a-day marathon runner, the iron lady gasped and spluttered as usual.

If the fens are flat, what the hell is this? I wondered. We could see for miles across the hazy Dutch landscape, and field upon field with few trees left us badly exposed.

It was Cartwright who queried this. Caddick quickly batted it back. 'Local intelligence tells us there is nothing much to worry about here, young man.' That word 'much' was interesting.

More Dakotas and Whitworth Whitley bombers roared over, and streams of parachutes continued to spew out of their backsides as they passed above Eindhoven. In the distance a deep rumble of gunfire and muffled explosions was a clear reminder of things to come. My knees and hands began to tremble again and a more worrying feeling returned as the ever-present knot in my stomach tightened.

As part of the Second Army Battalion, we were heading towards what would soon be named Hell's Highway. This road was the main link between Arnhem and Eindhoven and was strategically critical to both sides. A northerly breeze was building, bringing a smell of burned wood and ruptured industry. Through my field glasses I could see Eindhoven ablaze. Across the horizons on either side, an orange glow throbbed as the Battle of the Road began.

'I need a piss,' grumbled Cartwright. 'Desperately.'

'And I think I need a crap.' The knot got tighter.

'Okay, stay safe, chaps. Morton, get a brew on.' That was Caddick's farewell instruction as he slid off the tank on his way to another O-group briefing.

'What does he think we're going to do? Tiptoe through the effing tulips?' Nigel asked.

I laughed. Tiny Tim had an incredibly stupid novelty hit by the same name in the late 1960s. As a mischievous teenager, I remember slipping a 45rpm vinyl copy into the cover of one of Pop's favourite records, Ray Conniff's 'I'd Like to Teach the World to Sing'. Bland at best, the song was used for the television Coke advert of the day. Pop was not amused, Mum found it funny and I temporarily converted to a fan of the falsetto-voiced ukulele player.

I slipped into a shallow ditch to find somewhere to do my business and thought more about Pop and the Paras. Why he chose tanks was curious; being on top of other people would have been suffocating for him. I was different; horrendous situation aside, I quite liked the camaraderie of five people working hard as a team to stay alive.

In my other life, the reality was a different story. As senior years crept in and 'life's winter' approached, as my charming wife put it, I morphed into preferring my own company too. People have a habit of pissing me off, mainly selfish and entitled ones who irritate me so easily now compared to my youth's 'I love everyone' persona. Maybe it shouldn't have surprised me because most of my career involved working with sales teams. Like them, some of the characters around me here could perhaps provide the answer to my growing de-sensitisation to the human race.

'Five minutes and tea's up,' sang Morton, interrupting my multi-tasking of thinking and having a crap.

I zipped, buttoned and buckled up my overalls. Doing anything remotely discreet, especially number twos, was almost impossible in tankie overalls. 'Coming, darling.'

'Hurry, it will get cold,' he sang back.

Throughout the summer of 1942, Pop tasted tank life in the 54th Training Regiment at Barnard Castle, Teesside. That probably caused him to have a significant change of heart and, according to his war record, take the opportunity to transfer out of the RAC into the Parachute Regiment.

'Brew's up.'

I scrambled up the muddy bank and gratefully accepted our surrogate mother's mug of steaming tea. I laughed out loud when he held out what looked like a hub cap full of misshapen but neatly arranged biscuits. They looked tasty and, even more unbelievably, homemade. To complete this homely picture of domestic bliss, a frilly white apron contrasted magnificently with the length of fag ash hanging precariously over the plate.

'Thought you might have found a proper doily,' I said, thinking of the sort our grannies used to catch the butter icing and strawberry jam oozing from their Sunday-tea Victoria-sponge cakes.

'Do you want one or not?'

I grabbed a handful of the sugary beige delicacies and shoved them into my top pocket. Like sharks sensing blood, it wouldn't be long before the other reprobates in our gang got a sniff and snaffled the rest.

'Know what? You're not as bad as they make out,' I said.

'Very funny,' he clucked. 'You can say thank you to the locals for these.'

Morton shuffled off to look for the boys who were still nowhere to be seen. I dunked a biscuit into my tea and remembered how much Pop hated me doing that when I was a kid. But he did like a particular scene from Candid Camera, an early 'fly on the wall' television series of the seventies. The setup was simple: a man dunks his cream doughnut into another man's coffee on an adjoining cafe table and a camera records the coffee-owner's startled reaction. That was one of the more conservative sketches. The bottom pinching 'pretend it's not me' one, was more typical. Can you imagine the outrage if they made those programmes today? How we and most of the unoffended viewing public laughed back then, though.

I climbed back onto our tank, which was still spluttering as it cooled down, and dropped through the driver's hatch onto my seat. It was time to reflect on Pop's skydiving days – and I also needed to read that letter again.

209

'Ready for Anything' is the attitude the Parachute Regiment's motto demands, and there are three other important principles to consider before joining it: self-discipline, self-reliance and aggression, controlled. Pop had them all. He was also tough, so when you add to that his superb physical and mental fitness, he should have been a shoo-in – on paper at least. Even the controversial and brutal practice of 'milling' wouldn't have phased him if it was around in those days.

The 'milling room' is the final field test, and probably the most telling for accurate character assessment. Under the guise of 'controlled aggression', a sixty-second contest of fighting ferocity is unleashed and every trainee has to participate. This is not a time for clever boxing styles, dancing and defending; it is about destroying your opponent and punching yourself out. The conqueror, whose lungs feel ruptured at the end, is often more battered than their foe. Ultimately, controlled aggression and winning are the only things that matter. Paras are elite soldiers and passing that test might demonstrate enough character to survive on the battlefield. Pop would have relished it.

But sadly, it wasn't to be. It wasn't that aspect of the training package that let him down; something more serious sent him back to the Royal Armoured Corps into the confines of a tank, wedged into a driver's seat belonging to the 44th RTR.

My eyes felt heavy as exhaustion from the last few days hit me. I carefully unfolded the letter and read it again. The handwriting was a flamboyant swirl of dark-blue ink on white parchment paper. I held it up to the light and could just make out a watermark: Jarrolds of Norwich. That warmed me, but the neatly scribed words were depressing.

'How unkind was that, Pop?'

The short missive on a single sheet of paper was devoid of love or any parental connection; it must have been painful to read as it reopened a wound that was to become a lifelong secret.

My dream was vivid in its colour, reality and smell. Instead of being curled up like a fossil or wedged somewhere uncomfortable, I was sitting in an aeroplane, probably an Armstrong Whitworth Whitley. These were huge twin-engine bombers converted to offload paratroopers during their training.

The pungent odour and straining engine noise alarmed me at first. I estimated that about thirty paratroopers were sitting in two lines, and the bright yellow scarves around our necks caught my eye. 'To be joined up and used as a flag in an emergency,' was someone's explanation.

The ominous red and green light bulbs set high above an open trap door in the fuselage floor were unlit; that was good news. A static line stretched the length of the fuselage towards them. The order to 'hook up' would soon be given, prompting our penguin-like shuffle and subsequent oblivion. Luckily for me, my location was towards the end of our stick, so I couldn't see the chasm that would eventually suck me into the growling, grey void.

With nearly 150lbs of kit bolted, clipped and strapped around me, I perched on the edge of a long wooden bench and waited my turn. God help anyone underneath when I landed. And how would I get up?

Something else troubled me: the pitch of our two 795 horsepower engines was another reminder that it would soon be time to jump.

'We need to gain more altitude,' our jump master said as he tried to ease our anxiety. I adjusted the angle of my Sten gun, slanted across the front of my body, and checked the safety catch again. The fact that I had already completed two descents was little comfort; they had only been baby drops from barrage balloons. I clearly remembered being hoisted up to 1,000 feet in a swinging reed basket. Four of us, plus an instructor, waited. 'This is *only* the beginning, boys.' Came his comforting reassurance.

Here, it was different. When an instructor barked his orders we only heard the sound, not the words. We heaved ourselves up and faced left. Tormented by the dormant lights, we watched and waited.

'A balloon jump is far worse than falling out of a Whitworth,' I tried to convince myself. As a supplement, 'The height is the same, but the exposure in a gigantic party balloon is far worse.' It wasn't.

I remembered the last time out. As we fell through what was little more than a long-drop shit hole, the speed of sixteen feet per second seemed endless. It was far worse than my first jump.

Eventually the static line tugged at my canopy release and out billowed the parachute. Finally, as the brakes came on with a jolt, it felt as if I were ascending for a few seconds.

Not only were my guts left in that swaying gondola basket but also my misguided desire to ever jump again. Nevertheless, now I found myself in an aeroplane, the real deal. Five 'proper' jumps and the coveted maroon beret, wings and badge would be mine.

Getting that whiff again, I wriggled my backside on the hard bench to confirm that it was someone else guilty of accidental defecation. The post-drop investigation would be horrific for that person.

'Remember, boys, if you get it wrong, you'll slice off your ugly noses against the trap door.' Our jump master was reading my mind. Another instructor, strutting up and down the line checking harnesses, reinforced the consequences of 'jump hesitation'. A heavy silence followed, and the looming trap door looked bigger. 'Do you hear me?'

'Yes, sir,' we acknowledged him, all of us like zombies in our mindful chaos.

The gagging smell continued to waft around, and the avoidance of any eye contact made it difficult to ascertain who the culprit was. Usually a cigarette eased the nerves and served as a timely distraction but sadly our fag stash had been confiscated earlier that morning (with a degree of relish, it has to be said). A couple of brave lads also had to surrender their hooch-filled hip flasks. Why hadn't I thought of carrying one of those?

Apart from head-to-toe numbness and shaking knees, the only other feeling was the acidic sting of bile as it crept up my throat.

'Okay, you horrible lot. Two minutes.' With a knowing smirk, the jump master tried to find a couple of us to eyeball. Thankfully he missed me when I pretended to recheck my harness and Sten safety catch.

'Remember to bring it back if it doesn't open,' the other instructor said. The wit of their double act was hysterical; we'd heard it all before in training, and no one laughed then either.

Somewhere I'd read that the British MOD refused to pay £30 for reserve chutes due to cost. Perhaps the adage 'right first time' came from this?

'This, gents, is when you pray you packed properly.' Would they ever give up? But it was true. Parachutes in 1942 were made of four-ply silk and had twenty-four shrouds that connected them to a leather body harness. It was an expensive kit, so they liked to remind us, and we needed intimate knowledge of how to pack it properly.

Things began to move fast and all the moisture in my mouth evaporated. We were ordered to check the man's harness in front. This was it then: the time had come. 'Okay, gentlemen. Hook up to the line.'

The red light came on – panic time. The jump master went to the leading man in our stick. 'Ready?'

Green light on. Tap on the shoulder, and the first in our line dropped out. Next man out. Nightmare. We shuffled forward and I knew it would be my turn in about thirty seconds. A stick of eighteen men usually took about a minute to exit, and unlike a Dakota C47, there was an added complication. Because the jump exit was not a door but a nose-smashing hole in the floor, you had to drop onto your backside first. Time was running away from me now.

And then it was over when Tony Auden woke me up. 'There you are! You missed the snacks, mate.' His narrow head looming through my driver's hatch, complete with beret and dark glasses, was an unbelievably wonderful sight. He lobbed me a couple of Morton's delicacies and immediately waved goodbye.

'Thanks, Tone. Any news on what's happening?'

'Nope, not yet. I'll let you know.'

Being woken from a good dream, just as you are about to roger Julia Roberts for example, is terrible; being rescued from a nightmare like the one I'd had is good. But, as always, good was quickly tempered with bad out here. A wave of depression hit me when I saw the letter in my lap. I heard Tony's size tens slide down the side of the tank and picked it up again. The last sentence said it all.

Not wanting to jump is perhaps understandable, son, but refusing an order from a superior officer and your subsequent prison term has disgraced our family.

So, there it was: Pop didn't jump. My grandfather's sentiments disappointed me and made me sad. Until I'd read his war record, I knew none of this. Pop had always told me that he made three parachute jumps; maybe the third was from a C-47 or Whitworth, after all, but he couldn't face another drop.

His official charge was refusing to jump and his sentence was eighty-four days' detention served at Fort Darlan barracks in Chatham, Kent. With remission, he served six weeks and was then 'Y' listed back to where he started, the Royal Armoured Corps. On one of his service forms, under the heading of 'Qualifications', it proudly states 'Parachutist'. In another box, under the title of 'Courses of Military Training', the note is sadder: it simply says, 'Deprived of Para wings, 3.1.44'.

For my father, prison would have been easy; the real struggle would have been failure and the dishonour that went with it because he was a proud man. I'm not too sure about family disgrace, however. That said, we never lived near any of the family in Norwich; there lies a clue, perhaps.

I think the reality was more heartening. Pop might have landed in Normandy's killing fields if he had passed the last training phase and gained his prized maroon beret. Thousands died there and also at Market Garden, the calamitous Monty operation. Thirty-four thousand Allied paratroopers attempted to secure several strategic bridges and the critical crossing at Arnhem was the big prize. This transport vein across the Rhine fed Germany's primary industrial production zone in the Ruhr and, as in Normandy, another catastrophic death toll resulted in only 25% of our Paras returning home. Would Pop have made it that far? If so, would he have gone on to survive this diabolical one-week mess of a battle?

'That's war, my son,' he once said. 'It's a messy old business.'

Pop would not have wished me to say this but, just like my old friend Clint the Action Man, his Para days in the airborne infantry were thankfully short-lived. I'm not sure he would have seen it that way, though.

From Peter Meadows' war record

Disobeying a lawful command given by his superior officer, i.e. In the field on 23 December 1943, when ordered to draw a parachute, did not do so.

Battle of the Road

Following a compo-pack breakfast, Padre Huggins conducted a short service. We sat on our tanks and listened to his sombre words; we all knew he was more informed than us about what was coming our way.

Heavy rain again worsened the miserable ambience. Some chuckled as Huggins unfurled a black, bank-manager-style umbrella with a curved wooden handle. The service lasted about fifteen minutes and finished with a louder and more heartfelt rendition of the Lord's Prayer than usual. In conclusion, he saluted us crisply, swivelled on his heels in the squelching mud and went off to do the same for A and B Squadrons.

'Thank fuck for that,' moaned Tony.

'I thought it was very nice,' said Morton, who had made notes. The rest of us said nothing. It was teeming down now and we were all relieved to be back inside – except me. I had managed to leave the driver's lid open.

'You absolute twat, Meadows,' I admonished myself. The saturated seat was haemorrhoid-inducing cold as I slid onto it.

'Okay, chaps, listen up,' our commander's voice boomed through the headphones. I adjusted the volume knob but I already knew the plan. As usual, the day's route map had been completed over an uninspiring breakfast of dried biscuits and insipid morning tea. It didn't make me feel any better knowing what I did, and my stomach did its somersaults.

'Our slippery little Hun friends have blocked the road North of Eindhoven.'

'Cunts,' said Tony.

'Our job now, bow gunner, is to relieve our boys of this little niggle.' The C word was not used often.

'Any support?' asked Cartwright, putting on a weirdly camp Geordie voice.

'Yes, we have the infantry girls with us, plus the pleasure of our American cousins later.'

'Cunts.' Tony said it again.

215

The 101st Airborne Division, led by Captain Dick Winters' second battalion of the 506th Parachute Infantry Regiment, had landed in drop zones northwest of Son and the Wilhelmina canal. They were defending about twelve miles of road flanking the river Dommel that ran parallel on the east side. This had to be kept clear because Hell's Highway was the main artery connecting Eindhoven with Arnhem. Our task was to support the Americans in pushing back the Panzer 107th brigade, remnants from Falaise.

'All eyes are on us now, chaps,' concluded Caddick.

Great. Clearing German blockades and maintaining that status was critical and would be an ongoing project for some time. Success meant it allowed our troops free movement up the road, over the bridges and then onto our final advance into Germany.

C Squadron hit the road early on Wednesday, September 20th. Not exactly raring to go, we were ready for the start of another foray into the only certainty in our lives: uncertainty. Second in line and miserably wet, our convoy battered through another heavy storm that hurled stair rods of rain down on us like spears.

At least it won't kill us. On second thoughts, we might drown, I thought.

It took all my concentration to keep us in line and I could see virtually nothing through a blanket of spray and muck thrown up in front of me. The usual tank rumble and clank of tracks on the tarmac led to a crescendo of mechanical noise. It reminded me of Depeche Mode and their distinctive, industrial music of the early 1980s. An occasional roar from a Typhoon enhanced the orchestral blare as it buzzed us on the way to bomb enemy flak gunners in the north. The sound of these planes lifted our spirits a little and helped ease the churn of nausea that was slowly building.

Depeche Mode? How could an electronic band from Basildon feature in my thinking right then?

I thought about Pop and his brushes with authority. Paras aside, there were his infamous schooldays and his regular exclusions for fighting, all absorbed into family folklore much later. Most recently was his (and now my) battlefield altercation with Padre Huggins. Old Farmer Giles and his stupid cornfield were another that came to mind. On a scale of one to ten, though, surely they couldn't be considered outrageous? At best, they would come in at five on my personal Richter scale.

In comparison, I must have been an absolute saint and model son to my parents. My indiscretions were few and far between, except for occasional boss disagreements in later life.

Conveniently forgotten was one worrying moment for my parents: a brawl outside the Dog Inn. It ended badly when I found myself being catapulted skywards by a car drag-racing from the battle scene. The sceptical doctor at A&E told me it was a miracle that I'd stayed in one piece; he then noted diplomatically that alcohol and the resulting 'looseness of body' could have contributed to my survival. I like to think my natural agility and all-round toughness saved me that night. Witnesses later claimed I went over the car, somersaulted and landed on my feet!

Alcohol and being banned from a couple of hostelries were the only other brushes with authority I could recall. A dispute – or was it 'a debate' – with a landlord was one heinous crime. The bastard short-changed me and he knew it.

In another Cambridge establishment, my misdemeanour was to dare to possess a shiny, newly shaved head. 'And rugby shirts aren't allowed here either, you prick,' the cocky Australian barman concluded as he opened the door and invited me to leave. It wasn't even an England shirt; granted, one of those might irritate an Aussie convict with a chip on his shoulder. My response along those lines would have upset most Antipodeans.

It wasn't the pub full of Tarquins and Ruperts that I'd miss; it was the injustice of his decision that pissed me off. In no way a fashion statement like the perm was, my glossy new pate had been acquired in the name of charity, Children in Need to be exact. But I got the last laugh, though I'm not very proud of it. I told the bonehead that cancer treatment had caused my follicle demise and the shirt was a goodbye present. I can still see his face in meltdown.

Impulsive – that was always my problem. The more I thought about Pop's confrontations with authority figures, the more I worried about my own. Being banned for half a season with the rest of our football team didn't ease those concerns much. Our disciplinary record was not good, and when one of our star abusers knocked the referee out on a soggy afternoon in

November, we were hauled into the Essex FA to face an inquiry. The interrogation was brief and conducted on a one-to-one basis by a panel of decrepit old silver foxes.

When I was asked, 'So why do *you* think the referee got a punch, son?' I replied, 'Because he was rubbish.' That was the wrong answer.

We all said similar things and a six-month ban was duly imposed on us. My mate Alun Farley and I went off to play hockey for a local team but gave up quickly; it was too hardcore for us, and people got hurt – especially if you headed the ball as a joke.

More flabbergasted than proud, Mum kept the newspaper cuttings, including one from the *Daily Mail*. I suggested we frame it but Pop refused, adding, 'You stupid boy.' I hadn't heard that one before.

We got through our morning's work unscathed apart from a Panzerfaust shot bouncing off the front of our tank, which took out a slice of armour a foot long on its way past. At around noon, we made contact with a group of German artillerymen guarding a bridge over the Wilhelmina Canal, but a combination of our high explosives and infantry close-quarter combat quickly nipped things in the bud. Due to our superiority in numbers, this encounter was short-lived and a few shell-shocked prisoners were soon rounded up.

As the day progressed into afternoon, more enemy soldiers surrendered. Almost too willingly, they handed their weapons to our foot soldiers who escorted them to the holding cages in town. By late afternoon, and with the bridge open again, the flow of military traffic had increased dramatically. All these vehicles were headed in one direction: north. That included us, who had been ordered to laager at Sint-Oedenrode.

As days go, it was one of the easier ones, but easy was a word that would disappear for a while. From September 21st, things ramped up, and for the next five days, we plied on around the clock. They were the most intense so far; if there was such a thing as human autopilot, we were fully plugged into it. As exhaustion followed, our need for sleep was forgotten. Our brain's need to reboot was also ignored and all thoughts of rest and recuperation became a fantasy. We would not experience that luxury for many days.

Even our reliable Shermans struggled as they strained to achieve maximum output hour after hour. The Royal Electrical and Mechanical Engineers or cohorts from the Light Aid Detachment worked miracles to keep us going.

We had one memorable fright when the breech on our main gun decided to seize up just when German tank destroyers were spotted nearby. These colossal Jagdpanthers were manned with a Tiger tank gun and had the skin of a Panther. Confronting a JP usually ended badly and our only encounter with one was a dangerous experiment. Because their massive 88mm gun was fixed into a non-rotating mantle, it could only point forward. A good shot from behind was the only chance you had.

'Okay, nice and slow,' ordered Caddick as I manoeuvred us towards the rear of our prey.

The first AP round bounced off the weaker 40mm rear-armour plate. Cartwright's high-explosive follow-up exploded on the ground like a frenzied Catherine wheel. That alarmed me more than the rebound.

'Get us the fuck out of here, driver! NOW!' Caddick screamed. Our experiment had failed badly, and we hastily made ourselves scarce.

As our tanks seized up – or worse – the number of effective ones in our squadron gradually dwindled. We rarely left the confines of our rancid vehicles, but Major Foster was a stickler for maintaining a 'clean workplace' as he liked to put it. Although we ate, drank and fought from these stinking places, we rarely laagered long enough to clean them.

There was one small upside to our misery, however: rum. 'Work hard and play hard, boys,' Foster said as he issued it to our troop leaders and commanders. After necking a shot each, we added our bottle to an impressive collection in our drinks stash, otherwise known as 'the den of paradise'.

'And remember, chaps, cleanliness is next to bally godliness.' We all loved Teddy Foster and his cliches.

And then there were the drugs. As minutes turned to hours and then into days, battle fatigue must have been a genuine concern for the commanders of Operation Market Garden. This must be the case not just in north-western Europe but across all the other war theatres, including Africa and the Far East. The Germans, perhaps influenced by Hitler's use of stimulants, issued Pervitin (known as Tank Chocolate) to their troops; it was said that this crystal-meth-like drug fuelled the Blitzkrieg rampage through Belgium and France in 1940.

'Okay, boys, take one of these.' It wasn't an order, more of a gesture as Caddick passed a tube of them around.

'What are they, guv?' asked Cartwright, rolling the small white pill between his fingers.

'Pep pills, son.'

My father had told me that he used pep pills to keep him awake, and I'd thought nothing of it at the time. What about caffeine drinks, a staple diet for late-night driving and morning-after hangovers in my other life?

The Allies' equivalent to the German methamphetamine was Benzedrine. As with Pervitin, it was introduced primarily to prevent exhaustion and mental fatigue and, like speed, it detonated the nervous system with a rush of euphoria. It could also give its users a misguided feeling of invincibility. Maybe some of my Moroccan Gold wacky-baccy would have gone down better.

While pep pills were a valuable aid for tired armies, drug-crazed men indiscriminately firing weapons of mass destruction was an interesting concept. British pilots also popped smaller 10mg doses as they strafed or bombed the enemy – which occasionally included us. Looking at the innocuous tab on offer, it seemed that the Royal Tank Regiment, far more hardcore than the posh-boy pilots, were on double measures.

I took one and flipped it into my mouth.

'Do we have to, sir?' Big Nige was whining now.

'Yes, you do.'

Whether it was due to exhaustion or they didn't work, the Benzedrine didn't do much for our happy band of users. We unanimously agreed on this over a bedtime cocoa, heads buzzing and eyes as wide as barn owls!

If I had to choose, my preferred drug had always been beer, so when someone lobbed me my first can of Schlitz I was stumped on two counts. First, its weight because the can wasn't made of modern-day aluminium; second, how to open it when there was no ring pull.

'Use your teeth, twit.'

Big Nige threw me a bottle opener called a Church Key by our American cousins. At the other end was a triangular punch you levered into the can. The important thing was that two holes were necessary: one let air in and the other poured out the amber nectar. Actually, it tasted watery and weak, but most beers across the Atlantic did – and perhaps still do.

I felt no real buzz from pep pills, just more 'wired' than usual. My levels of alertness were higher; they had to be because the fug of one battle was merging into another. Most were tank-versus-tank mêlées; although we didn't knock out many, we were fast and agile compared to the lumbering might of our enemy. The cocktail of amphetamines and adrenalin made coping easier; it numbed our thinking and our fear of getting hit.

'Nice driving, Meadows, I taught you well.' Agreed. Caddick was an excellent commander who was decisive in his decision-making. His orders were always clear and all I had to do was respond quickly and things generally worked out okay. Standout mentors like him in my business life have had the same philosophy; they taught me the importance of meticulous planning, having strong people around you and being brave. It seemed that nothing was different on a battlefield.

September 21st fused into September 22nd, later known as Black Friday, and the Battle of Veghel. Accompanied by our American cousins from Dick Winters' 506th Parachute Infantry Regiment, we flushed through the town and headed towards Erp, another Wehrmacht-held stronghold.

The day started badly as the washed-out winter sky filled with scudding black clouds started pelting rain again. A heavy mist, combined with incessant shelling from our German friends, was made worse by the quick loss of three tanks to a roaming Panther.

Our sky troopers' friendly bonus also added to the excitement. 'More icing on the fucking cake,' lamented a disgruntled Valentine Caddick from his perch above.

The German attacks came from their heavy Panzer division, which now boasts 'King' Tigers, a new experience for our regiment. It was said that fewer than 500 of these monsters were built; as always, we seemed to face them all.

'Slow down; we don't need to squash the fuckers,' Caddick ordered.

That was a reference to the prisoners shuffling in front of us along the bank of the river Aa towards Veghel. The plan was for the 2/60 KRRC to relieve us and then move them into the bulging PoW cages erected on tennis courts in the town.

Luck had been with us for some time but, just as we congratulated ourselves again, it finally ran out. The hit came from our starboard side and jolted us violently to the left.

Caddick spotted it immediately. 'Panzerfaust. Across the river.'

We knew these deadly anti-tank guns had only one shot, but how many of them were there? Apart from the fact that we couldn't shift in any direction, our turret appeared undamaged and our gun was already pointing towards the river. While a short but noisy retaliation from our turret guns kicked off, we had a severe mechanical problem: there was a lack of track issue and the transmission seemed knackered.

There was *some* positive news. According to my dashboard dials, the engine was still working and all levels were in good order. Better than that, our cabin was free from smoke or fire. That probably meant the strike had hit us at lower-ground level and, although it had stopped us, it confirmed that our luck was holding out.

'Anyone hurt?'

'No, sir.'

It's funny how 'boss', 'guv' or even 'gaffer' would be the usual informal response to a senior rank, but when trouble or any formality beckoned, it soon became 'sir'.

'All out. NOW.'

We lined up in a tight row along the tree line, away from our incapacitated tank, in less than thirty seconds. All eyes scanned the river's north bank, including our commanders with the added benefit of binoculars. At the same time, we got our first sight of hundreds of British gliders as they swooped overhead, crammed full of men and fighting equipment. Their destination points were the allotted landing zones between Eindhoven and Arnhem. The

American 101st and 82nd landed in two zones south of the British. It was simple. That was the plan.

For now, here on *terra firma*, it was time to refocus. We hugged the ground tightly, expecting another rocket, waiting for it to happen; it didn't.

'What do you reckon, sir,' asked Tony.

'Kraut flying solo. Let's hang on a bit.'

And so we waited. I was at the far end of the line and noted that all our prisoners had taken the opportunity and hightailed it; all of them except one.

'Jesus.' Inconspicuous until now, he lay about ten feet away. He was much older than us and resembled a man of the cloth more than a Nazi killing machine. His round, gold-framed spectacles looked ridiculous. Snapped in the middle, a crude repair using black tape barely held them together. He was looking at me.

'Look who's here, sir.'

'Je…sus.'

The others became more interested and Cartwright generously offered to put a bullet through the 'effing Kraut's head'. None of us was too worried about the other escapees because the group of ten were unarmed, but one had decided to stay for some reason. Maybe, unlike some reports circulating about Allied soldiers, the British treatment of PoWs and our reputation for fair play still held firm. Then I remembered mental Moxton and his antics and cancelled that stray thought immediately.

'Fritz. Stay where you are… *Bleib hier*,' Caddick ordered.

'*Ja* … having no fears,' he replied.

'What do you reckon, Meadows? Damage wise?'

'Could be front bogies or just track,' I replied. 'I can't see.' I didn't tell him about the gearbox. An M4 was relatively easy to repair in terms of track replacement, but transmission issues would be more challenging for the engineers.

Caddick pondered his reply, then looked up and gestured to our new friend. 'Okay, Fritz, go and check out our tank.' It was an interesting request. Any enemy on the opposing riverbank would likely reveal themselves to their comrade; we would then understand the problem we faced. On the other hand, they could shoot him.

'*Kaput*. Look.' Caddick pointed to his eyes and repeated the order with the addition of some, improvisation that only the English could do. '*Kaput*. Lookinzee vaht hast happened. *Danke.*'

Brilliant! There was no movement on the other side of the river except for an occasional wisp of blue smoke as it drifted up from the receiving end of our missile barrage. Becoming mildly irritated at the German's lack of urgency, Caddick waved his pistol at him.

The German hesitated then quickly scrambled into a hunched jog. He reached the good side of our tank in rapid time. Stooping, he edged towards its front end, dropped onto his front and looked back at us. Caddick waved him forward impatiently. A second later, the man was out of sight.

'What if he warns them, boss?' asked Morton.

'Well, let's just hope he doesn't.'

We needn't have worried; our roving Jerry was back with us, all smiles, in just a few minutes. Lots of gold teeth and one missing at the front; a clergyman, perhaps, but a dentist most certainly not. He looked pleased with himself as he began his report. 'Spur *gebrochen*. Broken.' He proudly swirled his forefinger in a slow, clockwise motion. We all understood.

'*Gut jetzt verpiss dich.*' Our sergeant's response sounded rude and the German's smug smile evaporated.

'Go on, now fuck off,' he repeated. 'It's safer out there. Especially with the Yanks about.' He could not translate that into German, but our friend seemed to understand the sentiment and nodded. He still seemed reluctant to go, which was endearing, so I threw him a packet of Woodbines and my Zippo lighter.

'Ta, Tommy.' He gave me a half-hearted thumbs-up, and that was it; stuffing the cigarettes into a pocket, he shuffled away in search of his comrades. The whole episode had been surreal, and we let it soak in and said nothing.

It was Caddick who finally broke the spell. 'Okay, there's some good news, lads.'

'Good news?' We all looked at him.

'We've got the grease monkeys behind us.' That was indeed good news – and a surprise. 'HQ is about thirty minutes behind us, so go and tidy yourselves up, girls.' I caught his wink; the others didn't.

There was no question that we had it bad in the Battle of the Road. Tacking up and down Hell's Highway in a blaze of intense and relentless action was literally hell on wheels – but the Paras had it worse. Our job was to keep the corridor open and allow Allied reinforcements clear passage. They had been given just forty-eight hours to liberate the Dutch and to support our soldiers, including the British 1st Airborne at Arnhem. It was a stretch, and it failed. However, the 'ubiquitous' 44th RTR played an essential role in trying to achieve this goal. In the end, though, we were left with just thirty operational tanks out of seventy. The cost of failure to the regiment was huge.

In the final analysis, the history of Market Garden made grim reading. First of all, and usually forgotten, the Dutch people faced terrible repercussions from the German army in its galloping retreat. As they fled homeward, as always in war the mark they left behind was horrific. Not only did these invaders loot possessions, steal food and rape women, but 400,000 civilians throughout the war – mainly young men – were rounded up and sent to the Fatherland as forced labour. It is estimated that nearly 4,000 civilians died in Operation Market Garden alone, and that does not include those maimed for life and the thousands who died from German-enforced starvation.

As for the soldiers? Maybe perdition is the best description for what the Allied Parachute Regiments faced in the Battle for the Bridges. At a time when morale in the German army was at its lowest, this hapless campaign strengthened their resolve and probably extended the war in Europe by several months. While the US Airborne lost nearly 4,000 men, the British death toll was well over that with 6,000 soldiers captured. If you add the loss of 260 planes and 700 aircrew, plus Polish and Canadian casualties, Operation Market Garden was a catastrophe.

We stayed around Veghel until 30th September, still under the command of the 101st US Airborne. Promised some R&R, we laagered in a small village called Volkel east of Uden. We'd been promised four weeks but knew better; it would not happen.

However, a turn-up for the books did greet us in the guise of heavy tank replacement. It didn't happen. The flow had slowed, so our crew was back in Honeys, and that meant frontline reconnaissance duties again until more Shermans arrived on the scene.

From Peter Meadows' memoirs

Sometime in September, we linked up with the 101st US Airborne Division on the road to Arnhem from Eindhoven. This was in effect a narrow corridor and, as we neared Arnhem with the enemy on both sides, we lost and had many tanks crippled, quite apart from so many lives. We tried, but it became quite impossible to advance further to relieve the troops there. It became necessary to rest (battle weary), collect new tanks and completely re-equip for the winter campaign in Holland. Our losses in officers and men were replaced by all ranks from the 42nd RTR, including some old friends from past battles in Libya and Palestine.

Autumn

A devastating piece of news greeted us just over a week into our break. It was announced that the recce team had a new troop leader named Sergeant Billy Moxton. I was less concerned about him being back in the mix and more interested in one of his cronies, the lance corporal who had attacked me.

Noting my concern, Caddick took me to one side and whispered earnestly that my recent sparring partner was, in fact, dead. 'Brewed-up in Eindhoven.' It was a shock but I felt no sympathy, just relief. Having to look over my shoulder every five minutes was not a desirable situation.

A week later, the regiment moved north across the Maas River at Grave and onto Men's Island in Betuwe. Our new Honey was much more cramped than I remembered, made worse by the two stalactite-positioned steering levers dropping down from the hull. Neither was it new. A recent dollop of white paint hastily sloshed around the inside was still fresh and sticky; we would never know how much blood it covered. 'It's still fuckin wet, guv,' grumbled Morton.

'White paint reflects the light, son,' Caddick said. 'You'll see better.'

We were also down to a foursome: Tony had been seconded to RHQ to drive a half-track, which he claimed was a promotion. 'Halfwit in a half-track,' chuckled Big Nige to my right. That made him my bow gunner. God help us all.

'Master that toy, big boy, and maybe you can drive with me one day,' shouted Nige as Tony left.

'Gunner, loader and now demotion to co-driver. What a career you've had!' Replied Tony lifting a middle finger.

Unlike a Sherman, a Honey had a set of dual controls used for emergencies, which was generally only in the event of the driver's demise. I'd forgotten how luxurious a Sherman M4 was compared to this heap of rattling tin that required excessive right-hand leverage to keep us straight. On the upside, we had the benefits of an automatic transmission again; this, technically speaking, would give us a smoother ride, and it seemed to tick my boss's box, too! 'And I thought kangaroo petrol knocked my front teeth out!' he jested.

Famous for grazing land and Leerdammer cheese in my other life, Betuwe was an awful place in October 1944. Because of heavy shelling from both sides, the Dutch communities plonked in the middle of this firing range were the ones who suffered. To make it worse, history later showed that they were severely abused by the occupying army, something that was already a recurring war theme. These heroic farming 'Islanders', at a tremendous human cost, were eventually evacuated to safety by the Allies, but it took time and some chose to stay behind. Mostly, they were too old to fight as soldiers but stubborn enough to put their bodies on the line instead. All this sacrifice to protect their family's shattered livelihoods: it was a scene of utter devastation when we arrived on October 10th 1944. Most of the livestock was dead, their skins scorched off by rocket fire and bombing; the next foul breath of battle would also topple the few buildings left standing.

Our job – to hold the line and wait for orders – was the easy bit. Apart from random bouts of mortar stonking, the absolute misery was the weather worsening and turning cold. With plummeting temperatures and driving rain, life in our tanks, or foxholes when out on foot patrol, was wretched.

After a week, we moved back across the border into Belgium and took up a position in a small village called Poppel. Our orders there were the same: hold the line.

Our regiment's role was a familiar one. Thrusting forward on a broad front and harassing the Germans with sporadic shelling and machine-gun fire was straightforward enough, but apart from the atrocious weather there was something more sinister to contend with now: land mines. The road into Tilburg, ten miles away, was rash with not only mines but booby traps. On the last day we lost one tank to a tripwire triggered by a Panzerfaust mounted to a tree and also the life of an inexperienced sapper who tried to lift a strategically placed body off the highway. His reward? An S-mine that sprang up four feet and split his body into two.

'Okay, listen up.' That was how each morning briefing usually started; we would then try to figure out from Caddick's nasal tone whether the day was likely to be good or bad. Good meant we were out on a recce; it was better to meet a Tiger tank on a recce than lie in a slit trench filled with ice-cold water. That would be a terrible day.

'Okay, listen up,' repeated the sergeant. He deliberately held the pause. 'We're back on the road!'

Our mission this time was to check out an area around Roovert on the Dutch border and, if we played our cards right, it would fill the whole day. Like kids on a school outing, we eagerly got our stuff together and waited for further details.

'Good news and bad news, gentlemen.' Why was there always a spoiler? 'We are checking out alternative routes to Tilburg. We may run into some Jerry.'

'And the good news, guv?'

'That was it.' His face remained blank. 'Oh, and we've got Moxton with us on this one.'

'Fucking hell,' we all said simultaneously.

Moxton held our troop briefing in the pouring rain: same Mohican hair strip, a bushier beard than I recollected, and black sunglasses. Why always the shades? It was pissing down. He did have a particular style though and, like the London East End gangsters, he was always smart and his boots were impeccably clean. He also lectured us about respecting your family and hating your enemy: that was the essence of his code. The man was complex but at the same time he captivated me.

'Any questions?' He didn't want any. The three other tank commanders, including our own, shook their heads in unison. 'Excellent. What about the girlies?' Transferring his attention to us, he caught my eye. 'Joe Louis over there – if I catch one, you can have him.' He laughed.

I couldn't determine whether he was taking the piss or showing me a sign of respect. But why should he? I nodded back. His gaze held mine for an uncomfortably long time before he bent forward and dramatically spat out a glob of green phlegm. Then he gave us the order to mount up.

'Careful, Meadows. He's watching you.' Those comforting words confirmed that I had to watch my back while Moxton was in charge.

'The guy's a cunt, sir. I'm not worried.' Pop never used the 'C' word, so this spontaneous outburst surprised everyone in earshot; I'd said it, though, and it felt good.

Pop constantly reminded me that bullies were useless when isolated. 'Divide and conquer, son.'

'Meaning?'

'Just that. And always remember, get your punch in first and make it a hard one.'

We headed out of our camp bog with us at the rear. Our orders were to split up and, in our case, investigate the village church at Roovert; the tower and its graveyard were all great places for snipers to do their dirty work. The trip took longer than expected due to the accompaniment of a solitary sapper doing his minesweeping bit on foot. These men were fearless, and our more cautious approach than usual was welcome. But once again, the promise of Yankee Para support fell short; they were nowhere to be seen.

'You never read that in the history books, do you?' was another Pop quote and a reminder to me.

We arrived late in the morning as a bone-chilling, grey drizzle replaced the heavy rain. Eventually the outline of the church came into view. After some prolonged scrutiny through his field glasses, Caddick gave me the order to move forward slowly. 'Gently, driver. Treat those controls like you would Lana Turner's breasts.'

Lana Turner? Pop fancied Rita Hayworth, and let's not forget the sex goddess Hedy Lamarr, too!

Given that places of worship were home to snipers on both sides, I would have lobbed a couple straight into the tower. But there were rules to obey, namely those in the Geneva Convention. You could shred, scorch and dismember your enemy to death, but there were *rules* about how to do it.

Caddick dismounted about two hundred yards from the church's back door and disappeared. The object of attention crouched amongst a cluster of trees on a slight hill to our right.

'Thanks for the warning,' muttered Big Nige.

'Did he say anything to you?' I asked Cartwright.

'Just that he'll be back in ten.'

We felt uneasy and grew increasingly agitated as the minutes ticked. 'Shall I go and see?' offered Sid. It was down to him anyway because he was now in charge. Then, before we could answer, our absent hero stumbled into view with his thumbs held high.

'Thank fuck for that,' grumbled Nige. 'I've been desperate for a brew.'

Caddick clambered onto the tank, flopped down, and took a long draught of water from his canteen. 'No peace for the wicked chaps. Bring your side arms; we're off on a little walkies.' Only Sergeant Caddick could make a foot patrol feel like a Boy Scout romp in the woods.

'Have we got a picnic, sir?' His look said it all; I didn't follow up and when he gave us the order to split, it came like a punch as thoughts of Ian Taylors' demise hit me. I was going solo on this one. My orders were to survey the graveyard while the others went the other way. Holding my Schmeisser in a white-knuckle grip, I edged through the conifer trees circling the cemetery. With my tongue wrung out and stuck to the roof of my mouth, I crept through the trees towards what looked like a clearing ahead. The splashing sound from my water canteen broke the silence and was matched only by my heart as it hammered against the inside of my rib cage. I wanted to puke and felt faint at the same time, and then there was my tinnitus which screamed like a transistor radio playing at volume eleven.

The foliage eventually cleared to expose a small circle of granite headstones; the nearest one looked more recent than the others. Still half-crouched, I listened for any misplaced sounds. Because my bursting lungs hadn't breathed for a while, I exhaled as quietly as possible. The follow-up inhalation was extended and raggedy. I could hear blackbirds. Yes, that was it: birdsong, white noise and my raging heartbeat.

I continued to scan my new surroundings. 'Where are you, you Jerry bastards?'

It was interesting that I was thinking that way because any sniper worth his salt would have plugged me by then. The danger was real and I was alone. Once again, I thought about the stalking and failed assassination attempt on my mate's brother all those years before. Or perhaps I should say in the future.

The gravestone was relatively new and the inscription carved into the front was simple: a name, Adeline Benoit, and the here-today, gone-tomorrow dates that bracketed her short life. She was just thirty-five when she died in 1939. If I'd been looking at this headstone in my other life, it would be heavily weathered, covered in bird shit and considered old.

I noticed a larger stone towards the back of the graveyard and decided that would be a great place to hide for a while. It was also a good vantage point to look out for any two-legged foreign predators lurking nearby.

Our orders were to return to the tank at 14.00 hours, giving me just over forty-five minutes to rest. 'Resting peacefully' in a graveyard? The thought made me chuckle.

Bright autumn sunshine drenched me now instead of rain. Whilst not warm, it was great to feel the sun's rays on my face. As warmth soaked into my bones, I felt my body begin to wind down.

Food? I found some at the bottom of my day pack. One tooth-busting biscuit and two boiled sweets, hardly Mars bars or Jaffa cakes, Pop's snacks of choice, but we were always hungry and any supplementary food dampened the hunger pangs – except for American chocolate. Everyone agreed they could keep that shite. The Yanks were forever trying to trade their K-ration chocolate. Apart from its dreadful taste, it was also rock solid, so hard that our hammer had trouble breaking it up! And it didn't even dissolve in boiling water to make a hot drink!

The Brits generally stuck to barley-sugar sweeties for their sugar rush and traded other things instead. Tinned treacle pudding was a good one. The Septics (my name for them, the others wouldn't have understood) loved to exchange this for cancer-enhancing Lucky Strike cigarettes.

'If bullets didn't kill me then lung cancer will in later life.' I thought about that, as well as Pop's lifetime habit, which seems to have had few adverse effects on his long-term health. I lit up and looked around to see if any fruits or berries could make my snack a real feast; sadly, there weren't any.

It's not strictly true about Pop's smoking habits and his health: it could have finished him off on Guy Fawkes night several times. The Dollimores' fireworks party was always a highlight on the social calendar. My mates and I would sneak into the garden shed where the grown-ups thought they'd hidden the dangerous fireworks, to acquire some. Their garden was long and narrow with lots of cover, so we did our stuff behind the compost heap at the end. Whilst the elders oohed and aahed over Catherine wheels that never spun properly and Roman candles that spat out pretty colours with a limp *phut*, we were more hardcore.

Big rockets, Consulate menthol ciggies and cans of Harp lager 'borrowed' from the kitchen table formed the backdrop to the only party in town. We swapped legendary stories like: 'Did you know that Billy G strapped his hamster to a rocket and launched it into space?' All urban myths, of course – I think. Eventually, cold and out of munitions, we crept up behind our mums who were warming their hands with cups of hot tomato soup. Seeing them skip around the bangers and jumping jacks lobbed between their legs was always funny!

Back to cigarettes and his health. I remember Pop being a big kid at these events and he loved to light the blue touch paper, as instructed on all the TV ads, but with the glowing end of his cigarette clamped between his teeth. Perhaps the daily stonking of German artillery made this once-a-year whizz and pop of crayon-sized bangers insignificant. The Standard Fireworks taper stayed in the box for another year. What a hero and what an idiot. Happy days.

Like all cemeteries, the atmosphere in this one was calm and spiritual. The tranquillity bit was hardly surprising – but the sound of snoring was a new experience for me. This startling new sound came from somewhere nearby. I held my breath again to try and confirm the source of the strange snuffling rattle; it was coming from behind the headstone propping up my back.

'Jesus Christ.'

My heart rebooted again and I quietly got to my feet, simultaneously releasing the safety catch on my gun. Like a Chad cartoon character, I peeked over the large granite slab that separated me from the intriguing sound below. The shiny top of a large black helmet greeted me, unmistakably German.

Nothing can explain why I reached down and tapped the side of his lid with the barrel of my Schmeisser; it was the equivalent of tugging on a sleeping dog's tail. The snarling German was on his feet in an instant flurry of athletic contortions. Shocked at my stupidity, I froze as he faced me less than a yard away. That was bad enough, but at waist height, he held a pistol in his very steady right hand, and it was pointing up at me.

Stalemate, was all I could think as we stared each other out. But although he was young and fit, he looked frightened and didn't appear to know what to do next. Just like me, then.

'Drinken?' I asked.

'*Trinken*,' he laughed and corrected me.

'Yes, *trinken*.' I smiled back at him. He was about my age – 'war age' – and much taller than the new me. He had blue eyes, and we continued to scrutinise each other closely.

'*Wie lautet dein Name?*' he asked.

I understood this; among the few things I remembered from German lessons at school was how to ask someone for their name. Another was how to say I was twelve years old. '*Ich bin Zwolf jahre alt!*' How obscure were those memories?

We were still pointing our guns at each other and quickly needed some common ground to get out of this fix. Then a strange thing happened: my German friend made the first move by pointing his weapon downward. I followed suit and waited. It was my turn to lead, so I made an exaggerated demonstration of flicking my Schmeisser's safety catch back on. Instantly, like making a stupid chess move, I cursed myself; all he had to do now was lift his pistol and shoot me.

He looked down at his gun and flicked on the safety catch. '*Gute waffe, Schmeisser?*' His voice was deep and wavered slightly.

I guessed what he meant. 'Yes, much better than our shite. *Sehr gut.*'

He laughed again; it was genuine, and we both smiled. The icebreaker seemed to work. Like two people at a work conference, we gestured for each other to take a seat behind the gravestone. It was surreal. As we introduced ourselves, I chuckled when he told me his name was Wolfgang. What was my name going to be, Calum or Peter? I offered the latter, and he replied that his father's name was also Peter.

'Wolfgang, all I have on me are sweets.'

He took the barley sugar. '*Danke*. Sank you, *muchen*.' Mindful of offending my new friend, the enemy, I restrained my snigger. 'Schnapps? You like?' he asked.

'*Ich* loven Schnapps. *Fantastique.*'

Wolfgang was not as polite as me and laughed loudly. He reached into his pack; his fingernails were caked with dirt, and he didn't smell that fresh, either. Hygiene aside, my main concern was how he had found himself alone. Or was he?

A small liquor bottle distracted me. Unscrewing the bronze-coloured top, he passed it over to me.

'*Danke, Wolfgang, Sehr muchen.*' The hit worked its way down my throat, warm and strong. I wiped the top as kids do and passed it back.

We spent the next ten minutes attempting to communicate, and his English was vastly superior to my feral-pigeon German. Fumbling around in his wallet, he proudly presented me with a photograph of his girlfriend. Waiting for me to replicate this gesture, he seemed surprised when I couldn't.

'I have no one, Wolfgang.' I shrugged my shoulders. 'And certainly no one as beautiful as…?'

'Erika.' He kissed the photograph tenderly and put it away. His next move made me jump as a large army knife appeared in a black-leather sheath. I recognised it immediately. The dagger that had spent most of my childhood as a paperweight was now back in my hands.

'*Bitte, nimm das.*' Holding the sheath, Wolfgang offered it to me handle first.

'For me?' I replied. He nodded enthusiastically. So this was how Pop had obtained the infamous knife? Running my hands over the sheath, I asked Wolfgang if I could take it out.

'*Ja, bitte.*'

The ten-inch blade was razor sharp with a groove that ran its length on either side. All of us in the family suspected the knife was war loot; later, as the retired war relic gathered dust, Pop occasionally greased the blade with Vaseline. 'To protect it from rust,' he would say.

Scraping my thumb over its cutting edge, a sinister thought briefly crossed my mind as I held the weapon ready for its intended purpose. Wolfgang was unphased. He would never know about its future or the emotional significance of his gesture. He also seemed to trust me unconditionally as I played with the knife like a sword.

Feeling an urgent need to return his faith, guilt hit me when I emptied my Webley 38 chamber before handing it over. '*Ich habe* something *fur dich.*'

I would have to explain its disappearance from my kit, but I parked that concern for now. I also had my Luger, a German sidearm, to explain too. 'It takes the same ammo as yours.'

My attempt to appease my overt display of distrust became even more confusing when I dropped the extracted bullets into his other hand. To deflect the moment, I asked him another question. 'Why are you here, Wolfgang?' My elaborate hand gestures supplemented the words.

He understood because all British people liked to talk loudly and play charades when they spoke to foreigners. '*Meine freunde sind weg.*' He ran his hand across his throat. That was easy to understand. His friends had gone – dead, I guessed, and he was lost.

'Wolfgang, it is dangerous for you here. Soldiers are looking for Germans everywhere.'

Before I could offer him the sensible option of surrender, which should make it safer for him, he gave me the answer. 'Peter, I'm not surrendering to you,' he said in perfect English.

I could say nothing in return. We sat in silence until the voice of someone unwelcome called out my name. 'Meadows. Where the fuck are you?' Half-whisper, half-call, it was coming from the other side of the graveyard. I pressed my hand against Wolfgang's chest. He had to stay down for both our sakes.

'There you are.' Moxton, about twenty yards away, ambled towards me with his Sten gun ready.

'Having a shit, sir. Got terrible diarrhoea.'

The last word made him stop abruptly; for such a hard man, mentioning diarrhoea had a surprising impact.

Wolfgang had to stay still; his life, possibly mine, was on the line here. I glanced down, and all I could see was the top of his helmet and my Webley in his hand. He was also trembling.

'On a fucking grave?' Moxton asked.

I nodded.

'You dirty bastard.'

'A man's got to do what a man's got to do, sir.' I wondered how familiar the classic John Wayne line would be. The film *Stagecoach* came out in 1939, so he may just have seen it. I was also sure the Duke used that line in it – he always did.

Moxton grunted, unimpressed. 'Five minutes, son. They're waiting for you.'

'Yes, sir. I'll clean all this mess up first.'

He looked at me like a piece of the subject matter in question. Before turning away, he said something profound. 'The Duke is a fucking poof anyway. His real name is Marion, for fuck's sake!'

Please don't tell my father that, I thought. *He idolised the macho man of movies.*

Content that he was out of range, I held up both hands in front of Wolfgang. 'Wait ten minutes, Wolfgang.' We shook hands firmly and that was it. It was the most surreal experience of my life, and there had been many.

Our men were on seek-and-destroy missions for the next couple of weeks, in army parlance 'engaged target requests'. We enjoyed support from the infantry on these forays and things went well. Sometimes we led by blasting our targets, primarily buildings, and the infantry boys tidied up.

Even though churches acted as a sanctuary for enemy snipers – they had religious dispensation – though some mistakes were made. On other occasions our foot soldiers swarmed over the identified objectives, and we followed up by crushing everything in our path. I had no problem doing that: these people were not human, just abstract objects. It was simply a matter of 'them or us'.

On occasion, I thought about Wolfgang and hoped he was safe. I would never know.

Snow began to fall on November 9th and probably the best present ever was issued to our tank crew: Pixie suits. These were khaki-coloured padded overalls festooned with zips and pockets, and they had a hood. Big Nige called them 'walking sleeping bags' and he was correct; worn over everyday battle dress or overalls, we lived in them day and night. The cold was insane, especially after sunset, and these gifts from the MOD lifted our morale at probably the most miserable part of the campaign so far.

It was worse for the ground troops, especially the Paras, who had to travel light compared to everyone else. A chilling thought struck me: had the old man completed his training, it could have been me out there in his body. It was not unusual to see the infantry trudge through the quagmire of mud and ice with the frozen soles of their feet replacing the worn-out soles of their boots. The lucky ones only had trench foot and parasitic illnesses like scabies to contend with. Mercifully we remained healthy in our regiment, apart from hunger and the constant threat of being brewed-up into a mulch of scorched flesh and bone.

On the 22nd of November, we left the tank laager near Maasbree, a municipality in the Netherlands. This time we were on a solo reconnaissance mission minus our intrepid leader, Valentine Caddick. Somehow he had managed to wangle home leave but there was no animosity from us, just a desperate hope that our names would fall into the frame soon. So far our sergeant was the only one in our group who had achieved this; sadly, I knew it would stay that way for me. I wondered how Pop must have felt. Had he obtained home leave, would he have tried harder to rectify things with his wife and baby?

'Believe it or not, chaps, I'll miss you all.' Caddick sounded sincere. 'And promise to be good.' He jumped onto the tailgate of his departing wagon and gave us the thumbs-up.

'Bring us some rock back,' whined Big Nige.

'I'm going to bleedin' Romford, not Canvey Island.' The truck revved its engines and lurched off out of sight.

Just before he left, Caddick informed us that Sidney Cartwright would be sitting up top. I was pleased for Sid, but he wasn't so chuffed at the proposition. 'Fucking hell, lads. That's my nuts shot off, then.' He looked distraught. 'It's lids down from now on, boys.'

It was a valid point. There were other, more dire ways of getting home leave, including being pushed on a stretcher or being stuffed into a sealed body bag like a chicken wrapped in giblets. So far, we had been lucky on both counts.

There were three farms in the immediate area and, as our troop leader succinctly put it, they needed 'some serious scrutinisation'. Disparate clusters of the enemy separated from their divisions had been observed by the Resistance; experience told us they usually comprised one tank and a dozen foot soldiers in support. Our troop, creatively named the 'Searchers' by Moxton, was to split up leaving him back at base. That, for me, was a significant result.

Our crew's task on this assignment was to visit a smallholding near the village of Erp. Getting there should be easy, with only a shallow river and narrow sandy track to navigate the three-mile trip there. Ultimately, the trail dropped down through a pine forest surrounding a small stone-built farmhouse and outbuildings. I tucked my pencil away and wedged the folded route map behind the instrument panel.

Usually we went with infantry support on deployments like this and, supposedly, the American Paras had been promised – but again there was no sign of them. We later discovered that a 'slight communication breakdown' had prevented them from appearing. Of course it had, and it didn't do much to ease tensions between their rest-ridden Airborne soldiers and us. Most of us in the RTR had been combat-active since D-Day on June 6th. No recharging of batteries for us in Blighty like the Airborne, and no chance of enjoying a warm pint of mild and bitter in the Dog and Duck either.

I smiled as I remembered learning to drink on pints of light and bitter; mild was usually a drink for older men. While my underage mates and I were in 'beerage training', the old men sat on *their* bar stools and supped on small glasses of barley wine, sickly sweet, powerful stuff that weighed in at a mighty 10.6% abv. It was a serious, hardcore drink.

Our tipple of choice was only L&B because of one crucial factor: you always got served more than a pint – you did in The Bell, anyway. First, Big Beryl the barmaid drew a generous half-pint measure of Greene King best, then she topped up our glass-handled pint pots from a bottle of pale ale, leaving plenty to spare. An important thing to note was the added thrill of a crafty look at her ample tits as they jiggled with each tug of her exaggerated pint-pulling efforts. She loved the young lads, did our voluptuous Beryl, and rumour had it that she occasionally did!

Our tankies and the infantry boys had little luck in getting home leave for R&R. All we had to look forward to in our battle groups was the persistent and unrelenting grind of one battle after another with nothing to enjoy except the biggest prize of all: survival. We tallied the human cost at the end of each day and desperately hoped our luck would stay with us.

'Fucking glory hunters,' muttered Cartwright. That was a common sentiment about the Airborne infantry, but later analysis confirmed it was probably a misguided thought considering what they had faced during Market Garden, especially at Arnhem.

So far, so good. Because of the lush tree canopy and its sniper potential, we were 'closed down' as our newly promoted commander promised. It was still early morning and we hadn't travelled far, so the heat and body-odour levels inside the tank were almost bearable.

'Please halt, driver.' The unusually polite Sid had slipped into his new commander role nicely.

I eased back the paddles. What had he seen? Scanning through my periscope, I saw a large farmhouse with a wooden barn to its left. A few hens and a pig bustled around in the dusty front yard. The front door was open. Nothing too unusual – it was a lovely day, after all – but then two piglets appeared in the doorway and were chased into the yard by an agitated cockerel.

'Where would you hide your tank if you were a Jerry?' asked Sid.

'In the barn,' Tony replied.

'Correct. And don't forget, it's "guv" now.' A few seconds passed. 'You're coming with me.'

Tony was back in the bow-gunner seat after his short sojourn, and we were four up, unusual for a British-leased Honey tank. Maybe he'd failed his driving test? The smug teacher's-pet grin vanished when the reality of Sid's order set in.

'We'll head for the back of the barn,' continued Sid. 'Wait thirty minutes and if I haven't signalled, send a big bastard in.'

'What signal, sir? Guv?' asked a flustered Morton.

'I'll wave my arms and do the fucking tango. Idiot.'

None of this was in any training manual, but with our enemy on the run, the prize was too big to worry about much now.

'HE or AP?' Big Nige asked.

'High explosive, the full Monty.' Sid paused. 'Any more questions?'

There were none from me, but I wondered whether our pea shooter could reach the barn door, let alone hurt anything behind it.

Within seconds, the guys had gone. Cartwright departed via the turret, ignoring any sniper threat, while Tony used the driver's emergency exit below decks. It was probably sensible given the amount of huffing and puffing it usually took the traditional way.

We closed our lids and waited. I kept the tank ticking over but being stationary on a track lined by tall conifer trees made me feel uncomfortable. We had all seen what could happen if enemy artillery targeted treetops. They were called 'tree bursts' when javelins of wood and shrapnel exploded downwards onto their victims. It was usually okay for us but not for the infantry boys in support underneath.

'What can you see, Nige?' I asked. It was always dim inside with our lids down, made worse by the thick tree cover.

'Not a lot. Can you see any chickens?' Our gunner was thinking about our culinary options for that night.

'Not a dicky bird, fella.'

Morton chuckled at my little joke. I fixed my eyes on one half of the barn door, which was now slowly opening. 'Nige. Barn door?'

'Got it.' I heard him sigh, and it crossed my mind that he had misunderstood Sid and might let one go.

One side of the wooden door was already open but it was impossible to see if anything sinister was hidden behind it. Then the other side began to move and Tony appeared; he was dragging the door open and the barn seemed empty.

With his gun held aloft, Sid Cartwright stepped into view, attempting to do a tap-dance routine with some Michael Jackson-esque moonwalk moves to conclude it. If only he'd known that some sixty years later something akin to these moves would become legendary. He beckoned us forward and then approached the farmhouse door, which was still open and framing its owners and a dog.

It only took us a few minutes to reach the barn, where I pulled up in a cloud of dust and waited for my next instruction. Sid motioned me to back our tank into the cover of the barn. Done easily, I closed the engine down and dismounted. The four of us looked up as two Allied bombers, supported by a couple of noisy Typhoons, chose that moment to cruise noisily overhead.

'More mess for us to clear up later,' grumbled Cartwright. 'But the good news is I think breakfast awaits!'

He gestured towards the small family gathered soberly in the wide doorway. After introducing his wife, Mrs Kuipers and their daughter Ellen, the farmer invited us in and revealed various food items tucked in different hiding places around the kitchen. Methodically, Mrs Kuipers placed them in the middle of a large pine table, leaving just enough space for seven place settings: jars of Pickles, fruit marmalades, and a strange, grey-coloured loaf of bread soon dominated the table. It was not exactly multi-grain, but flour was scarce, and what little they had was probably infused with weevils.

As always, and on cue when any food was presented, Morton's eyes lit up as she placed a small basket of brown eggs beside the log-burning stove. A pot of boiling water was burbling away on top of it.

'Can we help?' I asked.

'No. Sit relaxing, please.' The stern but friendly reply came from Mrs Kuipers, whom we now knew as Mary. She eased me gently back towards my chair.

The couple seemed genuinely pleased to see us. Through broken English, sign language and charades, they described how the 'Moffan' had recently been unwelcome house guests. They had left when the Allied presence arrived two days earlier. The shocking part of the story was that their son had been taken prisoner. The farmer and his wife were incredibly stoic about it and seemed confident he would escape and get home. We had our private thoughts and politely said nothing. The son's name was Henk. To have hope was everything in this war; that and survival dominated everyone's thoughts most of the time.

Ellen was not so forthcoming, though, and it was soon apparent why. Her closely shaved head meant just one thing: fraternisation with the enemy. Collaboration was forbidden and sleeping with a German soldier had severe consequences, especially for the locals. The punishment for such a crime, usually administered by Resistance fighters, was marked by the symbolic practice of 'head shearing'.

She bowed her head to avoid eye contact, which made the direction of our conversation awkward. We didn't know if the girl was a rape victim or whether sexual relations had been consensual. She was around our age, tall, fair-skinned and probably blonde. She smiled. 'He was not a bad man,' she said. 'He was a boy, lost just like me.'

Her parents wanted to say something but didn't, and the room went quiet.

'Collars and cuffs?' whispered the Geordie, not that quietly. He winked and leaned over me to grab some bread; it was a cringingly embarrassing moment.

'Anyone for marmalade pudding?' Good old Nige jumped in and attempted to deflect the subject away from Ellen's possible rape and the colour of her pubic hair. Desperately rummaging around in his kitbag, with a massive sigh of relief he eventually plonked a tin of pudding onto the table. Ellen smiled again as I added a can of American Spam. A feast was in the making – WW2 ration style.

The mood lightened as the afternoon wore on and the hospitality got even better when a bottle of something homemade and mind-numbingly alcoholic appeared at the end of the table. It did not have quite the same pedigree as Poteen, the illicit Irish hooch, but it was equally throat-stripping and did amazing things to our brain cells in precisely the same way.

We stayed for the day before reluctantly leaving for our laager in the late afternoon. During our farewells and fuelled by alcohol, we stupidly agreed to look for Henk. We said we would, but we avoided eye contact when they asked us to bring him back home when we found him.

From Peter Meadows' memoirs

I think this must have been sometime in late November because there was snow on the ground and it was very cold. We were near Nijmegen, and I remember being invited into a Dutch home where we shared our rations with the family (a large tin of marmalade pudding and a tin of bacon to go with their potatoes, which is about all they had). After passing through the last of the Siegfried Line, we headed for our next big adventure: crossing the Rhine in amphibious tanks. Yes, that is perfectly true and as Michael Caine would say, 'Not a lot of people know that.'

Premonition

We spent the next week or so clearing mines and sorting out other hindrances left behind by the retreating German army. We didn't face them again until we neared Blerick, a fortress on the Siegfried Line known as the West Wall, running 390 miles from Kleve on the Dutch border to Weil am Rhein in Switzerland.

Our next objective was to get over this obstruction on Germany's western edge and cross the Rhine. To achieve this would be a monumental psychological victory over the Nazis; the 'grown-ups' in their briefings truly believed it would bring the war to a swift end.

Together with the infantry, and at limited cost, we mopped things up quickly in the German-held areas of Venlo and Blerick. Then came the unexpected news: six weeks' rest and recuperation. Nailed on, guaranteed, was the promise.

'After some rest, we'll prepare for our final assault in their back garden,' said the CO in one of his upbeat pep talks.

Someren is a small town between Venlo and Eindhoven. Two things happened soon after our arrival on November 25th 1944. Firstly, we were directed to our billets, which meant proper beds for once. Following Sid's instructions, we parked in the front garden of a small house on the edge of the town. I tried to imagine what my father-in-law would say had my car been left on his immaculately manicured lawn. As I looked at the higgledy-piggledy line of military vehicles squeezed into postcard-sized gardens, I noted that several brick walls and once-neat picket fences lay crushed in our rush to grab the best digs.

Secondly: 'And boys, I have some more news.' Silence followed. 'The sergeant is back!'

This was good to hear; we liked Caddick, and Geordie Boy would be ecstatic. His temporary post as commander was going back untarnished to its rightful owner.

Driver responsibilities meant closing down engines, which took time, so I was the last inside the house and ended up with a mattress flung haphazardly onto the slatted wooden floor of the landing. It was damp and smelled of disinfectant. We were all upstairs; the owners, an old couple, occupied the ground floor and cellar, which all houses in the Netherlands seemed to have. With good behaviour, I hoped our noisy and uninvited intrusion would be accepted as time passed.

Besides Sergeant Caddick's welcome return, the next few days were remarkably uneventful. However, we did get to know Mr and Mrs Kruppe and their strict house rules: no noise, no parties and absolutely no women.

'As if?' smirked Tony.

Like most Dutch people, they were accommodating and highly appreciative of their liberators. The couple also knew that circumstances could change quickly, so they kept to themselves most of the time. 'Walls have ears': this time-worn phrase was accurate and potent because the Nazi threat was always there. Like a grim reaper, it hung over everyone we ever liberated.

'Respect, boys. Show respect. These people are the real heroes,' was Caddick's constant reminder.

It was a sobering reminder; we had guns and the might of our military, but these people had nothing. They relied on us to protect them as they watched the feuding armies dismantle their country brick by brick. In addition, there was the depressing expectation that we would be gone when it came to rebuilding their lives at the end of the war.

Dinner time was when we got to see Arend and Lotte Kruppe, and it was Big Nige's opportunity to entice us with his limited haute-cuisine repertoire. Mrs Kruppe liked him, and together they fussed over various concoctions made from our rations and her meagre pantry supplies, mostly pickles, jam and stale potatoes, to name nearly all of them. We also had the NAAFI kitchen option to supplement our mealtime choices. Located in the market square, it was a great place to meet up with the other crews though, like most, we preferred doing our own thing.

The surprises kept coming. A few days later we got an order to collect and commission our new tank, an Easy 8 Mark 4 Sherman.

'Wait till you see this beauty.' Our sergeant was triumphant about this upgrade. It seemed the same as any other M4 from the outside, except for a slightly larger 76mm main gun. The subtle difference inside was her ammunition store, now technically called 'wet stowage'. The idea behind this better-late-than-never evolution four years into the war was to improve our less-than-slight chances of survival!

'When hit—' said Caddick: there was no 'if' about this possibility '—the chemicals will save us.' Water and antifreeze sloshing around our missiles would prevent them from igniting.

Judging by the reaction, our illustrious leader's selling job impressed no one. 'Why "Easy 8" then?' asked Tony, unconvinced.

'V8 engine,' replied Caddick. Too easy, I thought!

I noticed two large drums of what looked like white paint sitting to one side of the tank and four brand-new Kentucky mops propped up alongside them.

'Your job, chaps, is to whitewash her!'

'Paint her, sarge?'

'Yes, Cartwright, all over – lady bits 'n' all.' The recent cold snap and snow showers had made it necessary to update our camouflage, so our tanks' regulation olive-green coat had to go.

God, how I hated the cold. Pop did, too, and I wondered whether the intensity of this bone-numbing weather had led to his genuine hatred of winter.

Having enjoyed the baking heat of Africa, he took every opportunity to sun worship in our dumbed-down English version of summer. Work trips to Mersea Island near Colchester were excellent opportunities for this, and often meant a lunch break sprawled out on a stripey deckchair plopped on the beach by his red Morris 1100. Sometimes I accompanied him to work, and the added attraction of a Cornish-pasty treat made these days seem like a holiday.

I would listen intently to his description of the objectives of his visits and waited excitedly for his return to the car with their outcomes. Were these the seeds that sowed my career in sales?

I also remembered that he never used any lotions or potions for skin protection. On the other hand, being fair-skinned and adolescently vain, I worked endlessly hard at 'bronzing-up' mine. In those days, a mixture of lemon juice and olive oil helped, though the result was painful. Fried, red-raw skin served me in later life with several basal cell carcinomas. Pop was literally thick-skinned; he had the hide of an elephant and never suffered any such inconvenience.

The regiment received a fleeting visit from God himself: Monty. That done, news soon filtered through that we were about to get a visit from one of his disciples, Brigadier Carver. That was bad enough but made worse because he would stay for the best part of a day. His visit signalled that something big was brewing; more worrying than that, it meant a dreaded inspection. All subsequent activity leading up to his visit on December 13th would now focus on presenting the 44th RTR as an efficient, well-ordered and ready-for-action fighting brigade.

'Gentlemen, "simply the best" is what we'll be.' These were the colonel's briefing words to the regiment.

I wanted to laugh; Tina Turner sang those exact words forty-five years later, and it became my employer's (and others, I'm sure) rousing conference theme.

After relentless scrubbing down of our bodies, kit and tanks (white ones now), everything that moved eventually gleamed, both men and machines. We completed our work in a frenzy of activity that, combined with our new tank and Pixie 'zoot' suits, left us surprisingly revitalised. Preparing for the Brigadier's visit motivated everyone and, more importantly, it made us feel human for a change.

'I'm actually looking forward to it,' dared Big Nige.

'Knob,' was our unanimous reply.

They say the Queen smells nothing but fresh paint on her official engagements; the Brigadier's fragrant memories of the 44th must have been carbolic soap, axle grease and freshly applied whitewash. Everything went off pretty much without a hitch.

He wanted to see improvement in our gunnery techniques, so we were immediately sent off to Lommel to practice. This was depressing, and confirmed our fears that we were being primed for the advance sooner than expected. Nevertheless, despite our uncertainty our gaffers seemed happy, which was important; extra supplements of liquor and cigarettes soon found their way to us before the inevitable bad news landed as it always did when things were looking up.

'I knew it,' moaned Cartwright. '*They* knew it; that's why we got a fucking audience with God and old Carve Up.'

'We're on standby, Sid, that's all it is. Just forget it,' countered Caddick as he departed for the umpteenth O-group meeting of the day.

The Ardennes Offensive started on December 16th 1944. Long in the planning and preparation, Hitler decided on a surprise German counter-offensive; his key objective was to capture the port of Antwerp, a major supply route to the Allies' front line. This came as a surprise to us – and certainly to his generals. Hitler knew we had significant aerial superiority, but his army had men and hardware in the right place. Choosing a weather window to prevent the Allies from getting airborne, he planned to strike through the Ardennes Forest. Antwerp would be his before Christmas.

The only evidence that another battle was brewing was the increased number of Allied warplanes trawling over us daily. Then the weather changed for the worse again, and what had been a motivating few weeks stopped abruptly. The build-up of troops increased; many were on Kangaroo armoured personnel carriers slowly snaking their way towards the new frontline south of us. We waited for our call to arms, which would be to tag onto this mass movement comprised mainly of American troops.

'Pack your bags, chaps. You won't need any aftershave.' Our Commander nodded towards the pristine white Yank tanks as they trundled past. What a joker.

'Wank Yank tanks,' someone said.

We didn't get that fateful call. Christmas Day came and went much like any other day, and Teddy Foster took over temporary command from the Colonel as CO on New Year's Eve, 1944.

Eventually news came through that Jerry was on the run again. Stubborn USA resistance, supported by the British XXX Corps, slowly began to turn the tables on a rampant but short-lived German offensive. As the dense cloud cover lifted, hundreds of our planes took to the air again, terminally disrupting the enemy's supply chain serving the bulging Ardennes front. Adolph's desperate plan, after some early success, lay in tatters; it was to become one of the worst strategic blunders of his war. Diminishing resources, diverted from the vastly important

Russian front, poured into his 'hole in the bucket' initiative in the West. This last-gasp, catastrophic mistake opened the door and ultimately allowed an invigorated Soviet Army to cruise into Poland and onwards.

More than one million troops fought in the Battle of the Bulge: some 500 thousand Americans, 500 thousand Germans, and 55 thousand British. Approximately 20,000 Allied troops were killed in action. Fifty thousand were wounded, and half that number went missing. On what we called the 'dark side,' around 100,000 enemy soldiers were killed, wounded or captured. Each side lost over 800 tanks and the Germans lost 1,000 aircraft. Whilst the strategic cost to Germany was a game changer, the humanitarian cost to both sides was appalling and ridiculous.

We'd had our six-week 'rest bite', and it ended in early January when we were back on the road again in our new white tank, creatively called Snowflake. The roads were frozen solid, and I saw several tanks slide into the deep ice-covered ditches. Each morning, once the sun came up, a gentle thaw allowed us to move on without too much drama, and eventually, we found ourselves in Ophoven, situated on the river Maas.

'Not just a pretty face, Meadows.' The compliment, an expression often used by our sergeant, came from above. Our drive had been the most arduous in terms of concentration so far; all of us were amazed that we hadn't joined the others who regularly skated off-piste into the frozen gulleys around us.

'You've either got it, or you haven't, boss.' I felt chuffed about this achievement. It struck me that 'pretty face' was a phrase my father often used; perhaps it had originated from this very exchange?

There was another expression Pop found amusing, and it usually came in response to my mother's occasional nagging: 'Your wish is my command, dearest.' I'd heard Caddick use it in an off-duty moment with Teddy Foster, but with the added prefix of 'my dear boy'. It made me think of Jimmy Yule again.

RHQ was ensconced in Maaseik, the main town, and our supplies echelon was three miles west of us at Neeroeteren. C Squadron's job on our front-line section was to patrol a five-mile stretch of river with us on one side and the German 7th Armoured on the other. Tipped off by the outgoing infantry, we knew that the Boche liked to be nosey and would attempt to cross over. Our task was to give them a good old-fashioned stonking or return the favour with rubber-dingy patrols to lay down mines on their side of the river.

'This is infantry work, surely?' whined Geordie Boy, who was promptly told to 'wind his neck in' by Caddick.

'They are doing their bit upriver,' he explained to pacify his loader. 'And at least we can stretch our legs a bit.'

Wearing newly-issued white overalls over our Zoot suits, our first night was grim and uncomfortable. Fresh from the arduous trek, C Squadron was ordered to dig in and stay on guard in hastily scraped slit trenches. When I was a kid, we'd had a long chest freezer in the garage and, on this particularly miserable watch, I imagined lying in it.

In front of us was the smooth, slate-grey river shrouded in a heavy January mist. Any black blobs that attempted to move across its marble sheen got a fierce blast of lead from our Browning machine guns, which had been dismantled from our tanks. They had a greater range than the hundred yards expected from our standard-issue Stens, but their tracers fell well short when called into occasional spasms of action.

After six hours, we were ordered to stand down. The brew that Nigel Morton greeted us with was by far his best of the war. We were too cold to talk much and scrambled underneath our tank into the relative warmth of our frozen bed rolls.

This routine was repeated through a snowy January as our squadron rotated with the others between Ophoven, Kinrooi and Aldeneik. Time was split between river-bank patrols, where we saw some light action, and firing range practice at Lommel, a potent reminder of things to come.

Light action typically meant snuffing out German patrols that crossed over to capture Belgian citizens for interrogation. They weren't particularly successful, so we took many prisoners. We liked to call our version of interrogation 'cross-examination interviews'; after these, the Krauts were packed off down the line and held in PoW camps, often school playgrounds and sports pitches.

If we couldn't see our enemy, we often heard them. They had a habit of singing what we thought were patriotic German folk songs late at night, but they were actually songs of hate-filled propaganda designed to dishearten us. Few of us spoke the lingo, so as their words drifted over the river these male voice choirs had a reverse effect; they actually soothed our homesickness and anxieties.

'While they're doing that, we know they're there and not here!' said our sergeant profoundly.

'Unless they sing as they paddle,' grumbled Tony.

Being British and reserved, we rarely countered their vocal efforts, but occasionally when the rum rations were plentiful we gave it a go. 'Blaydon Races' was one favourite. It struck me that this could be how the Eurovision Song Contest started; however, it was more likely that in my other life it would bring out the hooligan in us. 'You're gonna get your fuckin' head kicked in,' would probably be our eloquent football chant riposte.

On February 18th we pulled out of the Maaseik area and headed towards Tilburg, where we waited for more orders. They weren't long in coming; a few days later, the whole brigade was on the move again, this time to Kleve in Germany.

We had to push a couple of feisty Boche paratroop divisions back towards the Rhine before we could cross over the north end of the dramatic-looking Siegfried line. 'Dragon's teeth. That's what they look like,' announced Tony, pointing towards the rows of huge triangular-shaped concrete barriers running left and right as far as the eye could see.

'Giant chunks of Toblerone,' was my thought.

Bulldozers and converted Sherman tanks smashed aside mountains of shattered masonry. Now and then a pill box with its doors blasted open came into view, so we sent another rocket in to make sure.

'We are now entering the Reich's inner sanctum,' announced Caddick. He made it sound vaguely sexual.

On February 28th, in a battle 'like World War 1' as Colonel Hopkinson later described in his report, we lost our tank, and with it we lost Tony.

A loud *krummp* and a blinding white flash preceded a cloud of blisteringly hot smoke as it coughed its foulness into the driver's section to my right – Tony's side. My eardrums popped first, and then the smell of grease and forged metal was overridden by the repulsive but familiar hit of roasting human flesh. It overwhelmed me as bile coursed up my throat. Tony died quickly. The new wet stowage worked well, but the situation was hopeless. What remained of my friend began to bubble and cook in what had already become a giant barbeque beside me.

The flames on Tony's side soon grew intense and, with no time to hesitate, it was essential that we 'hauled arse, fast'. Tony would have liked that. The missile had pierced our hull at shoulder height; I'd been lucky because APs tended to fly around like crazed pinballs. It was unlucky for Tony, though, because this one must have ricocheted around the bow-gunner compartment.

Nothing followed the initial strike. In less than a minute, we were facing the ruptured side of our tank where a deceptively small entry hole made by an 88mm AP was clear. Puffs of grey smoke filtered from it making it look benign, but the flames lapping around Tony's hatch told another story.

I thought about the previous night. We had been chatting about our hopes, wishes and dreams, but the conversation was more stilted than usual. Tony had lobbed me a direct question that made me sit up. 'How do you predict it will end, Pete?'

I knew the answer but couldn't confirm something that hadn't occurred yet. Perhaps a prediction was different. 'Hitler will commit suicide and the war will end in May. How about that?'

Tony looked at me and laughed. 'Mate, if only that were true.' He had already told us about his death premonition. 'I won't be around by then.'

I remember Pop discussing comrades who experienced premonitions before a battle. I was interested because a teacher of mine once told us about African witch doctors who influenced vulnerable tribespeople about their impending demise. Ultimately brainwashed, some of these poor souls believed in the shamans' powers and died.

Jonesy was our general-studies teacher, a scruffy little man who smelled of fags and bad breath. He was clumsy in his explanation and told us that if we said the same thing to ourselves and believed it, we would succumb, too.

This worried me, and I asked Pop if it was true. The conversation was memorable as we mucked out the horses one morning; that would make me about twelve years old. Pop could see my concern and quickly dismissed it, but being as clumsy as Jonesy, he ruined things. 'Soldiers were very often correct in their death premonitions, son.'

Tony was not a philosophical man and seemed casually calm when he told us, 'Chaps, I'm going to die today.'

'My cooking's not that bad, surely, Tone?' said Nige.

Huddled around a small campfire, supping the usual brew and warming our hands at the same time, we laughed it off, but it was not good karma and the mood changed. No one said anything. I flicked half a ciggy away and lit another.

Twelve hours later, I looked back at the tank and the smoking hole left by the missile that had killed our bow gunner. Tony, our brother and cheeky Cockney geezer, was no more; our bubble of invincibility had been burst.

'Today, chaps, I'm going to die.' I thought about what he'd said as we passed through the West Wall. Then I remembered the last thing he ever said. 'Every pitstop now will give us an excuse to piss on the Krauts!'

Coming down from a high is easy; recovering from a low like that can be tricky. Pangs of doubt and self-loathing cloaked in a wrapper of guilt and despair were hard to shift. We called depression 'dark times'. Some coped by drinking too much, others popped pills; closer to home, Morton cooked, Tony wrote letters, and I thought about the future and how to get back there.

Those had been surreal moments, but were they? Like a floating entity looking down, I felt detached from everything around me. Could all this be happening? A wave of homesickness hit me. I missed my wife, friends and sons; to see them again, my sole task was survival. It was critical to keep reminding myself of that, which was precisely what Pop said to me at Amblie. But what would happen after the war? Would I have to relive my father's life again, or could I jump to where I'd left off?

Thinking of Tony again, I felt the loss but it was only superficial. I couldn't find any depth of emotion or show any genuine grief outwardly. Was it because I didn't really know the man, or because this whole mess was unreal? Questions flooded my mind, but one worried me the most: how could I be so easily de-sensitised to another man's death?

Pop could be aloof and sometimes alarmingly cold in his attitude to life events, perhaps because of traumas like this. What we were now seeing in his war together was devastating, and it caused serious mental-health issues for many veterans years after. My father never struggled in that way; like many combat soldiers, he chose to park his demons in the backwaters of his psyche.

Little help was offered; in those days there were no PTSD programmes to defrag the human brain. The MOD tentatively played around with medication but it did more harm than good and wasn't progressed much.

I wondered if de-sensitised emotions could be passed down through family genes. In corporate life (and in no way comparable to battlefield experience), dehumanising business situations were relatively straightforward to deal with. Some managers agonised but I didn't; perhaps that was genetic.

A good example would be restructuring sales organisations, which often involved redundancies. I found it easy. I told myself to be as compassionate as possible but always to remember that protecting the wider business was my prime duty. Darwinian and corporate, yes, but also valid. Foremost, as a 'people person', like my father, I could also be cold and remote, and I never lost a night's sleep in my business life. As for my thoughts about Tony, what sort of person could be like this? It frightened me more than ever.

From the regimental book *A History of the 44th RTR*

On the 18th of February, the regiment moved to Tilburg and, on the 23rd, was on the move again towards the Siegfried Line and Germany, concentrating near Goch on the border. There was much fighting in this area between the 26th of February and the 3rd of March. Captain Bill Watkins and Lieutenant John Hamilton were killed. The regiment was withdrawn to Nijmegen on 7th March to commence ten days of training on 'DD' Amphibious tanks ready to cross the Rhine.

Into Germany

On March 7th I heard those words again. This time they came from Teddy Foster introducing the crew – specifically me – to our new tank named Donald Duck 1. 'One tank is unfortunate, two tanks concerning, Meadows.' He paused. 'Three? Well, that's downright careless!' Thank God he was smiling this time.

Our new tank was different; it was a Sherman M4, but it wore a skirt, making it one of the infamous DD tanks. We had heard much about Duplex Drives from the Normandy landings, where 290 converted M4s were used in the initial invasion thrust.

'I heard most of the fuckers sank,' Cartwright said.

'No, Sid, they didn't,' corrected Caddick. Only those used by the Yanks.' He smiled broadly.

The Americans' landings on the northern beach, Omaha, had gone worse than those of the British further down the coast. Hindered by rough waters and an intensive artillery barrage from the Germans, many DDs shipped from offshore landing craft, especially those from the US 741st Tank Battalion, failed to reach the beach.

'Shame.' Our reply was quick, spontaneous and insincere. We all laughed.

This was to be the first day of an intensive ten-day training period. While the others fussed about plugging holes and waterproofing gaps with tape, it was my job to work out how to drive this weird-looking machine.

Getting to grips with a new-fangled tank was not the only introduction to our lives: Tony's replacement had arrived, and he was odd. Most tankies were on the small side and fit, like me, but he was a rotund little chap wearing his green army trousers high above his waist, almost to his chin. His name was Billy Webster.

'Good afternoon, gentlemen.' His handshake was vigorous and almost too eager as he shook our outstretched hands in turn. His hand was clammy, and I watched Nige wipe his thigh when Webster eventually let go.

All we could see of our latest tank was its tracks and a wall of canvas about eight-feet high wrapped around it. 'You must be joking,' exclaimed Webster, who snuffled up to it like a foraging sow. Pork-Belly Webster would have been a better name because he did look like a pig. 'You must be joking,' he repeated.

The rest of us looked on and said nothing; we all agreed with him.

To Sidney's obvious delight, Webster's dialect signified something else: Another Geordie was about to join the team. But there was one crucial proviso: the fat little porker had to get on board first. When he did, all sweat and very little swagger, he told us that 'butchers weren't made for climbing on tanks'. It was no surprise.

'That's not proper Geordie – he's a fuckin' Smoggy,' complained Sid when our new friend revealed that his home town was Middlesbrough.

'Smoggy?' I inquired, although I knew the answer.

'Smog Monster,' raged Sid in mock anger. 'Ask him who his team is.'

Billy Webster's chubby round face broke into a broad, goofy smile and he looked triumphant. 'Actually, it's the Magpies.'

'Really? Well fuck my old boots! We've got things to catch up on, my old fella.' With that, they wrapped their arms around each other and wandered off.

I glanced at the operating manual for the hundredth time. The mechanical workings of a DD tank were heroic, and I hoped the colossal beast slumbering in front of me would play by the rules. The page headed 'Roles and Responsibilities' made for interesting reading. Two of us would do the work: I would drive, and the commander would steer. To do this, he had to stand behind the turret and use a tiller to move two big propellers.

The others had it easy: they stood on the deck, hopefully not a burning one! But they did have a simple job of the structural kind: they acted as support struts. All they had to do was lean against the posts holding the beige-coloured sides in place and pray they stayed up and the water stayed out!

A separate drive sprocket at the tank's rear end, driven by the revolving tracks, worked the propellors. This invention was ingenious, thanks to the ultimate 'blue-sky thinkers': Percy Hobart and his friend, the engineer Nicholas Straussler.

Back to Billy. He was strange in many ways and we soon found out he was superstitious, too. His quirky behaviour inside the tank was to wear his black regimental beret back to front. No one knew why because it exposed the waxy slope of his forehead, making him look even piggier, if that was possible.

'If Jerry gets hold of him, he'll be served on a plate,' whispered Morton the first time we saw him do this.

That was true: Webster could indeed find himself on the menu. I recalled that pork knuckle and sauerkraut is a German delicacy, and I also remembered Schumacher's bar in Dusseldorf. We regularly feasted on this dish during our football trips in the noughties. It was ironic, because at that moment Dusseldorf, a city in the industrial Ruhr, had already been flattened by Lancaster bombers.

Many tankies had superstitions. I didn't think I had any until a gleeful Big Nige, now freshly educated on the subject, pointed out mine: I always squeezed into my driver's hatch, facing left and outwards. How strange of him to notice that, but I'm sure it was more a physical necessity than a superstitious act.

I soon discovered that we all had them: Morton wore his socks inside out; Sid always had a Swan Vesta match tucked into his cigarette pack, red tip up, and Caddick repeated the Lord's Prayer to himself five times a night. 'You faithless fuckers need all the help you can get,' he confessed later. 'The fifth one is for me!'

As far as I recollected, Pop never admitted to any superstitions, nor can I remember any irrational habits, though some could happily argue the latter point.

Operation Plunder was about to start. We crossed the Rhine from Xanten early on March 24th, 1945, but only after each troop had charged their mugs of morning tea with carefully measured rum shots. It was 03.30 hours, freezing and very dark.

Caddick's words were ironic: 'I have a job to do first. Then we can all get slaughtered.'

We finally mounted up at 05.15 hours, but not before a bombing barrage detonated over 1,000 tons of explosives onto Wesel, just across the river. Like skeins of geese screeching across the North Norfolk sky, two hundred Lancasters from Bomber Command completed the deed.

So far the whole pattern of my war had been RAF strikes first, followed by heavy artillery from the guns behind us. After that, it was our turn with the infantry boys. We were the cleaners; it was tidy-up time when we got the signal. Nothing was different as the 44th RTR mounted up at 06.00 hours, except it was now broad daylight and we felt exposed. The plan was for a two-squadron front to ease into the water, but we had to wait for our turn in the queue.

To get on board, we had to climb a ladder running up the outside of the inflated skirt and then drop down onto the deck beside Caddick. It didn't take long and soon we were lumbering slowly towards the banks of the Rhine to begin our crossing. A squadron went off to the right and we chugged off in the same direction as the earlier departed recce troop. Colonel Hopkinson and RHQ were to follow the others in support, while the remaining B group waited on the bank to see what transpired. We were out on our own. To add more weight to an already heavy mood, news got back to us that the recce party was in trouble as it tried to find suitable exit points.

'Just some unnecessary irritation,' was how Caddick put it. Interpreted differently, Spandau machine guns and Nebelwerfer mortars had caused severe casualties.

'But presumably, we snuffed them out?'

There was no answer. Our boss was concentrating on steering our new vessel. As we bobbed along, the gentle side-to-side rocking motion worsened his erratic control of our ship and made me feel queasy. It also dawned on me then that our new sea captain was the only person on Donald Duck 1 who could see anything.

'Concentrate Meadows. DO NOT fuck this up,' I said to myself over and over again. All I had to do in the spooky darkness was keep my revs steady and not stall the damn thing.

It was eerily dark in what was, for me, a submarine, and only a dim orange glow pulsed from two electric light bulbs hanging from the bulkhead.

Despite nature's elements and the risk of a bullet or two, I still thought that those on deck were lucky. The buggers could quickly abandon ship if necessary, and all they had to do was lean against the sides of our floating bathtub while Caddick and I did the work.

'Welcome to the Wavy Navy, Meadows.' Our captain seemed happy, which was positive. He decided to give me a running commentary on what he could see, which sounded more like a migration of wild animals crossing the Serengeti's Mara River than an invasion into Germany. Weasels, Buffalo, and even Kangaroos were just some of the names he recited, all forms of amphibious troop carriers accompanying us on our unorthodox trip across the river.

'So far, so good, Meadows,' Caddick said.

Then, like a kiss of death, the enemy aerial barrage began. The only good thing about my predicament was that I couldn't see it; instead I got the throb of heavy shelling as it vibrated through our hull, and then the *krrrumph* of missiles as they torpedoed into the water like lunatic gannets. This commotion made Donald rock violently, bringing with it other aquatic problems. We would sink if we took on too much water, and a tear in our flimsy makeshift hull meant *curtains* – pardon the pun!

I felt the tank lurch suddenly to the right, and our course changed dramatically. Had we been hit? 'Boss. You okay?' I asked. There was no immediate answer.

Then Caddick said, 'Keep your foot down, Meadows; we're getting the fuck out of here.' We were told our proposed exit ramp on the other side was no longer functional, so our revised orders were to follow B Squadron, who were on the water now and trailing RHQ and A group.

'The new course *should* put us out of range,' was how he confirmed our new circumstances.

I didn't want to spoil his convivial mood by mentioning the minor fact that the Rhine was introducing itself via a so-called watertight, waterproofed escape hatch on my right.

Another explosion, very close this time, made us buck violently. A few cooking utensils and items of crew paraphernalia slid onto the deck with a splash. 'Calvados – please not the Calvados.' Forget the AP missile surfing around my feet; saving our hooch was the only worry.

Unaware of the fracas below, our jubilant, Rhine-faring captain then declared, 'So, we are tail-end Charlies. That suits me fine.'

Things soon quietened, but what was quickly becoming a paddling pool was becoming a concern. Just as I started to plan my evacuation and to worry that my sergeant hadn't given the order, I felt us beach smoothly onto something soft and giving. 'Already? Are we nearly there, boss?'

'We are, son. Give it some welly when I say.'

It seemed to take hours to cross four hundred yards of water, but it took just forty minutes, slowed by our tacking and jiving. Any longer, and the Rhine levels inside the tank might have impacted our floating ability more negatively.

The river bank was made up of soft bog and clay, and I felt the tank slide and skew to the side as Caddick bossily guided me shoreside. Donald behaved brilliantly, and after a bit of straining we extracted ourselves and made our way over a carpet of logs towards the tank concentration area. We heard through the radio that the mud later trapped several tanks permanently.

'Bad luck, boys,' jeered Caddick as we ground our way past them.

'Careless,' was my smug contribution. But some had been hit. 'Sad,' I said. How fickle was that?

Once stationary, the canvas skirts quickly collapsed down the sides of the tank, freeing us for land duties again. 'I knew a girl who dropped her drawers that easy.' It was more Tony Auden than a comment our sergeant would typically use, but it lifted my mood. We were safe – for now.

Simultaneously with our crossing, Operation Varsity kicked in when thousands of Paras dropped behind enemy lines. There were two parachute divisions in this advance: the 17th US Airborne, which came from bases in France, and the 6th British Airborne, which had come from England. The mayhem they caused was significant and, unlike Market Garden, Varsity was a victory. It came at a cost, though – it always did. Enemy flak guns downed more than one hundred Allied aircraft, and thousands of our ground troops were killed and maimed.

'Final statistics didn't reveal the true picture,' Pop once told me. I think he meant the genuine casualty numbers could never be measured, including the many who suffered life-changing injuries and psychiatric damage. But the doors to victory had been kicked open; Allied troops could swan onto enemy turf and finally conclude this godforsaken war. At least, that was the plan.

'The end is nigh.' Teddy Foster believed it, too and said so in his debriefing. It was a great message to hear, but the grown-ups wanted to play it down. Any complacency or cavalier approach now would be madness; equally, no one wanted to put their life at risk so late in the day. This worried the powers-that-be. Despite the overwhelming certainty of victory, everyone had to remain engaged and positive; consequently, our regiment was expected to continue as a dynamic fighting force until the end. There was still a job to be done.

'If a job is worth doing, it's worth doing well,' was another well-used Pop expression in my stroppy youth, one possibly borrowed from his squadron commander at the time.

Mac Beanland, the farmer with the thick arms and my first boss, also used this expression out of frustration. Ricky and I once got caught red-handed clearing – or possibly not – a field invaded by wild oats. The pesky weeds grew taller than the crop, making them easy to see. We were to navigate the wheat field carefully and systematically pull them out. Once gathered, we had to squash them into empty pig-feed bags stacked on a flatbed trailer on the edge of the field.

This was an ominous prospect because there were thousands of weeds. The first part of the task was easy: all we had to do was tug them out of the soft soil and we didn't even have to bend down to do that! But the next part of the process was the hard bit, which we didn't like much: you had to fold the oats in half and stuff them into a bag.

'It's important you get them sacks first,' Mac Beanland nodded towards the trailer, 'then fill 'em and drag them back.'

Richard and I looked at each other. Our boss was very serious during his briefing and, sensing our lethargy at the prospect, he continued, 'I don't want another crop of weeds next year.'

We nodded and looked at the empty trailer taunting us from the side of the field.

'When that's loaded, I'll take the bags away for a burn-up later.' That bit sounded like fun, but it would take us years to fill the damn things. That was not good, so once we got going, we pulled up a few and left most behind, trampling their seeds into the ground as we went.

Now and then our toil deserved a break; more accurately, our breaks were occasionally interrupted by exertion. When this happened, we sat down in our little corn circle hidden from the inconveniences of the outside world and discussed important matters like bicycles and football.

It was not as secluded as we'd thought because Mac took it upon himself to disrupt one of our sojourns. To paraphrase what he said without using Anglo-Saxon: 'he was not happy; in fact, he was very disappointed in us.' In addition to the 'if a job is worth doing' mantra, he shook his head and said, 'One boy is a boy, two boys are half a boy, and three boys are no boys at all.' It was profound when you think about it, and I will never forget it.

I blamed my friend for this state of affairs because I loved everything about the farm before he arrived on the scene. Scraping pig muck off the walls, driving tractors and even plucking turkeys for Christmas were great fun. But I, perhaps naively, worked for the enjoyment of the job and Ricky wanted wages. Mac Beanland shook his head again and muttered something to himself.

Feeling embarrassed at my adolescent shirking, I picked up an empty sack and returned to the field. Ricky, who had attitude, slouched off towards his bike and peddled off into the sunset. He never returned to the farm, though I did every weekend when the jobs got better – and so did the pay. Those were the happiest days of my life.

At around 10:00 hours, we met up with the 7th Cameronian infantry and headed for Mehr. Each tank in C Squadron, now devoid of canvas skirts, carried about ten infantrymen on its deck. Our job was to seek out and destroy everything German and anything that tried to block our way.

We had new energy and zeal, but something numbed me: I had to drive over bodies, both alive and dead. I also went through houses that we suspected hid the enemy. We often had it wrong, but this was war and I followed orders.

The Krauts were more stubborn now they were on home turf, and the civilians, unlike other Europeans we had liberated, hated us. We understood why: to these people we were invaders. But it became evident that the retreating German Army was not that kind to its own either; homes were looted and, more disturbingly for me, horses were deliberately blinded, making them useless for anything but being eaten.

Soon we found ourselves dispatching groups of prisoners towards hastily built holding cages on the banks of the Rhine. To describe them as defeated and discouraged would be an understatement, except for what was left of the SS and the highly charged and motivated Hitler Youth groups. They were still full of fight, and both groups made things exceptionally difficult during our final swan through Germany.

'Look at that little fucker,' Caddick muttered.

As we trundled alongside a row of tiny, terraced houses, a young boy – no more than ten – ran towards the tank in front of me. There was no blemish on these neat dwellings; they were untouched by this war, and the boy looked like any innocent child from any peacetime community.

Everything happened quickly. He held out a hand and made to throw a piece of what looked like bread towards the tank commander staring down at him. In the next second, his little body lay in a carrier-bag-sized bundle of blood-matted shreds, gunned down by the tank's bow gunner. The driver didn't stop, and the boy's kind offer of food lying next to his remains erupted in a blue flash of smoke, dirt and bones. Too young to be a member of the Hitler Youth, this lad had already been indoctrinated into their ranks. I wondered if his trick of lobbing grenades into tank turrets often worked.

'Little fucker,' muttered Caddick again. We looked on in despair.

There were other tricks that the SS liked, and a favoured one brewed-up two of our regiment's tanks soon after the Rhine crossing. Surrendering with a white flag aloft and hands held high, a group of PoW wannabes approached one of our M4 troops. Confident that an Allied tank or soldier would not gun them down, the bedraggled group reached an agreed point and then dropped to the ground. Hidden out of sight at 1100 yards, an infamous Jagdtiger tank destroyer did what it said on the label. It fired over the prostrate group of Germans and two lumps of flimsy Allied tin were promptly dispatched.

Our successful crossing of the Rhine led to several glowing citations; the 44th RTR had once again rightfully earned a place in military history. Not for the first time the BBC got it wrong in their reports about Operation Plunder, which annoyed my father. In his view, they did the same with the 'African situation' later in his life. After our mission's success, and with all routes open for our soldiers and armour to flood into Germany, it was difficult to hear on the radio that the 4th and 5th Royal Tank Regiments had led the way across the Rhine and taken the glory.

But we had to put vanity to one side as we swung across Germany towards our final destination, Hamburg.

Letter from Comd 12 Corps to Comd Armed Brigade Received from Comd 4-Armed Brigade

Now, we are well beyond the RHINE; I would like to congratulate you and all those under your command on the way in which you carried through the extremely difficult operation of crossing the RHINE. In particular, I would like to congratulate the 44th RTR on my behalf. There is not the least doubt that the presence of DD tanks on the far bank so early in the proceedings did, in my mind, materially contribute to the enemy's break-up on the line of the RHINE.

The above speaks for itself. I should like to add my own congratulations on your regiment's performance in the RHINE crossing, in the training before it and in all the operations since. Well done, indeed.

Apart from the BBC's and other press correspondence inaccuracies, the regiment's overwhelming feeling was pride in having done its job well. Major General Sir Percy Hobart felt the same in a letter he later published for all ranks.

I think 44 RTR deserve the highest praise. I was delighted with the keenness and efficiency with which they set about work on the specials. It is a great achievement to have mastered the equipment sufficiently in ten days to carry out what was almost an assault crossing thereafter. Only a very good unit could have done it.

From Peter Meadows' memoirs

These tanks were known as DD tanks and had been used successfully for the amphibious landing on D-Day, although not by us. They looked like mobile hip baths. Then followed a furious period of training. There was also the question of entry and exit from the Rhine. These tanks were basically the same, with a large inflatable skirt, extended exhaust above the turret, a propellor attached to the engine drive shaft and other refinements. The crossing was at XANTEN at about 4am at first light. Later on, we heard that, according to the BBC news and press, another tank regiment had crossed the Rhine first by a pontoon bridge. The following citation speaks for us all.

Commanding officer 44th RTR, Colonel Hopkinson

First across the RHINE is our Battle Honour and let no one dispute it. You have responded magnificently to all demands made on you, however adverse the circumstances, and I feel sure that during the past three weeks, the Regiment has very greatly contributed to the final crack-up of Germany.

Claus, Stranger and
the Slave Man

Back in a 'Honey', we trundled towards another farm and another recce mission on the day it decided to thaw. We were back in the recce troop attached to C Squadron, so everything was familiar apart from our new tank. And we were minus Billy Webster; his secondment to us had been brief. He now found himself attached to the catering supplies echelon for chilled food and meats. You couldn't make it up.

Grousers had been fitted to the outer track rims, and they strained and spun manically in the oozing black mud. It stank, and now and then, the secrets of past life offered themselves up to us, sometimes human, sometimes beast, and always rotten. We didn't look too closely. But grousers apparently made a wider track and gave us better weight displacement. That's what the engineers said.

'Handy to have as much grip as possible.' Caddick quickly endorsed this invention, trying to prove he knew something about it.

I really couldn't tell the difference. 'Apparently so, sir,' I replied.

'A good driver, Meadows, will make the most of his tools.' Of course, he would.

Our engines didn't enjoy the endless quagmire either; ours screamed at my boot-heavy treatment.

It was on this day that I met Claus Leuthold. We had already been introduced by three letters found at the back of my father's desk drawer during the customary clear-out following his passing. Written in perfect English, I subliminally knew they would be of interest later and had tucked them into the 'to keep' box in the corner of his office. There was little else in it.

It wasn't until I retrieved them for my project a few years later that I realised their importance, not just from a socio-historical viewpoint but also because they revealed a snapshot of a family in flight, this time from the Russian army in 1939. It was also about a mysterious friend of whom Pop had never spoken.

Cambridge, Mass, August 11, 1959

Dear Mr Peter Meadows

No doubt you will be surprised to receive this letter, so all of a sudden! Permit me, therefore, to bring back a few personal recollections that date back to the spring of 1945. At that time, one afternoon, you were among our liberators with your armoured car rolling through the Holstein countryside. It was then when I happened to run into you, my family being refugees from the former free state of Danzig. How happy we were to welcome you into our then so very modest 'residence' on a small farm! Since my mother is of English descent, I probably shared a great curiosity into you, our first 'natural' contact after that dreadful war and the hazards of living under the despised Nazi rulers.

Well, you agreed to stay with us that day, sharing your rations with us. As a token symbol, you asked for my horsewhip, which I still possessed since my happier days.

In the meantime, you have undoubtedly established your own successful career field. Myself, I graduated from Cologne, spent two years with the BAOR[1], five years with the US Army and am now a graduate of Harvard University.

Recently, I happened to discover your address which you gave to me before you left. As I am going to London next week to visit a young friend of mine (from Harvard), I thought it perhaps a good idea to call on you too and say hello.

I am not quite sure just how far you are from London, but if you can arrange it, I should like you to very much contact: Mr

---

[1] The British Army of the Rhine was an occupation force set up in Germany following the two world wars. Germany was divided into zones and split between the British, United States and Soviets. As the potential threat of Soviet invasion into West Germany increased, the BAOR became more responsible for the defence of West Germany than for its occupation.

Raymond Dish, 2, Hurst Road, East Molesey, Surrey.
(Telephone: Molesey 3874)
My plane should arrive on or about August 21; I plan to stay
for about three days before leaving for Munich and Paris. So, if
you do feel like coming to London for this purpose, I would very
much be pleased to meet you again.
Until then and with best wishes.
Claus Leuthold

I had a secret: it was the knowledge that our journey was to
end in Hamburg with the end of the war in Europe. This weighed
heavily; with no time for complacency from anyone, especially
me, I knew this nightmare had to end quickly.

'Don't fuck it now,' I muttered. Sometimes, the
communications mic was left open.

'Don't beat yourself up, son. Your driving is pretty good
today,' Caddick said. If only he'd known.

Apart from our detour to the farm where I met Claus, the rest
of our trip was a risky and arduous slog. Although rapid in the
grand scheme of things, the amount of ground covered by the
British Second Army still took us the whole of April to complete.
The main difference between this jaunt and our previous swans
was that we weren't chasing the mass of a German army in
retreat: most of them were actually behind us. Instead we faced a
small hardcore group of SS fanatics who just hadn't read the
script.

'Boche nutters.'

'Succinctly put, sarge.'

'All they want to do is fight.'

This was true, and to the death. Although an overused and
clichéd statement, it was undoubtedly the truth in WW2; nothing
could make them surrender. We lost a few tanks to mortars and
88s, but the overwhelming numbers of our infantry and heavy
armour meant that in most cases, we crushed their resistance—
sometimes quite literally.

'Oopsy, Daisy Meadows. I thought I heard him pop!' That
was a favourite line from Caddick's macabre joke-book. In truth,
it meant nothing to me; switched onto autopilot, I just wanted to
get to Hamburg alive.

269

When we weren't involved in skirmishes with fanatical groups of officer cadets, most of our time in the recce troop was spent finding travel shortcuts, avoiding roadblocks and clearing away land mines.

Our collection of PoWs grew by the day. Once processed, disarmed and plied with cigarettes, we sent them back down the line to British or Canadian holding camps.

If a bridge on our route had been blown, we called on an invention new to us: scissors bridges. These strange tank conversions unfolded a bridge before them; however, they had a shortfall, literally. If the river crossing was too broad, they became redundant, meaning the Royal Engineers swooped in like superheroes to build us floating pontoons instead. This was irritating because it took time and we were a regiment in a hurry.

The more sinister Crocodile, usually a flame-throwing Churchill tank, reintroduced itself. They could exhale flame over two hundred yards, and we'd last seen these monsters in France. The fuel used to ignite their evil breath was towed behind in a nine-ton, 400-gallon armoured trailer. And what a target they were; the light show was impressive, whether hit by an enemy missile or occasionally by friendly fire.

Bremen was the first significant city we reached during our German stampede, and it was our gateway to Hamburg. The town had been divided into operational sectors, each with a code name. Our sector was 'Marrow', and the job of the tank regiment was to systematically 'reduce' each one in an agreed sequence. As usual, the RAF had prepared things well; all that was left as we trundled forward was a compacted landscape of smoking desolation. Not a tree or living thing came into view, just a familiar smoking vista of unadulterated destruction festering around us.

It was April 26th, a warm day perpetuated by the usual death, dust and grime. We were ahead of schedule and took the opportunity to park up for a rest. About two hundred yards from the entrance of the central railway station, surprisingly undamaged by the bombing, a gang of about twenty men suddenly appeared. Oblivious to us, they made their way towards us. They seemed agitated and their conversation was animated;

to our uneducated ears, it sounded Russian. Something much more important than a British M4 had caused this.

A gangly, blond-haired youth was stumbling ahead of them. He was no more than twenty and almost naked apart from his boots and ripped military trousers.

'Stay as you are, chaps,' Caddick ordered. 'These look like slave workers from the eastern front.' It was a confident and knowledgeable observation; He knew everything.

We 'hatched up', and I watched intently as the group eventually came to a shuffling halt about ten yards from us. The gabble of conversation stopped as the men slowly tightened their circle around the boy, who could barely stand upright. He swayed sideways and muttered something in desperation; it was unintelligible but German. Then he dropped to his knees.

'This should be interesting. He's SS, and he's pleading for his life.' Caddick was also good at painting the picture and filling in the gaps.

I noticed that towards the back of the ring stood a stocky man carefully binding white bandages around his hands. This was not for medicinal purposes. He flexed his hands several times and stepped into the circle to face the young man. My other observation was the short wooden cudgel gripped in his right hand.

'This can't be right, sir.'

'Shut it, Meadows. Not now.'

The first strike, a short, sharp punch, felled the boy immediately. He rolled onto his back, clutching his face, a mistake that pre-empted his assailant's next move. The man jumped astride him and instigated a heavy bombardment of bludgeoning, left-right strikes to his victim's unprotected head.

They did not stop. Left, right club, left, right club, and on it went. I couldn't see – didn't want to see – but I could hear the metronomic roars of vitriolic approval as the German boy's screams synchronised in time with each crushing blow.

'Sir, we have to stop this!' There was no response. Was Caddick considering my request?

Then it came. 'No, son. Our orders are to seek out and destroy, just that.' Through the microphone, I could hear the tell-tale pup-

pup puffing sound of his pipe being lit. 'He is SS, and they're doing the job for us!'

'But it's a lynch mob, sir.'

'No, it's not. There's a back story here.'

Retribution: what else could rationalise such drastic action? But I knew this was naïve; the war was justification enough.

The beating stopped, and with it the pleading man's screams. When the pack parted, they were silent. There was no celebration, just a sombre acceptance that a man had been beaten to death. Apart from one foot twisted a complete turn, the bottom half of his body was still identifiable as belonging to a man. Above shoulder height, it was a different story: what was once a head looked like a crimson purée.

The 'slave men' didn't look back as they strolled towards the railway station. Stocky Man led the way and, as he did so he unravelled the blood-soaked bandages from his fists. They trailed like red and white ribbons on the ground behind him.

'Complete arsehole. We should shoot the fucker,' I said.

'You don't know the story, son.'

I still wanted to shoot him. I looked down at the boy. Enough to fill a metal bucket, a quantity of red, pesto-textured gunk splattered the ground around where his head should have been. Pulverised into a pulp and mushed into the ground, only a jackhammer should have been able to do this work.

'Do you think it was something he said?' Sid's attempt at humour wasn't funny, but we still laughed.

And then something strange happened. Throughout the war, until that moment, I had controlled my physical actions, albeit locked inside my father's shell, but now an outside force took hold of me. 'Oy, you! Come here and have a go.'

Without any effort, my body hoisted itself from the driver's seat onto the front deck. Caddick bent double and almost fell out of his turret in an attempt to stop me. 'Meadows. Don't you FUCKING dare!'

I ignored him and landed beside the tank where the boy's distorted body lay. He had been joined by an old silver-haired woman wrapped in a black shroud. She bustled around on a well-rehearsed mission and promptly disappeared after removing a signet ring from the man's broken fingers. A few more civilians surfaced from the cellars hidden beneath their trashed homes and picked their way through the rubble oblivious to us. It reminded me of a zombie movie.

'I said, "Come here and have a go".' My efforts to regain self-control were useless as the rage inside me intensified.

The man stopped and then turned around wearily to face me. Kerching. Result.

'Either get your raggedy arse over here, or I'm coming to you.'

It was my voice, but they were not my words. He probably didn't understand me, but he saw a British Tommy having some sort of meltdown in front of him. The man's comrades shifted uneasily and looked to their leader for his response.

'Meadows, this is an order,' Caddick growled. 'Get back into the fucking tank – now!'

I didn't reply. There would be consequences but I wasn't controlling this; was my old man?

Stocky Man made his decision and slowly made his way towards me. All I felt was anger; more importantly, his reaction didn't frighten me. An adrenalin-fuelled, pre-conflict battle rush numbed me as an immense power surge coursed through my body.

The man was at least fifty, much older than me. And he was fit. Although I sensed a reluctance, he walked confidently and stopped two yards short of me while his comrades remained where they were.

Eye contact was essential and ours were locked on. This man did not want to fight, not because he was scared but because he had done his job. The English soldier facing him was a mere irritation. I should have been relieved but I couldn't accept the injustice.

'Leave it alone, Peter,' Caddick said.

An internal alarm rang loudly. 'Big man, eh?' I sneered.

He said nothing but his gaze remained fixed on mine. Holding up his left palm, he gestured towards his back pocket with his other hand. I nodded. His black-leather wallet contained several scraps of notepaper; hidden amongst them was a small black-and-white photograph, which he passed over carefully. It was shiny with serrated edges; in it, a pretty young woman held two babies, one propped under each arm, twins, I assumed. He put two fingers to his forehead with his thumb cocked then pointed with his other hand towards the twisted corpse at our feet. She was beautiful; she was happy, and now she was evidently dead.

Perhaps the boy wasn't guilty, but he'd had to pay the ultimate price for another man's deed on the eastern front. I wanted to believe this. I looked back at the face of a broken man whose stare was now on the photograph in my hand.

Then I noticed the betrayal: a slight twitch in his right eye.

Fighting was pointless. I made the first move and stepped back, bowing my head. That was risky because losing eye contact meant his feet were now my check and balance. Thankfully, they remained still. The next thing that seemed vaguely appropriate was to salute the man. These were conscious choices; the power controlling me had gone.

He studied me for a second, went to shake my hand then changed his mind at the last moment. Nodding instead, he turned and walked away. It was over.

'And he who casts the first stone,' scrambled through my brain. How many men had I killed; how many had I driven over, knowing they were probably still alive?

Up in the turret, Caddick was steaming and the other two seemed to be in a state of shock. 'He was a fucking Nazi, Meadows.'

'I know, sir, but he didn't have a chance.'

That was it. There were no recriminations and Caddick let it go. He knew we were at the end of our war.

We arrived in Hamburg on ceasefire day, and a couple of days later, Victory in Europe was announced. With it came the official end of the war in Europe. It was May 8th 1945.

In the days of anticipation leading up to it, I knew what was coming but could not say anything.

'Boys, it's nearly over,' Caddick informed us.

'Really?' That was all I could say.

There were few celebrations and a numb acceptance of the end. We loosened up after a bottle of rum or two, and everything became a haze of adrenalin-stimulated partying. Many years later, they used to say that if you could remember the 1960s, you weren't there. Well, the same applied to our early days in

Hamburg. I doubt anybody remembered anything following VE Day. We certainly made our mark there. 'And let no one dispute it,' to quote the Colonel again.

Germany was soon split into zones, with the British responsible for Hamburg and Dusseldorf. Canada, the USA and Russia had the rest between them. We were based in Rantzau. After some training, I got my stripe back and was promoted to the rank of lance corporal.

My new job was as a gun mechanic. I was also asked to set up a riding school when Colonel Hopkinson collared me on a hot day in June. All swirling black cloak and tapping swag stick, he made me a proposition that I could not refuse. 'You are the trooper on the horse?' A statement of fact or question? I was unsure.

'Yes, sir. I remember it well, sir.'

He nodded wryly. 'I want you to set up a riding school.' He smoothed down each side of his moustache. 'To keep the men active and out of trouble, you understand.'

And so began my next project, one that I loved. He gave me the use of a Jeep and a private to drive it, and off we both went to take half-a-dozen horses from nearby farms.

'To be returned at a later date, of course!' Hopkinson said.

The Meadows School of Riding commenced operation two weeks later on July 1, 1945. To use a mixed metaphor, I was like a pig in shit – except this was horse shit. I loved their smell, even their dung, and the *clippety-clop* of newly shooed horses soothes me to this day.

One morning a new friend appeared as Big Nige and I were returning to our billet. All waggy tail, wet, black nose and bounding energy, he chose me of all people to latch onto. Pop's favourite animals were dogs and horses and they sensed this, just like the mutt that was nuzzling my crotch. Bored with that, he bounced up and grabbed the end of my scarf in his teeth. The dog was a male: I knew this to be a fact when he ran to a low brick wall, dragging my scarf between his legs and displaying a set of tight, hairy bollocks.

He stopped suddenly to look back my way, and I could swear he winked at me. Once he had my attention, a hind leg went up, and he peed generously over my scarf and the corner of the wall.

'Bet you wish you could do that,' laughed Morton. 'What are you going to call him?'

At first sight, the mutt looked healthy and seemed in good condition, but there was no collar or name tag to identify him. 'Stranger,' I replied.

I liked dogs, but in the aftermath of COVID and the fanatical obsession of the entire British population to 'own one', this loving feeling had been seriously tested.

From old photographs and Pop stories, I knew that Stranger became an inseparable part of his life in post-war Hamburg. I couldn't work out what breed he was; yellow in colour, with short hair, he looked more like a punk dingo than a dog.

It made me think of our once great nation, now attired in waxed overcoats and red-tartan waistcoats – and that was just the dogs. Brands such as Labradoodle-Poodle-Noodles and Cocker-Snitzy-Pitzy-Poos are paraded alongside matching dressed owners who dote on them like children. Ridiculous – and how deep must their pockets be? These spoilt creatures cost an arm and a leg to buy and maintain as they scoff a menu of fine-dining delights into their coiffured hairy guts. And how many are there? In my other life, as they gasp, fart and shit their way through the streets and once-glorious countryside of Great Britain, there seems to be a pandemic of them of Spanish flu proportions.

'You want to call him Psycho, Meadows.'

We watched as Stranger did what lots of male dogs like to do. He aggressively raked the ground behind him, each paw scratching backwards in a choreographed movement. That done, he dragged my urine-infused scarf towards the wall and attempted to hump it. 'Jesus, Stranger,' I said. 'Give it a rest.'

'Scarf abuser,' chuckled Big Nige.

Confirmation of the growing number of canines is evidenced by those little black plastic bags you now see festooned on our trees and bushes like Christmas-tree decorations. I wonder what goes through the minds of the morons who hang them there? 'I'll leave it here for now to collect later.' Or maybe, 'Doesn't this lovely poo bag look great amongst this gorgeous apple blossom?'

Selfish, elitist bastards. So much more can be said about the things that irritate the dog-less minority like me. Their leads, for example. They used to be two feet long and made of leather; now, they are stretchy, plastic things that can extend the length of a football pitch. If they don't garrotte you, they trip you up into – guess what? A steaming pile of dog shite.

Finally, my pet hate: pubs. To be clear, I love pubs but they all welcome these pests with open arms and jars of dog biscuits are where the pickled eggs used to be. If you don't tread in the obligatory water bowl, you'll eventually trip over them as you dare go near the bar to get served.

'Excuse me, please.' A reasonable request, I thought, but there was a startled look of entitlement on the red face of the fat man flobbed out on the straining legs of the bar stool in front of me. After an exasperated and elongated sigh, he attempted to drag an even more obese lump of furry blubber away from the hostelry doorway.

'Thank you SO much,' I said sarcastically. He nodded and took a deep, wheezy breath from the overexertion of lifting his pint. I looked around for the nearest defibrillator.

'If I was Dick *Fosbury*, I might have *flopped* over him,' I thought that comment was clever and congratulated myself. It was, of course, wasted on the prick in front of me; it did cross my mind that the dog might understand better.

'It's not Christmas, is it?'

It took me a second. I thought Fat Man was being philosophical. 'No, that's Bing "Frosby".'

When I was a kid, dogs were pets and there was a rightful place for them at the bottom of the family pecking order. And it was easy because there were only two sorts to choose from: Alsatians, 'dangerous' dogs often owned by the macho, numbskull types, and Labradors, docile hounds for the rest of us in the more benign owners' camp. Oh, and lest we forget, there were Poodles; apart from old ladies, anyone seen with this permed excuse for a dog was either a poser or queer.

Prince was the last dog we owned, and he was a mongrel. Today, he would be frowned upon due to the rampant sexual exploits of his Alsatian, Husky and Labrador descendants. That said, perhaps the modern craze for blending breed types started then.

Talking of sexual encounters, I had managed to avoid such possibilities and the subsequent feeling of betrayal that would no doubt follow. It was the psychological bromide that helped to dampen any such desire within, which was weird given that I was now my father and knew what would happen.

Since being stationed in Hamburg, the boys had certainly enjoyed the city's delights – and there were lots to enjoy. It wasn't just the men who had some catching up to do; the women had been experiencing a dry spell too, so to speak, including Sergeant Sarah Miles.

It was early February 1946 and the 44th RTR was disbanded, which meant a transfer to the 1st RTR, also part of the Desert Rats. We had been in Hamburg as an occupying force for nearly a year when I entered a NAAFI store early one morning. 'Little Pete? How can I help you today?'

The voice came from a pretty woman wearing bright-red lipstick with her dark hair tied tightly in a bun on top of her head. I had never seen her before, and she was lovely. I looked over my left shoulder and then my right, and realised the question was directed at me.

The three stripes on her arm quickly indicated that a proper response would be required. 'Sergeant.' I saluted. 'Little Pete?' I queried. She already irritated me.

'I've been watching you.'

'Have you indeed?'

Her accent came from across the Scottish border; it wasn't rasping Glaswegian, so it was probably from the other place. I asked her.

'Correct, little Pete, I am impressed.' An awkward moment followed.

'Are you hitting on me, ma'am?' It was a brave call, but she was pissing me off. Pop was indeed vertically challenged and, yes, she was taller than me, which was not difficult, but I felt her cheeky jibe was out of order.

'Stop being precious,' I told myself. 'Are you married?' I asked her. Go for it, son.

'Are you?' she replied.

And so, the table-tennis chat batted on. It was to be the conduit to an affair that lasted most of the following summer. While I ran my riding school she worked in the NAAFI, and all our spare time was spent with Stranger.

During a deep and meaningful conversation one day, I asked her what she liked about me.

'Well,' she said after taking some time to consider this, 'you are a charming man with good manners.'

Nice to hear, but it was not the romantic response I'd expected. 'Short, dark and handsome' was not forthcoming.

It was true, though; Pop was old school regarding manners, the first to open doors for ladies, and our car door always got the same treatment for my mother. Even in their later years, the finer courtesies stayed with him. As they held hands, probably to hold each other up by then, he insisted that Mum remain on the inside track of any path they attempted to navigate.

I guess you could also call this good etiquette, and it reminded me of Mrs Benn, who taught this subject to our group of unruly catering students in the mid-1970s. Honestly, most of us couldn't even spell the word, let alone understand what it meant. The reason for introducing this strange session to our hotel and catering management course was, she said, 'to teach you how to behave properly in fine-dining restaurants and hotel establishments.'

Being mature in years, she was a frightening cross between Margeret Thatcher and Mary Berry, the celebrity chef. Mrs Benn took absolutely no prisoners. Anyone who sat incorrectly or didn't focus intently on her lectures got the infamous side-on, one-eyed stare.

'Deportment is everything,' she would say. 'Ladies? Straight backs with hands on laps. And don't forget the knees. Keep them together, please.' We all laughed at this, especially the boys.

'And gentlemen, legs together, too. You are not at a rodeo.'

'Are you allowed to cross them, miss?' asked Bridget, a large girl with legs like tree trunks. I thought of Kenny Everett's character Cupid Stunt and his manic TV sketches of the eighties.

Again, we all laughed. After all, coming from her the question was about an impossibility. Bridget fidgeted in embarrassment and squeezed her chubby knees together tightly.

'Imagine them around your neck,' mumbled someone from the back.

'What's the proper drink to have in a restaurant, miss?' came a question from Nigel, supposedly the intelligent one in the group.

'Good question, young man.' Mrs Benn approved this smart-arse question from our group's mature student and elder statesman.

He quickly shrank back in his chair, regretting his promotion to class pet. 'Thank you, miss,' he mumbled, staring at the floor. That sycophantic acknowledgement didn't help his cause much, either.

'The correct beverage to consume at the dinner table is a small glass of wine.' She pondered for effect. 'Or even something non-alcoholic!'

'That means no Tetley's, then,' offered Janet, a voluptuous girl with big blue eyes who enjoyed a pint and occasionally more with the college rugby team.

'Unless you mean *tea*,' countered Mrs Benn, her left eye slowly turning towards the wider group. 'Then absolutely not. A glass of beer is for gentlemen and should ONLY be consumed in public houses.' The eye was entirely side-on now, and there was a sneering disdain when she got to the latter part of that sentence.

And then came Laura. All the lads fancied Laura, who was tall, willowy and beautiful. Her long, black, curly hair just touched the top of her perfectly formed backside. She was far too good for us, and she knew it. Her unapproachability was sheer torment, made worse because she had a dickhead of a boyfriend who drove a flash car. He was intelligent, good-looking, and one year ahead of us on the same OND course. With those big, brown 'cow eyes', as Nigel called them, Laura asked the second sensible question of the day. 'What should a woman wear for an important job interview, miss?'

'Huh, as little as possible,' muttered Ian to my left.

Mrs Benn's reply was boringly predictable: it went along the lines of being smart but not too revealing. She pointed towards her own once ample and well-covered cleavage. 'And definitely no red lipstick.'

What? Surely that was mandatory. I thought of the *Mayfair* soft-porn mags stuffed under my mattress, the ones we swapped like collectors' items.

Then came the last question from 'sensible Deborah', a quiet, conservative girl who lived in Colchester with her elderly parents. It was dynamite and blew the lid off proceedings for that particular lecture. 'Is sleeping with a boy on your first date okay?'

A stunned silence followed, except for the sound of shattered jaw bones being scraped off the floor. All eyes were on Mrs Benn, who didn't break a stride. 'Only if he brings a Durex to the party, dear.'

Like Vesuvius, the class erupted into laughter and Mrs Benn's steely composure melted slightly as her wrinkly old face broke into a sort of smile. She *never* smiled.

I wondered what she would have said had I asked her whether it was good form for me to elaborate on the carnal exploits experienced with Sergeant Sarah Miles. I can hear the answer now: 'Absolutely not, young man. Discretion at all times.'

On the 9th of December 1946, I was charged with stealing a silver spoon from the mess room and with this came demotion again. Soon afterwards Sarah returned to England and her other life, a married one, as it happens. It was a double whammy and I don't think there was any correlation between her decision to leave and my minor theft charge. She liked my manners, though; didn't that count for something? Trapped in a dual life, I honestly didn't care about her departure, but how I wished I could say the same about the charge. I vehemently opposed it.

'I've never stolen a thing in my life. It was just an accident.' That was my plea.

It fell on the hairy, jug-handled, deaf ears of a stuffy disciplinary committee. The truth was simple: looking for a table, I had slipped the teaspoon into my top pocket and forgotten it was there. But it was hopeless, so the charge of 'being in possession of a spoon, the property of the NAAFI' stuck. It didn't cause me too much collateral damage—just three days' pay and a demotion back to private, where I could be happily insignificant again.

When I saw the ENSA poster, I felt panic and joy simultaneously. The Entertainments National Services Association was coming to town, and Ivy Benson and Her All Girls Band were the star turn. Could this mean I got to see my mother again? This beautiful woman I knew as my mum was in her prime and at the place she wanted to be most: centre stage.

Then, like another dose of bromide, this initial jubilation slammed me back into panic mode. What would I say if I met her? The scenario was a possibility and it troubled me. *Jesus, I was Pop.* The ramifications were incomprehensible. How would I reach out to her – as a future son, or as her husband, my father? It would change everything. It was dangerous.

I remembered the BBC documentary about Ivy Benson called *Lady Be Good.* Mum featured; with her posh telephone voice, all actress, she recounted the story about one particular performance in front of the troops.

Ivy Benson remembered the strange encore request, too: 'I'd rather be in her than in the army!'

Although embarrassed by Ivy Benson's recollection of a soldier heckling, I'm pretty sure Mum secretly enjoyed the memory. Jean Peterson was a shining star and a bit of a diva – I've got the photographs to prove it!

I tried to ignore the strange euphoria surging through my veins and decided to deal with the problem/opportunity later.

'Meadows. Fancy a spin on one of your nags.' It was the voice of my foe, Padre Captain Huggins, and I hated the way he changed a question into an order. He was making his way towards me, pulling on a pair of elbow-length brown leather gloves; with his beige breeches flaring out like elephant ears, they combined to make him look ridiculous.

The nearest 'nag' fully tacked and ready 'for a spin' was Winston, huge and with a beautiful chestnut coat. Far from a nag, he was not only a good-looking beast and extremely intelligent but he also had aggressive tendencies. How wonderful was that? The padre didn't have a chance.

'Did you hear that, Winston? He called you a nag!' I whispered.

'Looking for an early morning "trot out".' There it was again.

'No thanks, sir,' I said, deliberately to irritate him.

'Not you, you fool.'

Having completed some elaborate stretches that included noisily straining down to touch his toes, Huggins eventually straightened up and waited impatiently for me to walk Winston around to him. Suddenly frisky and eager to 'trot out', the horse came to a stuttering halt. I did nothing to dampen his enthusiasm. 'Come on, Meadows. Get this damned animal in order.'

Captain Huggins was an experienced rider, but I doubted whether he had ridden a horse this size or with Winston's spirit. He often used his rank and status to jump the booking queue, too, which was another reason to dislike him. Everyone, whatever their rank, waited their turn.

'Need to get a ride in before the rigours of the day.'

Apart from his Sunday service and the occasional wedding, he did absolutely nothing. Every day was comfortable for him; his only rigour would be to wipe his lardy, fat arse. Known as Muggins Huggins, no one liked him.

I decided that today would be the day.

Like many horses, Winston mischievously blew out his tummy when he sensed the saddle going onto his back. That meant the girth strap should have been tighter; good riders always checked this before mounting up. 'Do your checks, sir, and he's all yours.'

Huggins looked at me and ignored my advice. Brilliant, bring it on. With an exaggerated huff and puff, he hauled himself into the saddle. Winston jigged around, irritated by his new passenger. An overly sharp jab of heels, followed by a nasty flick from Huggins' riding crop, set him off.

I could not believe it: the captain's direction of travel was towards the jumps. Even better, it was a triple-cross bar made from heavy timber poles that most riders would work up to. I could hardly believe my luck as Winston broke into a stuttering first-jump canter.

'Please, God, do your very best for me,' I prayed.

Up they went, and in mid-flight it happened. The girth clamping the saddle and its rider loosened and I watched in stunned ecstasy as the padre slipped round to Winston's left side in glorious slow motion. Off he slid, and he hit the ground hard – very hard. The accompanying 'Aaagh' was gratifyingly audible as he lay writhing on a cushion of horse poo and mud.

'Did you check the girth, sir?' I asked, rushing as slowly as possible towards the heap of breeches, boots and bilious gas sounds escaping from it. Sadly, the captain was only severely winded, and his injuries appeared minor, but the good news was that I never saw him again. Ever.

'Naughty Winston.' I gave him a firm thumbs-up. Was it a grin he gave me as he nodded back?

I also had a fall on March 17th 1947. The guys had been bugging me for weeks to take part in an army show-jumping competition. Various stables and riding schools from our zone had been encouraged to enter riders, and my sponsor, Colonel Hopkinson, was keen to see his regiment represented.

An offer I couldn't refuse was made worse because jumping was not my thing. My last attempt in my youth had not ended well. I'd cleared the jumps, which was good – but before the horse, who didn't. Laddie, our gentle and erratic New Forest pony, looked embarrassed, and so he should have done: the bar was only set at twelve inches!

So competition day arrived. My chosen steed, Adolph, was a different kettle of fish. With a name like that, the omens were dire. Everything about him was German: big, strong, well-made and unreliable; if Adolph had been a tank, he would have been a Tiger. Sadly, just like tanks, he couldn't jump. Being an optimist, I reckoned I might survive because he was a gigantic eighteen hands. He could have stepped over the jumps, but he didn't.

I remembered the approach vividly: the jolting, faltering canter, the red-and-white telegraph poles, and then Adolph's neck smashing into my mouth.

***

The young boy's eyes, framed by an old man's face, stared back at me. A younger man, probably his son, mimed an apology as I glared through my passenger window. I tapped the steering wheel and watched impatiently as he led the old man towards a bus blazoned with the name *Normandy Landings*. That made me feel guilty, so I acknowledged him with a thumbs-up and dropped the passenger side window.

Pop came to mind. 'Please tell him he's a hero. Tell him that they will never be forgotten.'

Both men turned to look at me, smiled and waved back. 'Silly old duffer,' the voice came from my side. 'See it all the time, mate. Those old buggers should be dead by now.'

I said nothing and handed over my ferry tickets and passport. I smiled, not at that comment but because this was Calais and my road trip of all road trips had ended. And because the idiot studying my credentials had no idea of my recent back story, all seventy-five years plus.

Was it over? Could this be a dream in wartime Germany? I rubbed my mouth to check for bleeding; there was none, and this was indeed my car and not a horse. Yes, it was over.

The officious individual continued to scrutinise my documents and began to hum the famous ditty, 'Hitler has only got one ball, the other...' What a prick. I imagined he was wearing what was now starting to replicate a Nazi uniform and decided to let him continue.

'Shame Adolph didn't wipe out the old bastards.' He chuckled, thinking I'd appreciate his amusing comment. Then, licking the tip of his pencil, he marked something onto the boarding card and handed it back to me. 'Soon, be on your way back to Blighty, guv.'

Yes, and probably greeted by ignorant prats like you in a country that will soon forget. Instead, I said, 'You, my friend, are a prize wanker.'

'Do what?'

'You're a brainless twat who'd be wearing a Nazi uniform if it wasn't for those old bastards.'

He looked up and winced; he got it. 'And what's more, you'd be going home to a wife called Ursula with hairy armpits and a fat blond kid called Fritz.' I snatched my passport from him and pressed the button to close my window. Winking, I put the car into drive and drove towards the ramp that led up to the ferry.

'Respect, boys, show respect.' Valentine Caddick's words rang loudly in my ears.

From Peter Meadows' memoirs

After a few more battles came the end of the war. We were billeted in Schleswig Holstein and a large schloss (castle) built in a square with stabling for several horses. I borrowed a horse from a nearby farm and took myself off for a ride across the countryside.

Lo and behold, who should I meet but the 6' 4" figure of the colonel walking towards me with a dog he had befriended? He reminded me of the incident in the tank laager earlier and suggested I started a riding school to occupy the troops who needed some form of relaxation. He gave me a scout car and a driver, plus the necessary requisition forms to gather a dozen horses from nearby farms. I was careful not to deprive any farmer of more animals than was justified. We were able to find hay and oats from local farms, and two prisoners of war helped with grooming and feeding.

I forgot to mention my dog, Stranger, who had attached himself to me sometime at the end of the war! Then followed some of my happiest memories whilst in the forces and, at the same time, I was able to improve my riding skills. However, when I was persuaded to enter the Army show-jumping event some months later, I succeeded in knocking down every jump!

Epilogue

What next? Pop was demobbed on New Year's Day, 1947. Although he was contracted to the Territorial Army Reserves until May 1951, he left Germany with a heavy heart. With his duty complete and his marriage over, an unknown future lay ahead and I cannot begin to fathom the toll it took on him mentally. We never discussed it.

His fruitless attempts to cultivate a long-distance relationship with his baby son, and the torment, must have been unbearable as he trained for D-Day at Bovington camp 300 miles from his home in Norwich. It was a futile cause anyway, because divorce proceedings were already in motion and his wife rebuffed all his efforts to connect with his son. The consequences were catastrophic and he rarely saw Anthony before he embarked for Europe in June 1944. Cruel, perhaps, but this was the harsh reality of war, and his son became another war-baby statistic.

But something magnetic pulled my father: Africa. Rather than staying safely bored and unwanted in England's post-war rebuild, the thrill of another adventure beckoned him. Through the 'jungle drums', as he put it, he heard about a small British-led expedition leaving Marseilles for Cape Town in South Africa. The cost of his passage was £100, and he joined two fellow voyagers, one related to the vicar of Cley, my parish church.

Was his decision to leave selfish? Probably, but forging long-term relationships with his wife and son never really started. Perhaps he was running away, though I don't think so. Pop was a man of principle; if the door of reconciliation had been open, I'm sure he would have dived through it.

His bruised life was destined to take a path fuelled by the drug of adventure instead. At only twenty-four and with few prospects, he looked towards the British Commonwealth for his destiny.

'I looked for the pink countries on my globe,' he once told me, and one caught his eye: a British government sponsorship scheme in central Africa to cultivate groundnuts. 'Monkey nuts, son, peanuts to you.'

Pop chose to be different by trying to make a difference in an alien country most people hadn't heard of. It meant a long journey, so the newly connected trio travelled from Algiers and traversed the Atlas Mountains towards Kano in Nigeria via the Sahara Desert. That was 2,500 miles and just stage one.

It was a new and dangerous experience for all of them; the Sahara was hostile and unchartered, and food and water soon became scarce. Modern navigational aids didn't exist in those days; there were no route maps because there were few roads. Instead they relied on obscure landmarks for compass bearings and the occasional nomadic warrior or camel to guide them!

Their chosen mode of transport was a modified Ford Mercury shooting-brake with specially designed off-road sand tyres. It was a good car and the plan to have sand tyres was excellent; however, there was a problem: the tyres didn't like heat and burst in one of the hottest places on earth. Despite this setback, numerous other mechanical issues and a trio of men who didn't much like each other, they completed the trip in a record-breaking ninety days.

North Africa in the bag, they prepared for a 3,000-mile trek through the jungles of Cameroon, French Equatorial Africa and the Belgian Congo. Their destination was Nairobi, Kenya, but my father decided to deviate from the plan. He said farewell to his companions, who continued their journey south, and made an audacious application to join the Kenyan police force. He had military credibility, but he was pushing it at just over 5' 4" tall when he claimed to meet their entry requirement of six feet.

'What's eight inches?' I can see the smirk on his face as he left the puzzled interview panel. They gently declined his application.

Back on plan and back on the road, he headed south in a battered old Land Rover acquired for a few dollars. His destination was a small mid-continent country called Nyasaland, now Malawi. This was where the groundnut scheme had been initiated, but he quickly saw more opportunity in water than in nuts.

With little knowledge but a strong desire to learn, he moved to Rhodesia to help drill for it. As he dug wells and arranged irrigation systems on tobacco farms, he decided that his future would be in the 'weed' itself; he was an expert at smoking it, but now he wanted to cultivate and sell the stuff.

After borrowing some money from his father, Percy, he acquired 2,000 acres of fertile land in the African central belt. The area was called Kasungu and was back where he'd started in Malawi.

With a combination of local knowledge, stubbornness and drive, he set about planning this new adventure. First he had to build a farmhouse, then outbuildings and eight drying barns. He knew absolutely nothing about this – and what would a former British army tank driver possibly know about farming? With no 'how to build a house' or 'grow your own' YouTube videos to help him, his unwavering self-belief got him through. It was a vertical learning curve but he was never short of advisors. Intrigued and sometimes bewildered, his native workforce was always there for that strange little white man from England. They called him '*bwana*', which means big boss or master in Swahili. Pop ignored that; he saw himself as a partner and custodian of the land for others to use later.

It took a few months before Sable Creek Farm was ready, named after his favourite African antelope with long, curved horns. Many years later, Sable Homestead was the name of our first family home in England. No farmhands watched him paint the sign that time, just intrigued neighbours who hid behind net curtains in suburban houses called Brookside and The Laurels.

In 1955, Pop took some home leave and boarded a ship in Durban bound for England. His primary mission was to buy a second-hand tractor; job done, his life was about to take another turn when he met a professional singer by the stage name of Jean Peterson. The story goes that this lady was on a date with her boyfriend on a Saturday evening in a cosy Norwich pub.

'I made my move like a cobra.' Pop's words, not mine.

Subtlety is not generally associated with my father. Still, the poor man on a romantic night out with his girlfriend was promptly evicted, watched by our mystified heroine.

'As luck would have it, son, it was Miss Jean Peterson's destiny that she met me.' His words again.

From 1947, Mum had been the lead vocalist with Ivy Benson and Her All Girls Band, a big name in their day. They toured extensively throughout occupied Europe and the Middle East in the post-war years. Her real name was Gertrude Lilian Bedwell, probably an unfortunate surname for a beautiful blonde singer performing for an overly appreciative audience of randy, sex-starved men!

By anyone's standards their courtship was unorthodox. It was only three weeks before Pop announced his imminent departure back to his farm in Malawi, and he duly set sail from Southampton with a second-hand tractor in tow but minus his newly acquired girlfriend.

But something significant happened before his departure. As they said their goodbyes in 'their pub', romantically called The Murderers, Pop went down on one knee. Alas for him, Jeannie (his name for her) did not readily accept his gallant proposal of marriage. Perhaps she had PTSD, or maybe it was guilt that she had allowed her ex-boyfriend to be blown away by a little piece of human dynamite. Either way, her answer took some time as she played an old-fashioned game of 'hard to get' for a while. As it happened, it took a long while!

Over the next two years, their only correspondence was through Wells Fargo telegrams and handwritten love letters, lots of them. Communication was even more difficult because Pop's nearest post office was eighty dirt-track miles from Sable Creek Farm. His occasional trips to Lilongwe for supplies now always included an eager visit to collect the mail.

Jeannie eventually succumbed two years later and set sail for Africa on the *Union Castle* cruise liner from Southampton. It was 1957, and late July. I can't imagine her trepidation in making this life-changing decision and leaving slow, safe Norfolk for a weird bloke who had gate-crashed her date! Plus she had only spent three weeks with him before he disappeared for two years. There were many things for her to consider, including the not-insignificant dangers of living in an unknown African country. All of this must have involved hardcore risk assessment.

Her decision surprises me because *Enter the Dragon* springs to mind. As my mate and I schemed how to get in to see this iconic movie, Mum fretted over which Borstal she would have to visit to see me again. 'It's too much of a risk, dear.'

'Don't be silly, darling,' piped up Pop. It was little help.

'You can be quiet! I won't be visiting you!'

Pop took us to the cinema – and that was when he made his first mistake. 'One and two halves, please, Miss.' The film was X-rated, and we were fifteen.

Alun and I quickly knew we had work to do.

'How old are you, son,' came a knowing question.

'Eighteen, miss, born on February 6th 1955.' My friend's confident reply and mental arithmetic stunned me.

It was my turn next. 'And you?'

'The same, miss.' Trying to sound like Lee Marvin, it came out more like Basil Brush.

The kiosk lady's doubtful nod worried me as she slowly tore off three adult tickets. 'The candy floss is over there, boys.' She pointed to where two eight-year-olds were waiting to be served; *Herbie Rides Again* was showing on the other screen.

'Don't worry, chaps, well played. You'll soon be old enough to buy a beer!' That was Pop's second mistake and from a man who allegedly never made mistakes.

My mother didn't view herself as a risk-taker, so I was always fascinated by her African story and once asked her in a moment of mother-and-son chit-chat why she'd gone there. For someone who took two years to decide, her explanation was as immediate as it was brief. 'It was so easy, Calum.' Her eyes lit up. 'I loved your dad the second I set eyes on him.'

That love never waned and it was mutual. Photographs may fade but memories last forever, and I remember one particular evening. Free from embarrassment and oblivious to me, they smooched around our kitchen table to the lounge-lizard crooning of Bryan Ferry singing 'Smoke Gets in Your Eyes'. Yes, it's in the playlist!

They were married on August 12 1957 in a small registry office in Lilongwe and enjoyed their honeymoon in Beira, a beautiful beach resort in Mozambique. They were apparently very busy because, nine months later, Mum gave birth to me, Peter Calum Meadows, on June 11, 1958 at Sable Creek Farm.

'My beautiful little boy.' That was how she described me, naturally.

In late 1959, civil disturbances and political unrest in Nyasaland meant that safety, especially for white farmers, was severely threatened. Pop was a consummate risk-taker and thrived on it, but this was too dangerous and he wouldn't compromise his family. As the Federation of Rhodesia and Nyasaland began to crumble, he had to make an important decision.

The world my parents wanted for our future had gone, so the blood, sweat and tears of their creation, Sable Creek farm, also had to go. He sold it for £1500, and my parents moved to Mashonaland in Rhodesia. Pop managed to slip in another trip to England, this time to buy a Land Rover, and took time to reconnect with his first son, Anthony, who was sixteen years old by then.

By now Pop had a network of contacts in Rhodesia and, like a true farmer, he prepared his ground well. He secured work managing a tobacco farm called Drumarda in a region called Centenary, a remote bushland area on the border of Mozambique. Although extremely isolated, the land was fertile and beautiful, and the place soon became an idyllic replacement for Sable Creek.

But déjà vu was around the corner. The 'federation' pot was simmering nicely again, African nationalism was growing and the warning signs were clear.

My parents' ultimate decision to leave Africa must have been heart-breaking, but it was to be a fortuitous one! Soon after we left, the Unilateral Declaration of Independence (UDI) led to Rhodesia's independence from Britain in 1965. Sanctions imposed by Harold Wilson's British government, and the United Nations hurt the country and its people badly, but that was nothing compared to what followed. The 1970s civil war between factions of Robert Mugabe's ZANU-PF and Joshua Nkomo's ZAPU was bloody and destroyed the economy, killing many black and white people.

I always think of Jan Leeming when I hear the name Joshua Nkomo. She was a BBC newsreader, and there were always two camps in our sitting room when she was talking about the 'troubles' in Africa. Mum and I would laugh at her jaw-dropping attempts to pronounce his name correctly, whilst Pop seethed with rage at this 'mad gorilla' and his terrorist antics. He despised Mugabe and Nkomo equally, with Harold Wilson coming in a close third. As for Mum and me, we just adored Jan Leeming.

In December 1972, African nationalism became personal when it made a brutal and direct mark on us. My godfather, Archie Dalgleish, was a dour Scot; I have only vague memories of him as a wiry, stern man who always wore a bush hat loosely flopping over his head and sported a long wooden pipe between his teeth to complete the picture. Chinese-backed insurgent guerrillas from Mozambique and Zambia were making sporadic attacks mainly on white-owned farms; their strategy of taking on the 'Rhodesian' army had failed, so they decided to pick off nominated farmers instead.

One such farm was Whistlefield, belonging to Uncle Archie and Auntie Agnes. The attack came via a mortar and AK47 strike; although miraculously no one was killed, it signalled the beginning of trouble ahead. Archie was Pop's best friend and mentor; they must have been like two peas in a pod, both stubborn and pugnacious characters, but both pioneers in a country they cherished deeply.

What came ten years later in 1982 ramped things up even further: Robert Mugabe's government-led massacres in Matabeleland. By then he was the elected Prime Minister of the first black-majority government, which had been formed two years earlier. These acts of genocide were repeated during a long reign of terror that sadly led to the destruction of a new and potentially wonderful country called Zimbabwe.

All this happened well before the infamous land grabs of 2000. By then Mugabe, trying to save face in front of a watching and wanting nation, had decided to appease his restless people by offering them white-owned farms. 'The whites who were here were mere actor farmers,' he said in justification.

Mugabe's subsequent land grab gained momentum with little discrimination between colours; all lives were cheap, and thousands were murdered during his tyrannical reign. My father hated Mugabe for his treatment of Zimbabwe and for cheating its people of everything good by promising something better,

'Liberation hero? Liberation from what, to what?' It was a rueful question to himself, a man who had liberated many people in his time, and something he said to others who tried to understand but couldn't… or wouldn't.

Ultimately, my parents' decision to leave Africa was quite simple. The love affair with the continent was over and the future looked distressing and dangerous. Pop was forty, living in a country he treasured but in turbulent times. It was time to leave; it was time to go back to England.

As another chapter in his life closed, we docked in Southampton on a cold January morning in 1963. I remember it well; it was snowing hard and, at five years of age, this new phenomenon was special. My parents put on a brave face as we walked down the gangplank to meet relatives. I dread to imagine what they were thinking; it must have been like 'walking the plank'.

Pop spent the second half of his life appearing content, but I suspect he was hiding a simmering frustration on the inside. After a brief trip to Canada like many exiled Rhodesians searching for work, he returned and went corporate, joining the Shell-Mex and BP oil company as an industrial sales representative. At least he found some continuity because he was a fuel-oil salesman to light industry and farms. We lived in a beautiful village in rural Essex called Great Bardfield, and Mum worked as a librarian at the local USAF base in Wethersfield. Part-time work supplemented Pop's salary and helped boost our fresh start in England. Life was certainly different for us all, but it was safe.

Despite using skills gleaned from Africa to build things like rustic fences and irrigation systems for our flood-prone garden, or constructing my much-envied tree house, my father missed another piece of African life: the expatriates' club. I think he visited one in Salisbury; I'm not sure if the gin and tonics or the emblem of a sable antelope attracted him most.

In an attempt to reintroduce something similar into our lives, we joined the Little Bardfield Country Club. We weren't rich, and the club certainly wasn't exclusive. I recall the small indoor pool with its murky green water, and the fusty oak-panelled billiard room (gentlemen only) smelling of stale cigars and farts. The place was tired and needed vast amounts of cash to bring in the other missing ingredient: people. Mum didn't like it much and Pop rarely went; even so, we were members for about a year.

The club struggled on for a little longer. There was an upside: I loved going there; it was where I learned to play snooker badly and squash slightly better with my newfound sporty chums from the village.

About this time, Mum returned to the stage, this time under the auspices of amateur dramatics, when she joined the celebrated Dunmow Players. She always performed in musicals because, apart from us, music was the love of her life. Classic productions such as *My Fair Lady, The Sound of Music* and *Doctor Doolittle* added to her growing repertoire, along with more high-brow comic operas like Gilbert and Sullivan's *HMS Pinafore* and *The Mikado*.

Mum suffered from anxiety and low self-esteem; much later in life, I learned she had a nervous breakdown after her mother died. She never took to the stage again professionally. Nevertheless, with this boost of confidence came a mother full of life and back at the top of her game, especially when an orchestra struck up. She only wanted to be in the chorus line, but we all knew that Jean Peterson could have taken any principal role. In many ways, she did. The transformation was amazing to see, and her presence lit the stage the same way as it did whenever she walked into any room. I was so proud of her and wished she could have overcome her nerves and taken on those lead roles so that people could see just how good she was.

But I'm not being totally sincere. When mates came around and her vocal gymnastics inevitably kicked in, particularly during rehearsal times, her embarrassed, Harry Enfield-like adolescent son became Judas!

Although Mum suppressed her mental-health issues well, I know this now: she was always happy raising her son and loving her soul mate, Pop. I loved her deeply and wished I'd told her so more often.

Pop broke up his mundane and safe corporate sales life by adopting some adrenalin-induced hobbies. He took up karate and quickly gained a second brown belt at the grand old age of fifty; later, he took up sailing and purchased his beloved yacht, *Vegabond*. This gave him freedom and seclusion, much needed to recharge the batteries of this human dynamo of a man. During his more cerebral moments, art, in the form of oil painting, returned to his life. Subjects ranging from wild animals and winter landscapes to nude ladies were occasionally exhibited locally. I recall the stunned look on the vicar's face and his bobbing Adam's apple when introduced to blonde Mary, legs spread akimbo over a red-satin chaise longue.

I also remember him taking on a challenging horse ride in the Spanish mountains, which was to be his last big adventure. We had three horses, a dog, a cat, and numerous pet rodents to keep everyone busy. But although family life was idyllic and safe, I knew there was a void; he got bored quickly and missed his real home, Africa.

Pop took a redundancy package and retired from Shell in 1980. My parents decided to return to their roots in Norwich about the same time I struck out in life and left home. He was just fifty-seven and enjoyed thirty-four years of retirement – not bad, if you can get it. They weren't wealthy in terms of money, but they were rich in terms of happiness. Theirs was a conventional retirement filled with gardening, coach holidays to Italy and churchy things for Mum.

Then came the grandchildren, my wonderful boys James and Dominic from my first marriage. Sadly, divorce is prevalent on the Meadows' side of the family but, unlike my father, despite an acrimonious parting I had some great years with my ex-wife, Susan. My parents doted on their grandchildren and, apart from some minor health issues, their golden years were kind to them.

Mum passed away in the early hours of August 13th 2004. It was one day after their forty-seventh wedding anniversary; how cruel was that? Cancer took her; it was an agonisingly painful death, but mercifully quick. In the end, she was pumped full of morphine and neatly tucked up in a hospital bed as the three of us waited for the inevitable.

It was my turn to sit beside her and I felt the faintest of squeezes as I held her hand. She was saying goodbye to me. I gently beckoned Pop over and a few moments later, his Jeannie peacefully slipped away, her hand in his. As the celebratory anniversary roses caringly put beside her a few hours earlier looked on, his heart was shattered then. The only woman he ever loved had left him forever.

The funeral was a celebration, if you want to call it that. I never understand the celebration bit: loads of booze and shallow chat. The deceased didn't choose to die, and you didn't want them to, but let's all have a good old knees-up because they would like it that way. Not me; chuck me in a box and let everyone be miserable for a few days. After that, you're just dust, and you're forgotten anyway.

Many friends were there, and there was lots of respectful laughter and a short eulogy from me, plus, of course, music. That and the dog were the only times I ever saw Pop cry, a heart-rending, inconsolable weeping as Louis Armstrong finished singing *Hello, Dolly*. I put my arms around his shaking shoulders, worried he would not last long without her. He thankfully proved me wrong and soldiered on for another ten years. I know he struggled sometimes but he never grumbled or complained about his life; his was a truly great one.

'I miss her son. I miss her like you won't believe.' That is the truth; he missed his Jeannie, his soulmate.

He did keep busy, though. There were letters of complaint, lots of them. The subjects of his ire were broad but typically concerned with what he considered to be 'injustices in the world', ranging from serious topics like the ivory trade in Africa to global warming, and banal subjects such as pop music, over-paid footballers and glam-rock pop stars! Recipients of his letters were numerous: newspaper editors, such as Charles Moore of the *Sunday Telegraph* and Cabinet politicians like William Hague couldn't escape him.

Targets of his wrath also included local hoteliers. It appeared that one particular victim seemed incapable of controlling 'unruly and feral children'. *These unruly mites run amok like monkeys in your 'over-priced', poorly managed leisure club.*

They all got the Meadows' treatment. Some replied, but most didn't.

Pop briefly went to South Africa on holiday but never returned to the central belt he called home. I did, though, and with my young family found Drumarda in 1997. It was still there but a mere shell of the place I remembered. The farm sign was the same, now rusty and bent with time; how amazing that it was still pitched on the edge of a narrow dirt track called the main road.

It led the way to my first memories of home. A long tree-lined driveway ran up to our farmhouse, though it now seemed shorter because everything is bigger when you are a child. As I drove up the bumpy track churning up clouds of red dust behind me, I recalled that the farmworkers' compound was at the end on the left-hand side. They had lived in circular rondavels pitched in a snug, neat row. I remembered the open fires with boiling pots of *sadza* and the stripped hides of antelope skins drying in the sun.

A flashback reminded me of when Pop and I went for an afternoon stroll not too far into the bush and only halfway down this driveway. We returned to where we'd entered the scrubby gauze a little later, chatting and holding hands. A shocking sight faced us: my mode of transport, powered by my tiny legs, was a small trike called Hercules. He looked in a bad way, upended and twisted into the ground, with most of his little black saddle missing. The twisted coil springs and ripped leather remains were covered in a coat of thick yellow gunk that smelt like bad breath.

'Probably a hyena,' said my father earnestly.

I looked up at my dad's pistol, which always seemed to be strapped to his side, and felt safe. For the inevitable debrief later, Pop calmly sat my distraught mother down. It didn't end well, and all future expeditions of this sort were banned instantly. A knowing wink confirmed differently as Pop walked out of the house and into the yard.

Opposite the compound was our farmhouse. Back in the day, it was whitewashed, roughly thatched and surrounded by a lush green lawn. This was a place where my minder Nelson and I lolled around together. Nelson was a Staffordshire bull terrier, cream in colour, with a distinctive eye patch and no tail; vets docked them in those days. I remember our days together in the endless sunshine, just him and me and my tortoises, Jack and Jill.

On a typical day, my friend Adsom, the garden boy, would carefully tend the flowers. I always felt safe with him as he kept one eye fixed on a curious and very mobile child and the other on possible dangers in the shrubs. Together with Nelson, Adsom was my chum and my guardian. And there were plenty of hazards for him to worry about, usually snakes, most of them nasty.

I remember one occasion well, the only time I remember Pop using his gun. I was playing with Nelson and my orange Tonka toy lorry on the lawn when a loud shout went up, 'Mamba! Mamba!'

Adsom was up the tree behind me in a flash. While he jabbed and poked around with the end of a broom handle, Pop stood beside me and carefully aimed at my friend's head. So much could have gone wrong! *Krack, krack*, and then the smell of cordite as blue smoke drifted out of the barrel. Soon two snake skins were stretched out on the grass; once dry, they would be given to Adsom (head still intact) to make belts.

'What's that for, Pop?'

'To cook something nice and stewy.' He was chopping through the pink flesh and making a small heap of snake meat on the lawn.

'We really should try it sometime, Peter.' I hoped this was Mum's little joke.

The ambience of Drumarda on my return visit was very different. The circular house and its windows were now boarded with sheets of corrugated iron, and an assertively high barbed-wire fence surrounded the garden. The lawn, my old playground, was a patch of dead grass and red dust. As for Jack and Jill, I wondered where they were; tortoises live forever, don't they? And what of my friend Adsom and his family?

The house's physical structure remained unchanged, but her cosiness was absent as she crouched sadly before me. Memories surged back and I trembled slightly. That had been my happy and safe place, my sanctuary; now it was lonely and derelict. Someone later told me that a family owned the property but did not farm there. What a waste of its history. Except for a pack of feral dogs chasing their tails and two large white birds circling above, there was no sign of anyone else.

It took me back as the dogs yelped and raced through the dilapidated buildings; these were once the barns, where rows of freshly harvested tobacco leaves hung in bunches on long wooden poles to dry. I will never forget tobacco's pungent sweet smell as it cured. In the foreground, another small building sheltered a few scraggy chickens from the scorching midday sun. They were skinny little things and their featherless bodies looked grotesque as they clucked, pecked and scrapped around for food.

I thought of roast chicken; with some basting, they'd have looked oven-ready.

Back to Robert Mugabe: It is true that in the beginning, this potentially dynamic leader offered big promises and, more importantly, real hope to his people of all colours. Predictably, he delivered absolutely nothing except corruption and despair. Although his former country was once called the 'breadbasket of Africa', with him and little bread, Zimbabwe instead became a 'basket case'.

Ironically, my research into our farm at Drumarda told me that after my visit it became the official residence of a ZANU-PF government official. It would have killed Pop to know that. Three years after my return, Mugabe's 'land-grab' programme finally claimed it.

Would a black *farmer* ever be the custodian of this land? If so, my father would have been delighted because so much of his time was spent encouraging and training his native farmhands to become self-sufficient crop growers. Pop never forgot his African roots. These wonderful people had shown him loyalty; he always remembered their open arms when he had arrived on their land many years earlier.

I'm so glad Pop didn't go back and witness the stark realities of this African tragedy; it would have broken his heart. I never tried to find Sable Creek Farm where it all started in Malawi, but maybe one day I will. If I did, it would be a tribute to my wonderful mother and remarkable father, a simple, understated man who lived a remarkable life in the most unremarkable way.

And finally, after all, what could a tobacco-farming, tank-driving art student ever achieve? Long live his memory. I love you, Pop.

From Peter Meadows' memoirs

As I was due ten days' leave, I elected to go to Chamonix in France and stay in a hotel run by the Army (a skiing resort) and took Stranger with me. There, I met and made mad, passionate love to a lady army sergeant and we went skiing together, which was not as demanding as the more intimate moments. Stranger did not approve!

It was not long after this that I was demobbed, but before this I had to find a home for my dog Stranger. He found a home with the quarter-master sergeant. I also had to dispose of a couple of German Luger pistols, although I kept a German sword marked with a swastika.

And so home to 'Blighty' to move on with my life. I had already decided that my future would probably be in Africa. However, I had no particular qualifications, other than being a student at art college and able to ride a horse and drive a tank. Not a great deal to offer a prospective employer, other than my natural charm and good looks combined with a certain modesty.

A letter from Claus Leuthold

Institut European
12 rue Royale
Fontainebleau
France
October 14, 1959

Dear Peter,

Today I have received your very nice letter, and I must say that I am really happy that I finally succeeded in finding you! When I arrived in England in late August, I was at first disappointed that no reply had arrived at my friend's address. But there remained a certain amount of hope on my part that I might be more successful in the course of time.

You know, Peter, all those years I had carried with me that same little piece of paper on which you had written your address – to me, it meant a souvenir of our first friendly touch with people, too long divorced. Perhaps that I still carry with me some traces of our partially English past which evoked such strong emotional sentiments. Since a certain attachment to that 'special island' and English ways have remained quite strong with us. Although I am now an American, there will always be that certain warm feeling for England.

But let me give you first a few more details which might 'bridge' the past 15 years. My father joined us on that little farm where you met us shortly after your departure. We all had a rather tough going, which did not change substantially when we moved to a small town near Cologne. In 1950 I graduated from the Gymnasium (comparable to a BA). For the next two years, I worked for the British Army of the Rhine (BAOR), a quite interesting experience. At that time, I received a letter from friends in America informing me about the possibility to make my way in the United States. At any rate, this required that I had to serve for 5 years in the US Army as a 'regular.' Well, it has not been quite easy sometimes, but I did advance and saw several interesting parts of the world.

In 1957, I received my 'Hon Discharge' and became a 'proper Harvardian', from which university I graduated this past summer. Earlier this year I learned about this new European Business Institute which seemed to me to be a good opportunity to prepare myself for a business career later on. One day, I hope a respectable American firm will take my services. That will be the time when I may become 'prosperous' (as you kindly wished it to be) and find the chance for responsibility. Until then, however, there remains a long way to further studies and the uncertain path of 'fortune's favours!'

Friends of mine often wondered why I chose to leave Europe, perhaps for no other reason but to combine the possibilities of an American with the elements of a European heritage!? You know how much these two continents – all part of one world – needs each other today.

In this respect, I think it quite courageous and commendable that you and your young English family took the precarious uncertainties of life in Africa, which too often seems to be swallowed up by its feverish nationalism. Unfortunately, certain ill-conceived measures of our own people tend to do more harm than good. I do regret very much that your own estate met bad luck but may I express my sincere hope that your new position does offer you a reasonable satisfaction and maybe the 'jumping board' for a new endeavour of your own.

It has been most kind of you to offer me the hospitality of your parents in England. This coming spring, I intend to take my sister Jutta (she was barely 13 years when you were with us) for a short trip to England, and perhaps I may take advantage then of the opportunity. As to the possibility of meeting you in the near future, I can just now only hope to find a way next year to make a trip to Africa (perhaps as a kind of fact-finding trip) or on my own if I can find the means. Needless to say, I would very much like to meet you and your, no doubt, charming family as well as that part of Africa where so much is at stake.

Thank you again for your letter and best wishes and greetings.

Yours sincerely,
Claus Leuthold
PS I hope you don't object to my familiarity of style (quite American!).
This picture must substitute for a family portrait later on.

10. Claus Leuthold, Harvard 1959

11. Jean Peterson, Belle, Germany 1948

12. Peter and Stranger 1946

13. Stranger on duty

**14. Peter, the lady Sergeant and Stranger with the crew
in Chamonix**

15. Skiing with the Sergeant

16. The Sahara 1947

17. Aboard the Union Castle ship heading for a new life in England in 1963

18. The author and Muggins 1967

19. Mum and Pop's Ruby Wedding Anniversary 1997

My Funeral Poem

Pop
May 4th 1923 – 26th November 2014

My Pop was a stubborn man.
A black-and-white, right-and-wrong type of man,
He was a passionate man,
A compassionate, sound and funny man.

My Pop was a naughty man,
A twinkle in the eyes, smiley type of man.
He was a glass-half-full man,
A small unit, but a dynamite man.

My Pop was a cheeky man,
A sometimes crude and 'laugh at his own jokes' type of man.
He was a straight and true man,
A 'give you his right arm,' generous man.

My Pop was a loyal man,
A brave and strong, 100% type of man.
He was an honourable man,
A positive and very happy man.

I loved my Pop; he was my hero and my Superman.

Road Trip Playlist

'Hello, Dolly' – Louis Armstrong (for Mum)
'Wonderful World' – Louis Armstrong
'Africa' – Toto
'We Have All the Time in the World' – Louis Armstrong
'My Way' – Frank Sinatra (for Pop)
'Up, Up and Away' – Ray Conniff singers
'Beach Baby' – First Class
'Going to Barbados' – Typically Tropical
'Siegfried Line' – The Two Leslies
'Darkness' – Be Bop Deluxe
'Panic in the World' – Be Bop Deluxe
'Northern Lights' – Renaissance
'Disarm' – Smashing Pumpkins
'Born Free' – Mat Monro (for Pop)
'Crime of the Century' – Supertramp
'Living Years' – Mike and the Mechanics (for Pop)
'Child of the Universe' – Barclay James Harvest (for me)
'Mocking Bird' – Barclay James Harvest
'There Goes My Hero' – Foo Fighters
'Wild Horses' – Rolling Stones
'You're so Vain' – Carly Simon (for Pop)
'Simply the Best' – Tina Turner
'Don't Stop Believing' – Journey
'Lay Down the Sword' – Wishbone Ash
'Stand Beside Me' – Hothouse Flowers
'Peace on Earth' – U2
'This Guy's in Love with You' – Herb Alpert
'I Am, I Said' – Neil Diamond (for Mum)
'The Pretender' – Jackson Browne
'One of These Nights' – Eagles
'Only Love Can Hurt Like This' – Paloma Faith
'Comfortably Numb' – Pink Floyd
'Wish You Were Here' – Pink Floyd
'Child in Time' – Deep Purple
'Song for Europe' – Roxy Music
'Songbird' – Eva Cassidy (for Mum)
'He Ain't Heavy, He's My Brother' – The Hollies (for Mum)

'Born to Run' – Bruce Springsteen
'Don't Let Me Down' – The Beatles
'Smoke Gets in Your Eyes' – Bryan Ferry (for Mum & Pop)
'Who Knows Where the Time Goes' – Fairport Convention
'My Wanderings in the Weary Land' – The Waterboys
'Stranger on the Shore' – Acker Bilk (for Mum)
'Adagio for Strings' – Samuel Barber
'Northern Sky' – Nick Drake
'If You Could Read My Mind' – Gordon Lightfoot
'Hounds of Love' – Kate Bush
'Stay With Me Till Dawn' – Judie Tzuke (for me)
'Joe Public' – The Rutles
'The World Goes On' – Barclay James Harvest

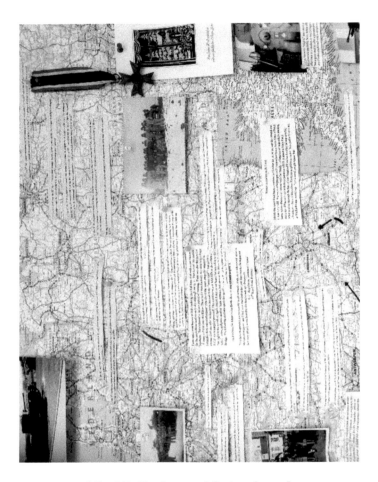

Me, My Father and I storyboard

Bernard Montgomery's letter translated into text
(the day Pop landed on Sword Beach)

My Dear Simbo
You may like the following news of our battle.
1. There is no doubt the Germans were surprised, and we got on shore before they had recovered. The speed, power, and violence of the assault carried all before it.
2. Generally, the beach obstacles presented no difficulty; where they were troublesome it was because of the rough weather - and on some beaches it was pretty rough.
3. D D Tanks
   (a) Used successfully on UTAH beaches
   (b) Failed to reach the shore on OMAHA beaches and all sank – too rough.
   (c) Were not launched on 50 DIV front as it was too rough; were landed "dry" behind the leading flights; casualties to AVRE sappers 'high' as a result, and to leading infantry.
   (d) Landed "dry" on Canadian front.
   (e) Used successfully on 3 DIV front.

generally it can be said that the DD tanks proved their value, and casualties were high where they could not be used.
4. As a guess prisoners about 6,000 so far. They consist of Germans, Russians, Poles, Japanese, and two Turks.
5. British casualties about 1,000 per assault Division. American casualties not known. High proportion of officer casualties, due to sniping behind our front. Two Inf Bde Comds wounded.
   a. Cunningham 9 Bde
   b. Senior 151 Bde

Good many Inf CO's killed, including HERDON, OC 2 Warwicks. No general officers are casualties.
6. The Germans are fighting well; Russian, Poles, Japanese, and Turks, run away; and if unable to do so, surrender.
7. Our initial attack was on a side front, and there were gaps between landings. The impetus of the assaults carried us

some way inland and many defended localities were bypassed; these proved very troublesome later. In one case a complete German Bn, with artillery, was found inside 50 DIV area; it gave some trouble but was eventually collected in (about 500 men). There is still one holding out – the radar station west of DOUVRES; it is very strong and is held by stout-hearted Germans.

8. Sniping in back areas has been very troublesome, as a result of Para 7. The roads have been far from safe and we have lost several good officers. I have been all right myself, though I have toured the area all day. There have been women snipers, presumably wives of German soldiers; the Canadians shot 4 women snipers.

9. The Germans are doing everything they can to hold on to CAEN. I have decided not to have a lot of casualties by butting up against the place; so I have ordered second Army to keep up a good pressure at CAEN, and to make its main effort towards VILLAGE BOCAGE and EVERCY and thence S.E. towards FALAISE.

10. First US Army had a very sticky party at OMAHA, and its progress at UTAH has not been rapid. I have therefore ordered it to join up its two lodgement areas and to secure CARENTAN and ISIGNY. It will then thrust towards LA HAYE DU PUITS and cut off the Cherbourg peninsula.

11. The two armies have now joined hands east of BAYEUX.

No time for more.
Yrs ever
B. L. Montgomery

PTO

PS.
The country here is very nice; green fields; very good crops; plenty of vegetables; cows and cattle; chickens, ducks etc. The few civilians there are appear well fed; the children look healthy; the people have good boots and clothing. The locals did not believe the British would even invade France or come over the channel; they say that the German officers and men thought this also – which may account for the tactical surprise we got.

B.L.M.
0900 hrs
9 June
PS.
I enclose a copy of a letter sent today to my chief of staff. This will give you my situation and my future intentions. It is of course very secret; please acknowledge receipt personally to me by wireless – of M500
B.L.M.

Milton Keynes UK
Ingram Content Group UK Ltd.
UKHW050122180724
445629UK00009B/89